# YAKIBA
## Grilling Techniques
—Shio-yaki, Furishio-yaki, Yuan-yaki, Tare-yaki, and Yakitori

THE JAPANESE CULINARY ACADEMY'S COMPLETE JAPANESE CUISINE

THE JAPANESE CULINARY ACADEMY'S COMPLETE JAPANESE CUISINE

# YAKIBA

## Grilling Techniques

Shio-yaki, Furishio-yaki, Yuan-yaki, Tare-yaki, and Yakitori

JAPANESE CULINARY ACADEMY

# CONTENTS

DISCLAIMER: All procedures described herein should be mastered under the guidance of a professional chef. The advice and strategies contained herein are based on the assumption of professional training and familiarity with the basics of Japanese cuisine. Neither the publisher, nor authors, nor editor shall be liable for any damages, special, incidental, or consequential, to health, reputation, or enterprise, resulting from reference to the content described herein.

Published by
Japanese Culinary Academy
office@culinary-academy.jp
https://culinary-academy.jp/
#305 Eiwa Oike Bldg. 436 Sasayacho, Nakagyo-ku,
Kyoto 604-8187, Japan

Distributed in the United States and Canada by
Kodansha USA Publishing, LLC.

© 2024 by the Japanese Culinary Academy
Photograph © 2024 Saito Akira and Yamagata Shuichi

All rights reserved.
Published 2025
Printed in Japan

31 30 29 28 27 26 25   10 9 8 7 6 5 4 3 2 1

ISBN 978-4-911188-10-1

**PREFACE**  MURATA YOSHIHIRO  6
How to Use This Book  8

## Chapter 1  Introducing *Yakimono*  11
Grilled Dishes in Japanese Cuisine  12
The Science of *Yakimono*  14
■ Salt-Grilled Striped Mackerel  Shio-yaki  18
*Yakimono* in History  22

## Chapter 2  The Basics of Grilling  29
Types and Methods  30
How Fish Changes Under the Effects of Heat  38
Hygiene in Preparing and Cooking *Yakimono*  40

## Chapter 3  Basic Types of *Yakimono*  43
■ *Yuan* Style Butterfish  Yuan-yaki  44
■ Grilled Salmon in Miso Marinade  Yuan-yaki  48
■ Grilled Marinated Barracuda  Yuan-yaki  52
■ Miso-Marinated Grilled Beltfish  Yuan-yaki  56
■ Salted and Grilled Tilefish  Shio-yaki  60
■ Grilled Tilefish Flavored with Sake  Shio-yaki  64
■ Overnight-Dried Whiting  Shio-yaki  69
■ Grilled Yellowtail  Tare-yaki  72
■ Grilled Eel on Rice  Tare-yaki  76
■ Grilled Quail  Tare-yaki  80
■ Grilled Sweetfish (Electric grill)  Furishio-yaki  84
■ Grilled Sweetfish (Charcoal grill)  Furishio-yaki  90
Eating *Ayu* Whole: An Experiment in Different Ways of Arranging Charcoal  91

Kishu Binchotan: Charcoal Production in Harmony with the Forests  96
The White Charcoal Production Process  102
Coppicing and Forest Management  104

## Chapter 4  *Yakimono* Variations  107

- *Awayuki* Grilled Sea Bream  **Shio-yaki**  108
- Salt-Crust Baked Sea Bream  **Shio-yaki**  110
- Grilled Sea Bream Head  **Furishio-yaki**  112
- *Kenchin* Style Grilled Sea Bream  **Furishio-yaki**  114
- Sea Bream Grilled with Oil  **Miscellaneous**  116
- *Yuan* Style *Sawara* Mackerel  **Yuan-yaki**  118
- Grilled *Sawara* Mackerel with *Natane* Topping  **Yuan-yaki**  120
- *Sawara* Mackerel *Hoba-yaki*  **Yuan-yaki**  122
- Sea Bass Roasted in Green *Hoba* Leaves  **Yuan-yaki**  124
- *Tade-Miso* Grilled Sea Bass  **Tare-yaki**  126
- Grilled Sea Bass with *Hosho* Paper  **Furishio-yaki**  128
- Tilefish Grilled with *Karasumi* Powder  **Shio-yaki**  132
- Tilefish, *Shiba-yaki* Style  **Shio-yaki**  134
- Grilled *Kinmedai* Marinated in Sake Lees  **Yuan-yaki**  136
- Koji Grilled Salmon  **Yuan-yaki**  138
- Rikyu Style Sesame-Grilled Flounder  **Yuan-yaki**  140
- Grilled Pufferfish  **Furishio-yaki**  144
- Grilled Pike Conger with *Tare* Sauce  **Tare-yaki**  146
- Grilled Conger Eel, Yawata Style  **Tare-yaki**  148
- Grilled Sea Bream and Shrimp Roasted in a *Horaku*  **Miscellaneous**  150
- Grilled Lobster in the Shell  **Miscellaneous**  152
- Grilled Cuttlefish, *Ro-yaki* Style  **Miscellaneous**  154
- Clam Grilled in the Shell  **Miscellaneous**  156
- Abalone Grilled in a Salt Crust  **Miscellaneous**  158
- *Tsubo-yaki* Style Grilled Horned Turban Shell  **Miscellaneous**  160
- Kamo Eggplant *Dengaku*  **Miscellaneous**  162
- Pan-Grilled Mallard Breast  **Tare-yaki**  164
- Roast Duck Breast  **Miscellaneous**  166
- Beef Tenderloin in Miso *Yuan-ji* Marinade  **Yuan-yaki**  168

### *Yakitori*—Cuts of Meat  170
- Breast (*mune*; *shio*)  171
- Boneless thigh (*momo*; *shio*)  172
- Boneless thigh (*momo*; *tare*)  173
- Chicken oyster (*soriresu*; *shio*)  174
- Chicken oyster (*soriresu*; *tare*)  175
- Chicken and long onion (*negima*; *shio*)  176
- Chicken and long onion (*negima*; *tare*)  177
- Tenderloin (*sasami*; *shio*)  178
- Wing flat (*teba*; *shio*)  179
- Neck meat (*seseri*; *shio*)  180

### *Yakitori*—Chicken Giblets and Rare Cuts  181
- Hearts (*shio*)  182
- Hearts (*tare*)  183
- Liver (*tare*)  184
- *Tsunagi* (connective tissue; *tare*)  185
- Kidneys (*segimo*; *tare*)  186
- Gizzard (*sunagimo*; *shio*)  187
- Skin (*kawa*; *shio*)  188
- Skin (*kawa*; *tare*)  189
- *Bonjiri* (uropygium or pope's nose; *shio*)  190
- *Nankotsu* (breastbone cartilage; *shio*)  191
- Meatballs (*tsukune*; *shio*)  192
- Meatballs (*tsukune*; *tare*)  193

Garnishes and Other Accompanying Dishes  194
Skewering Techniques (*Kushi-uchi*)  198
*Tsubo-nuki*  204
*Yawata-maki* (long-fish-wrapped burdock)  205
Types of Grills  206
Glossary  207
Causes and Prevention of Food Poisoning (Focus on "Grilling")  210
Index  211
Conversions  215

---

The jacket features the work of Yoshioka Sachio (1946–2019), the fifth generation of a lineage of Kyoto master dyers. Yoshioka was known for the finesse of his traditional vegetable-dyeing techniques. The jacket of this volume displays *hanadairo*, a hue of blue that is paler than *ai* (indigo) but darker than *asagi-iro* (light blue-green).

---

NOTE: Japanese names in this book are given in traditional order, surname first.

# PREFACE

## Murata Yoshihiro
Honorary Chairman, Japanese Culinary Academy

Since antiquity, Japanese have believed that the divine, called kami, is to be found everywhere in the natural world that surrounds us. Trees, waterfalls, ponds, and other notable places of natural beauty have been worshiped as kami and revered as embodying the divine. Human beings do not live by their own strength alone; like other living things, they depend for sustenance on the presence of the divine everywhere in the natural world of which they are a part. In agriculture, human beings are custodians who tend to the rice and other crops. In fishing, they are allowed to harvest the fish that have been nurtured by the seas. These beliefs have had a profound impact on traditional Japanese ways of thinking about food. Since we cannot survive without consuming other living things, we must give gratitude for the sustenance we receive. The relationship between human beings and food is not a simple one of hunter and prey, but one built on respect for other animals and plants. This view emphasizes gratitude for the blessings received. In Japan, people commonly say "itadakimasu" before each meal. This phrase, which means, "I humbly receive," expresses gratitude for the nourishment taken from other living things. Japanese culture teaches us to value these blessings: The traditional admonishment is that not a single grain of rice should be wasted.

This book introduces grilled foods (*yakimono*) and their place in traditional Japanese cuisine. Grilling itself presumably began in prehistory, when humans first learned to build fires and cooked meat and other foods over its heat. People have always attributed sacred qualities to fire, and the trees that provided the wood were also often regarded as sacred. People took these precious natural materials to make fire, which they used to cook the fish that flourished in the seas and rivers, and in this way took sustenance from nature's bounty. This sense of reverence is one of the characteristics of *yakimono* and its place within Japanese cuisine.

In traditional Japanese restaurants, preparation of food in the kitchen is divided according to process. The station called the *yakiba* is responsible for the preparation of grilled dishes. This is one of the major stations, alongside the *mukoita* (largely responsible for preparing sashimi) and the *nikata* position in charge of simmered dishes. These roles also correspond to a chef's progress through training. After an apprenticeship performing menial tasks and a stint serving in the *hassunba* position for preparation of the *hassun* appetizers, a trainee chef's first major cooking role normally comes upon assignment to the *yakiba*. Although there is some variation among restaurants, this generally takes place no earlier than the fifth year in the job. Here, while learning how to handle and cook the different kinds of fish in season throughout the year, an aspiring chef also learns about the calendar of traditional events and culinary techniques that reflect the changing seasons.

As well as learning the techniques that have been handed down over generations, the aspiring chef must also ensure that the food will please the person who eats it. Preparing food that will satisfy someone from a different cultural background sometimes requires the chef to alter the way the food is prepared to suit the expectations of the guest.

An important consideration here is that there are at least two sides to any kind of cuisine: cultural aspects relating to history and beliefs, and other aspects that can be explained scientifically. It is important to understand culinary techniques scientifically, without losing sight of the respect and gratitude for the bounties of nature touched on above. The two may not always be easy to reconcile, but it is by moving between these two competing priorities and learning to balance them that traditions evolve and develop.

This book introduces the steps by which *yakimono* dishes are prepared, and we have worked to produce a book that explains these processes as faithfully as possible. In a sense, the process of grilling food could hardly be simpler: "Put the ingredients on a skewer and grill them over a fire." But this basic process involves many techniques refined by generations of chefs, and numerous aspects that require expert judgment based on years of experience. In this book, therefore, as well as measuring and listing information such as the temperature of the heat source, distance between the heat and the ingredients, and cooking time, we have also tried to explain what chefs are looking for and what decisions they are making while grilling. For this reason, we have included photographs showing the colors and other attributes that a chef looks for when choosing the moment to turn food on the grill or deciding when the food is "done." In particular, the photographs showing how various ingredients should look when they are ready to serve will make this book a useful reference.

With *yakimono*, much of the important work is done before the food ever comes near a heat source. To understand these preparatory processes better, we have included the results of tests that show how the end results differ when the same ingredients are prepared under different conditions, photographs illustrating the changed condition of muscle fibers after cooking, and scientific explanations for why these changes take place. In many cases, Japanese culinary techniques have been handed down by practice and imitation. Part of our ambition with this book is that by explaining them with quantitative data, we can make them into techniques that anyone can reproduce.

Of course, the figures in this book should not be taken as a single, definitive "correct answer." Rather, our hope is that by reproducing the techniques introduced here, readers will come to understand the reasons for them and apply these lessons in their own cooking. Nothing would give me more pleasure than to see chefs and cooks drawing on the recipes and techniques in this book to expand their own creativity, thereby opening up new potential in this field of the culinary arts.

# How to Use This Book

Pages 18–21 of chapter 1, as well as most of chapter 3 and chapter 4, contain explanations with photographs of the preparatory steps and grilling procedures for a wide range of *yakimono* dishes. The book does not intend to dictate a single "correct" way of preparing these dishes. Instead, the aim is to show as clearly as possible how chefs achieve the desired results. We give precise data, including time and temperature measurements, so that readers can understand both the processes themselves and the thinking behind them.

Category. This book divides *yakimono* into four categories, according to the preliminary treatment of the ingredients before cooking: *yuan-yaki*, *shio-yaki*, *furishio-yaki*, and *tare-yaki*. (See p. 15 for more on these categories.)

This section includes notes explaining the purpose of the preparatory processes, as well as any other special points to note with the recipe.

Measurements of a sample cut are given as a guide to appropriate portion size.

In salting fish, sometimes you want to sprinkle salt evenly all over the fillets, while on other occasions some parts may call for more or less salt. The photograph on page 45, showing the salt sprinkled on the surface around the fish, indicates how heavily it should be applied.

Recipes for garnishes and other decorative accompaniments (*ashirai*) are shown on pages 194–197.

**Boxed texts**
These texts provide scientific explanations for important points in the preparation of each recipe, aiding understanding by explaining *why* certain steps are taken.

8

The entire cooking process is photographed at timed intervals using a fixed camera. This makes it easy to see how color and other aspects of appearance change from the first application of heat to the end of the cooking process.

This column shows the actions taken by the chef and the time for each action, from a starting time of 00:00. The photographs on the right show the color and appearance of the ingredients at the time of each action.

This section shows the type of heat used, as well as the direction of heat, temperature at the start of the cooking process, and distance from the heat source.

### Boxed texts

This section contains photographs showing how the end result differs depending on the preparatory steps taken, as well as scientific explanations and other information.

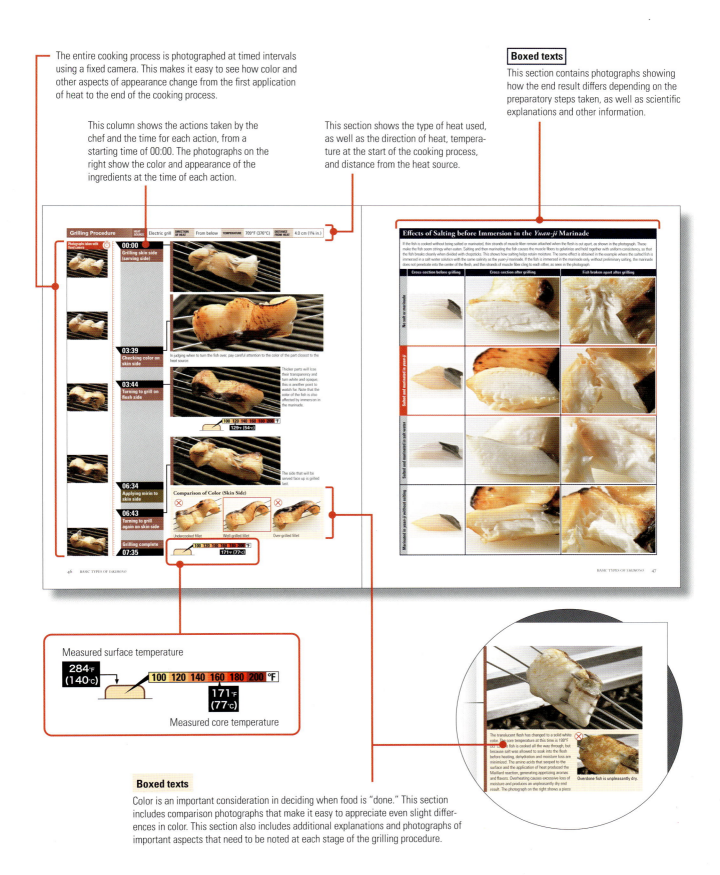

Measured surface temperature

Measured core temperature

### Boxed texts

Color is an important consideration in deciding when food is "done." This section includes comparison photographs that make it easy to appreciate even slight differences in color. This section also includes additional explanations and photographs of important aspects that need to be noted at each stage of the grilling procedure.

HOW TO USE THIS BOOK 9

Chapter 1

# Introducing *Yakimono*

Grilled fish and other ingredients (*yakimono*) occupy an important position in a traditional Japanese meal alongside *nimono-wan* (clear soup dishes). Blessed by the bounty of surrounding seas, Japanese cooks have developed distinctive tastes using the plentiful supply of seafood and salt and perfected ways to prepare different types of ingredients and adapt grilling techniques to suit the way the food is eaten.

This chapter explains the Japanese approach to grilling and the thinking behind it, and goes on to cover the effects of preparing the fish and some of the changes that take place during the cooking process, using salt-grilled striped mackerel (*shima-aji*) as an example.

# Grilled Dishes in Japanese Cuisine

The philosophy of Japanese cuisine is based on reverence and gratitude: Respect for ingredients and the natural bounty from which they come, and awareness that partaking of the life of other living things is what makes our own lives possible. This respect drives chefs to present ingredients in their original form and bring out the best of their natural flavors.

In preparing fish, for example, a chef might serve horse mackerel (*aji*) sashimi in such a way as to suggest the undulation of the fish's body, or prepare salt-grilled sweetfish (*ayu no shio-yaki*) skewered in the "dancing" (*odori-gushi*) technique, evoking the appearance of the fish swimming in a stream. These practices reflect images of the living fish and are an expression of respect for ingredients as living things.

Since ancient times, there has been a belief in the sacred nature of fire. Cooking life-giving food over fire therefore took on an aspect of ritual. It is likely that the first cooks grilled food over wood fires, but the short burning time of wood made this method ineffective. The use of charcoal, which burns more slowly and provides longer cooking times, gradually came to be favored. Charcoal has been an important source of heat and energy since ancient times, and is known to have been used as far back as the Jomon period (14,500–900 BCE). Of course, other heat sources are available today, but the association of cooking food over a charcoal fire with the sacred has survived and is still important in the world of Japanese cuisine.

## The Grilled Dish in a Japanese Meal

Within the menu of a Japanese meal, grilled dishes (*yakimono*) are one of the highlights, alongside the *nimono-wan* (clear soup dish, also called *nimono*). The importance of the *nimono-wan* comes from the intricate and time-consuming processes used to prepare it. It uses stock made from precious and painstakingly prepared ingredients like kombu (kelp) and katsuobushi (bonito flakes) and normally includes intricate and difficult-to-make processed items like steamed seafood balls (*shinjo*). The flavors obtained from these ingredients are an important part of a meal. Alongside these dishes, grilled ingredients (particularly fish) play the role of main dish and are the main source of protein.

The tendency to treat protein as the most important part of a meal is common to most food cultures around the world, and presumably comes from an instinctive human understanding of the importance of protein and fats as the building blocks that sustain our bodies. Humans everywhere share a preference for foods that have been rendered easy to consume by grilling or other cooking methods.

## The Tastes of Japanese *Yakimono*

Each cuisine has customs and preferences of its own, based on differences of climate and culture. The French approach to cooking fish, for example, makes use of oils and flavorings that have a decisive impact on the flavor of the finished dish. These flavors are naturally quite different from Japanese-style grilled fish. The practice of grilling food is common throughout the world, but different customs and preferences lead to considerable diversity in the taste of the finished dishes.

Japanese cuisine in general tends to minimize the assertion of fatty or oily elements. Grilling (*yaku*) is as a general rule done over a bed of charcoal embers, and refers to heating from below. This means that most of the fat will drip down from the fish or meat into the fire during the cooking process.

One of the aims of grilling is to impart the flavors created by the fire. In Japanese cuisine, that evokes the sacred associations of fire and celebrates the special flavors it imparts to precious ingredients. Among the attractions of grilling are the rich brown colors and toasty aromas it produces. These are the result of grilling directly over the fire. Food cultures differ somewhat in the flavors and aromas they perceive as desirable. In Japan, there is a preference for the crispy and aromatic surface of grilled dishes.

Since food is generally eaten with chopsticks, one requirement is that it needs to be grilled to a consistency that allows both the skin and the flesh of fish to be divided easily into bite-sized pieces using chopsticks. Around the world, people universally regard tenderness as a desirable quality in food, but Japanese cuisine prizes a wide range of textures and consistencies. Grilling fresh fish directly over glowing charcoal—bringing out the aromas of the fire, searing the skin to a crisp, and cooking the fish through—is one method that is felt to present the textures and aromas of the fish at their best. At the same time, the quite different, firmer textures of fish served raw as sashimi are also esteemed. This openness to different textures and different ways of enjoying natural ingredients (especially fish) is perhaps the result of a long history of consuming fish as a mainstay of the diet.

## Preparatory Salting of Fish

In the Japanese style of grilling, the flame is allowed to penetrate until the fish is well done. Serving fish "rare" is not common in Japanese cuisine. The basic approach is to slice the fish into servings of around 70–80 grams (2.5–3.0 oz.)—a convenient serving size that also allows the heat to reach to all parts of the fish evenly during cooking.

One characteristic is the preliminary preparation, in which salt is allowed to penetrate into the fish before it is exposed to the heat. As well as improving the flavor, this process also makes the flesh less likely to harden when exposed to high temperatures over a charcoal fire. This tradition of salting is thought to have originated with the method of drying fish. In coastal areas, people would gut fish after landing their catch and place them in seawater (approximately 3.4% salinity) before hanging them to dry. Immersing the fish in seawater allows salt to penetrate deep into the body of the fish, which would then be left to dry and bake gently in the rays of the sun. People would have discovered in the course of this process that adding salt helped to preserve the fish, and that removing moisture from the flesh would concentrate the umami-rich compounds within and increase its flavor. This later developed into the custom of preparing fish by adding salt before cooking.

## Development of Marinades

Seasoning of food would initially have been limited to immersing fish in seawater and allowing the salt to penetrate the flesh of the fish, but more elaborate modifications evolved over the years. In coastal areas, seawater was boiled to produce high-density salt water, while fish sauce and other seasonings were made using fish entrails. In inland areas, people learned how to use soybeans to make miso and shoyu leading to the development of marinades and shoyu-based flavorings. These evolved into a number of variations including *tare-yaki*, made with shoyu and a sweetener; *yuan-yaki*, made with shoyu, sake, mirin, and citrus zest; and miso *yuan-yaki*, made with *yuan-ji* marinade and miso.

# The Science of *Yakimono*

The major characteristic of grilling in Japanese cuisine is the use of charcoal fire. Burning charcoal releases far infrared radiation, which cooks ingredients at high temperatures. High temperatures can easily lead to overcooking, a problem chefs remedy by skillful use of salt and a nuanced understanding of its effects. This section looks at some of the changes brought about by the addition of salt, both during the preparation stage and in cooking.

## Preparation Mechanisms and the Uses of Salt

Grilled foods (*yakimono*) in Japanese cuisine can be divided into two main categories: those that use salt as a seasoning, and those that use salt chiefly for its effects on proteins. Miso and shoyu, which contain substantial amounts of sodium, are also used both as seasonings and for their effects on proteins.

As seasoning, there are two main methods of using salt. One is the direct application of salt to the fish, which is then grilled almost immediately (*furishio-yaki*). The other is the use of condiments such as miso and shoyu as a basting sauce applied in the course of grilling (*tare-yaki*).

For salt's effect on proteins, there are also two basic approaches. In the first, the fish is sprinkled with salt and left to rest before cooking or soaked in salt water (*shio-yaki*). In the second, the fish is marinated in condiments such as miso and shoyu and then grilled (*yuan-yaki*). Most other methods can be regarded as variations on one or the other of these two basic approaches.

If you sprinkle salt on a piece of uncooked fish in an amount equivalent to approximately 1 percent of the weight of the fish, the salt will gradually dissolve, producing an extremely high-density salt water. Since the muscle fibers (and muscle cells) of the fish have lower osmotic pressure than this high-density salt water, contact with it causes the fish to shed moisture through osmosis. The breakdown of the membrane of the muscle cells also brings amino acids and other substances to the surface.

The salt then gradually diffuses into the fish. By thirty minutes after the application of salt, the salt will have diffused over the outer surface; after around two hours, not only will the salt penetrate the surface but components such as amino acids that have leached out will be reabsorbed into the flesh.

As the salt diffuses through the fish, salt-soluble proteins in the flesh dissolve. This increases the water retentiveness of the muscle fiber even when grilled, limiting dehydration and preventing the fish from becoming too dry. In Japan, it is common to grill the fish at a core temperature of around 170°F (75°C), until the proteins become denatured.

Seasoning the fish with salt before cooking and dissolving salt-soluble proteins in this way increases water retentiveness and helps create a succulent texture. Since salt is not absorbed into the lipids at this time, it is necessary to use more salt in the case of oily fish. Seasoning with a generous amount of salt and leaving the fish for a certain time before grilling makes it possible to achieve the desired amount of toasty color and tasty aroma without losing tenderness and juiciness inside.

Many of the seasonings commonly used in Japanese cuisine contain salt, including shoyu and miso. When marinades combining shoyu, mirin, and sake (such as for *yuan-ji* marinade), or *shiro* (white) miso, shoyu, mirin, and sake (miso *yuan-ji* marinade) are used, the osmotic pressure of the marinade is higher than that of the muscle cells in the fish. After dehydration, these cells break down and the salt penetrates into the fish. The salt-soluble proteins in the fish dissolve, so that water retentiveness is maintained even when the fish is heated. The sugar content of the mirin also helps to increase the water retentiveness of the fish.

The surface of the fish is rich in amino acids and sugars from the shoyu and miso contained in these marinades, and this triggers the Maillard reaction, resulting in a deeper color and richer aromas during cooking than can be achieved by seasoning with salt alone. To prevent the

> ## Categories of *Yakimono*
> In this book, we divide *yakimono* into four categories, according to the way salt is used in the preparation process.
>
> ### Marinating ↔ Sprinkling
>
> **Shio-yaki**
> Fish or other ingredients are sprinkled with salt, which is left to penetrate the fish some time before cooking.
>
> **Yuan-yaki**
> Fish or other ingredients are soaked in a marinade such as *yuan-ji*, miso *yuan-ji*, or similar shoyu-, mirin-, or sake-based marinade, in such a way as to cause the salt to penetrate the fish.
>
> **Furishio-yaki**
> Salt is sprinkled on the fish mainly as a surface seasoning.
>
> **Tare-yaki**
> The fish is basted with *tare* sauce before and/or during grilling. If any salt penetrates the fish, it does so for a short time only.

surface temperature from getting too high, it is important to keep the fish an appropriate distance from the fire and avoid heating it too quickly.

## The Mechanisms of Heat in Grilling

When fish or meat is grilled over direct heat, the surface browns gradually. If the process continues unchecked, the high temperatures will cause a black carbonized deposit to form. Judgments on how far this process should be allowed to proceed—on when the fish or meat is "done"—differ somewhat from one culture to another. In grilling, it is important always to have a mental image of the end result you want to achieve.

### Surface changes

This browning is caused by the Maillard reaction that occurs when amino acids or proteins are heated at high temperatures in the presence of sugars. The higher the temperature, the faster this chemical reaction proceeds. Low moisture content also accelerates the process. The color of cooked food has an important impact on flavor, and determining when food is "done" requires quick judgments. Obtaining the desired color requires minute adjustments of cooking time and distance from heat to ensure that the Maillard reaction proceeds at an appropriate speed and to the desired extent.

The Maillard reaction not only causes browning on the surface, but also generates the rich aromas produced during grilling. For this reason, judgments about the extent to which the browning should be allowed to continue also affect the flavors and are of vital importance.

Preparing fish by applying salt before grilling causes the muscle cells to release moisture rich in amino acids and sugars to the surface, through the osmotic pressure of the salt. This makes it possible for an adequate Maillard reaction to be obtained by heating the fish to a surface temperature of around 175°F (80°C). If the fish is prepared by soaking in a marinade of condiments like miso or shoyu that contain large amounts of amino acids, or mirin, which contains large amounts of glucose, these ingredients will boost the process and stimulate stronger Maillard reactions.

Charcoal has long been the standard source of heat for grilling in Japan. A charcoal fire produces surface temperatures in excess of 1100°F (600°C), and radiates large amounts of far infrared heat. When these rays come into contact with food, they penetrate the surface and are transformed into heat around 1 to 2 millimeters (1/16 in.) beneath the surface, so that the surface of the food reaches temperatures of around 265°F (130°C).

The carbon monoxide emitted by charcoal when burned retards lipid oxidation, limiting the unpleasant smells caused by the oxidation of fats in fish and ensuring that the dominant aromas are those generated by the Maillard reaction during the cooking process.

When grilling fish, it is common practice to stimulate the fire with a hand-held fan. Fanning the fire supplies oxygen to the charcoal, increasing the radiant heat and raising the temperature inside the fish. Any oils that drip into the fire will be carbonized and burned off rapidly as smoke. When cooking over a fire, the smell of the smoke may cling to the fish; fanning directs the flow of smoke away from the fish, ensuring that the fumes do not spoil the flavor and aroma of the fish as it cooks. Fanning has two effects: It strengthens the Maillard reaction on the surface of the fish and ensures that the main aromas are the desirable ones.

## Changes inside the food

When grilling fish or meat, the temperature at the surface of the food rises as a result of radiant heat. The inside of the fish or meat is then heated by conduction.

Heat causes various changes in the muscle fibers of the flesh of fish. At 68°F (20°C), lipids start to dissolve, and at 104°F (40°C) the fibers and collagen shrink, squeezing out moisture. At 122°F (50°C), the fibers start to coagulate, and at 140°F (60°C) collagen turns to gelatin. Salting the fish and leaving it to rest before cooking, or immersing it in *yuan-ji* or a similar marinade, prevents excessive loss of moisture. In grilling, the core temperature can reach temperatures in excess of 175°F (80°C), but the fish remains succulent and juicy thanks to these preparatory steps.

With *yakitori* and other types of grilled chicken, on the other hand, it is common to use salt for flavoring only, or to baste the chicken in *tare* sauce while grilling, rather than relying on preparatory salting or marinating alone. The properties of meat mean that different changes take place when heat is applied compared to fish. In meat, fat starts to melt and muscle fibers shrink at temperatures over 122°F (50°C), and collagen shrinks at the same time. At 140°F (60°C), muscle fibers coagulate, and at temperatures over 194°F (90°C), collagen turns to gelatin.

These heat-induced changes affect the texture of the food, and it is therefore important to consider core temperature in deciding when to complete the cooking process and consider the fish or meat "done."

## The Role of Salt: Salt-Grilled Striped Mackerel

The following is an explanation of the method for preparing fish by applying salt and then leaving the fish to rest before grilling. For this example, we use striped mackerel (*shima-aji*), a fish that does not contain large amounts of collagen or fatty oils. The explanation focuses on the role of salt.

Japanese cuisine has developed a number of techniques

---

**The Science of Browning: The Maillard Reaction**

Complex aromas and browning play an important role in a positive taste experience. These changes are caused by chemical reactions brought on by the application of heat. Browning, which changes the colors of food during cooking, is well known. There are two types of reaction: enzymatic and non-enzymatic browning. Enzymatic browning is caused by a reaction between polyphenols and oxidizing enzymes contained in fruits and vegetables. Enzymatic browning occurs when you cut open an apple, for example, and the exposed part of the apple discolors, turning brown.

There are two types of non-enzymatic browning: the Maillard reaction (a reaction between amino acids and carbonyls) and caramelization. The Maillard reaction is produced when reducing sugars (for example, glucose, fructose, and lactose) react with amino acids and proteins at high temperatures and in conditions of low water activity. This reaction is extremely complex and is still not completely understood. Numerous chemical compounds are generated by the reaction. These include the water-soluble substances that give grilled food its distinctive brownish color, the aromatic compounds released during cooking, and substances that impart hints of bitterness. Since most foods and condiments contain sugars and amino acids, the browning that occurs during cooking is mostly attributed to the Maillard reaction. In fact, the Maillard reaction plays an important role in imparting desirable complex flavors to food.

The Maillard reaction proceeds more rapidly at higher temperatures, and the reaction rate can increase three- to fivefold with a 50°F (10°C) rise in temperature. When cooking at high temperatures, the reaction occurs quickly, producing rich aromas and browning. Even at lower temperatures, the reaction still takes place, albeit more slowly. The Maillard reaction also takes place during the slow simmer (approximately to six hours) involved in making stock from meat and bones, adding complexity and depth to the flavors.

One point that is commonly confused regards sucrose, or common table sugar. No Maillard reaction is involved here. Browning does occur when sucrose is heated at high temperatures, but this is caused by caramelization. This process, which produces a sweet smell, is a key technique in the repertoire of pâtissiers.

to make food easy to handle with chopsticks: Food is sliced into bite-sized pieces before serving, or is cooked until it is tender enough to be divided easily with chopsticks. In grilling fish, it is important to ensure that an appropriate Maillard reaction occurs on the surface, creating pleasant aromas, and that the inside of the fish is heated to a sufficient temperature so that proteins will coagulate, ensuring that the cooked fish is succulent and juicy, and tender enough to handle with chopsticks if needed.

The specific steps for grilling striped mackerel are as follows. First, apply salt to the uncooked fish, the equivalent of around 1 percent of the fish by weight. The salt is concentrated where it comes in contact with the fish but gradually dissolves and becomes a high-salinity solution. The osmotic pressure of the saline solution is greater than that of the fish cells, so water seeps out of the cells. The salt then permeates the muscle fibers. After about thirty minutes, the salt spreads over the entire surface of the fish. After around two hours, it soaks into the inside. The osmotic pressure of the salt causes moisture containing amino acids and sugars to seep from the muscle fibers onto the surface of the fish. This ensures that a sufficient Maillard reaction takes place on the surface of the fish when it is grilled, producing the desired colors and aromas. The diffusion of the salt also dissolves the salt-soluble proteins contained in the muscle cells. This increases the water retentiveness of the proteins when heated, and prevents the fish from becoming too dry.

As it is grilled over charcoal, with the heat coming from below, the food must be turned to ensure cooking on both sides, and the process is normally finished by grilling the side that will be presented face up when the fish is served. Salt-grilled striped mackerel follows this usual pattern, and the grilling ends with a final application of heat to the side that will be served face up until it presents a pleasing appearance of "doneness" (see p. 21).

During cooking, the temperature on the surface of the striped mackerel rises as a result of radiation heat. Next, conduction heat transfers these high temperatures to the inside of the fish. Heat causes various changes to occur in the muscles. Preparing with salt before cooking allows moisture to be retained and ensures a juicy texture in the cooked fish. The umami components do not dissolve into the melted fat in the fish, but instead remain in the juices of the flesh. Salting the fish to prevent loss of moisture therefore also prevents umami-containing constituents from escaping during cooking.

The toasted, charred, or browned effect and the colors imparted by grilling (Maillard reaction) are an important element in the flavor of the finished meal. To achieve the right level of coloring, it is important to adjust the cooking time and distance from the heat and ensure that an appropriate Maillard reaction takes place. This requires quick decision-making. As well as browning, the Maillard reaction also generates the desirable aromas produced during grilling. In judging when the fish is "done," it is important to consider grilling time as well as the extent of the Maillard reaction produced on the surface of the fish.

**Changes on the Surface of Uncooked Fish Fillets**
If fish is salted and left to stand, the surface of the fish gradually takes on a smooth, slippery appearance. For the striped mackerel in this example, after three hours too much salt seeped into the fish, making it unpleasantly salty, while one hour was not sufficient to achieve the desired effects.

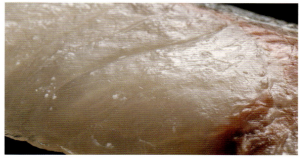
One hour after salting

Two hours after salting

Three hours after salting

### Shio-yaki
# Salt-Grilled Striped Mackerel
*Shima-aji no Shio-yaki*

---

Striped mackerel (*shima-aji*) is a large saltwater fish with a wide distribution in warm and semi-tropical waters around the world. It is prized for its flavor and attractive white flesh, and is widely used in Japan in a variety of cooking styles. The species is farmed and is now available throughout the year.

In preparing salt-grilled striped mackerel, salt is allowed to soak into the flesh of the fish before it is grilled. As well as adding a salty tang to the flavor, this prevents the fish from becoming dry when cooked. Collagen produces a succulent texture when heated. When grilling, careful overall judgment is needed to achieve the right degree of aromatic browning on the outside while maintaining the perfect balance of flavor, aroma, and texture.

SAMPLE CUT: Width: 5.0 cm (2 in.)
Length: 18.5 cm (7¼ in.)
Thickness: 1.7 cm (⅝ in.)
WEIGHT: 80.0 g (2.8 oz.)

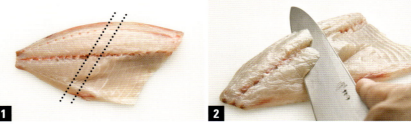

Striped mackerel filleted *sanmai-oroshi* style, is placed with the tail to the left, skin side down. Here the knife is shown cutting with the grain of the muscles (*junme*). Cutting in this direction ensures that the meat will be held together by the muscle fibers and will finish on the grill with a firm texture. Cutting against the grain (*sakame*) severs the muscle fibers and makes it more likely that the fish will crumble when heated. This direction of cutting is often used on fish with fibers that are tough. The chef chooses the direction to cut depending on the fish and the desired outcome.

### *Serves 3*

3 portions striped mackerel (*shima-aji*)
Salt, as needed

Garnishes

⅜ *sudachi*

¾ vinegar-pickled *myoga* (*su-zuke myoga*; see p. 194)

1. Clean and fillet a striped mackerel in the *sanmai-oroshi* style. Place the dressed fillet with tail to the left, skin-side down.
2. Cut the fillet into three portions, holding the knife diagonally to the fish. The skin side will be served face up (and grilled first).
3. Sprinkle salt (1% by weight) on both sides of the fish, and leave to rest for 2 hours.
4. Pat fish dry and thread each piece on three skewers, folding one end over in the single-tuck (*katazuma-ori*) technique (see p. 202).
5. Grill as shown on the following pages.
6. Transfer the fish to a serving dish, and garnish with the vinegar-pickled *myoga* and *sudachi*.

Fillet used in this example

Salting and resting the fish for two hours causes a high-density salt water to form on the surface. Contact with this causes muscle cells to shed moisture through osmosis. The cell membranes break down and salt diffuses into the muscle cells, causing salt-soluble proteins to dissolve. The dissolved proteins in the muscle fibers coagulate when heated above the denaturing temperature. Coagulated muscle fibers have good moisture retention even when heated. This minimizes dripping of juices from the fish during cooking and ensures a succulent finish. The moisture that seeps onto the surface of the flesh contains amino acids that encourage the Maillard reaction and produce rich aromas during cooking.

INTRODUCING *YAKIMONO*

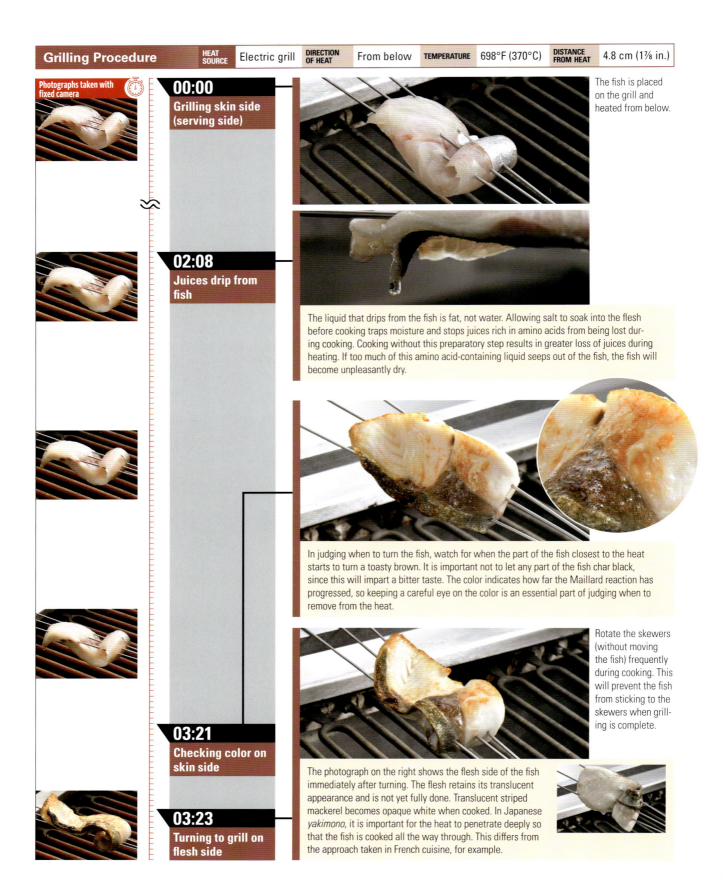

20 INTRODUCING *YAKIMONO*

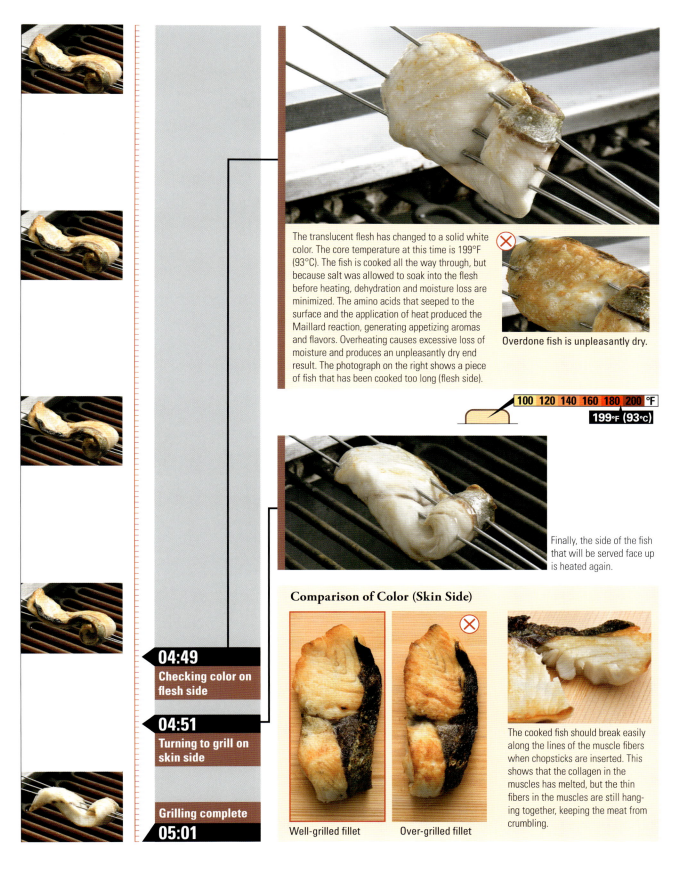

The translucent flesh has changed to a solid white color. The core temperature at this time is 199°F (93°C). The fish is cooked all the way through, but because salt was allowed to soak into the flesh before heating, dehydration and moisture loss are minimized. The amino acids that seeped to the surface and the application of heat produced the Maillard reaction, generating appetizing aromas and flavors. Overheating causes excessive loss of moisture and produces an unpleasantly dry end result. The photograph on the right shows a piece of fish that has been cooked too long (flesh side).

Overdone fish is unpleasantly dry.

199°F (93°C)

Finally, the side of the fish that will be served face up is heated again.

**04:49** Checking color on flesh side

**04:51** Turning to grill on skin side

**Grilling complete 05:01**

### Comparison of Color (Skin Side)

Well-grilled fillet    Over-grilled fillet

The cooked fish should break easily along the lines of the muscle fibers when chopsticks are inserted. This shows that the collagen in the muscles has melted, but the thin fibers in the muscles are still hanging together, keeping the meat from crumbling.

INTRODUCING *YAKIMONO* 21

# *Yakimono* in History

This section provides a brief history of *yakimono*, mostly based on early recipe books and similar texts. The commonest method of cooking *yakimono* in Japan today is to skewer fillets of fish and grill them over charcoal. How old are the earliest references to this style of grilling?

## *Yakimono* before the Edo Period

The earliest reference to what we would now call *yakimono* can be found as far back as the mid-Heian period. The *Wamyo ruijusho*, a Japanese dictionary compiled in the tenth century, includes a definition for the term *aburi-mono*, which it glosses as "cooked meat." There is no information about how it was prepared or the cooking methods that might have been used. The word *aburu* is still used today, but the verb *yaku* and its derivatives are more common in describing grilling techniques. One book printed in the Edo period, *Ryori momoku chomi-sho* (A Compendium of Cuisine and Flavorings, 1730), distinguishes between the two terms, claiming that *yaku* means to cook at high heat, while *aburu* implies gentle heat, applied from a greater distance. But most books from the Edo period and later use *yaku* without discrimination for all methods of dry-heat cooking, and do not seem to differentiate the term from *aburu* in this way.

The *Chuji ruiki* (Notes on Culinary Matters), a book on food preparation for court banquets that dates from sometime after the end of the thirteenth century, describes a method of cooking called *nukago-yaki*. This seems to have involved skewering fillets of carp, with the skin still on, seasoning by sprinkling salt and pouring on sake (known as *suri-bishio*) and then grilling them. A dish with the same name occurs in the fifteenth-century *Yamanouchi ryorisho* (Recipes of the Yamanouchi Household). Here, the dish is made by placing three small cubes of goose meat on a skewer, seasoning by *suri-bishio*, and grilling. *Nukago*, also known as *mukago*, originally referred to the round buds that sprout on the stems of Japanese mountain yam plants (*Dioscorea japonica*) and other species of wild yam. These were grilled on skewers before eating; the name seems to have been used by extension for dishes in which small chunks of carp or goose were skewered in a similar way and cooked over fire.

What other kinds of *yakimono* existed before the Edo period? The *Okusa-ke ryorisho* (Recipes of the Okusa Household), a text on cooking and banqueting etiquette apparently written around the end of the sixteenth century, contains a passage about a style of food called *ujimaru-kaba-yaki*. This seems to have been more or less the same grilled eel dish still popular as *unagi no kaba-yaki* today. Unlike today's *kaba-yaki*, however, in which the eel is divided into pieces before being grilled, in the description in this text the whole eel is skewered from head to tail, then dipped in a mixture of shoyu and sake before being grilled. An alternative method is also described in which the eel is prepared with *sansho-miso* (miso seasoned with Japanese pepper). At the time, sushi made from eel caught in the Uji river in Kyoto was particularly esteemed, and "Uji-maru" became a popular nickname for eel. *Ujimaru-kaba-yaki* was therefore an alternative name for a type of grilled eel dish.

For *tai no koke-yaki* (*koke* literally means "moss"), sea bream was cleaned by drawing the gills and internal organs out through the gill opening (*tsubo-nuki*, see p. 204). It was then wrapped in straw and covered with *kabetsuchi* (wall-clay) earth before being placed in the fire. Tubes of bamboo were inserted into the fish's mouth and shoyu poured through them to flavor the fish as it cooked. It is likely that this early form of *yakimono* is related to later *shiogama-yaki*, in which fish is cooked after packing with a layer of salt (see p. 27).

One example of a *yakimono* dish that used oil was *tai no nanban-yaki* (*nanban* being a reference to ingredients or cooking techniques introduced from overseas), in which sea bream was fried in sesame oil or lard. This was not a deep-fried dish; it seems to have been similar to *abura-yaki* or *iri-yaki* styles of cooking, in which the ingredients are sautéed using a small amount of oil.

## Heat Sources Used in Historical *Yakimono*

The cookbooks that have survived do not record what heat sources were used to cook the dishes they describe, but since these texts dealt mostly with meals prepared for the upper classes, it is possible that they used charcoal, which was still an expensive commodity in this period.

Production of charcoal in Japan is thought to date

From volume one of *Shiroto-bocho* (The Amateur Kitchen Knife), by Asano Kozo, with illustrations by Hokyo Gyokuzan (1803). The illustration shows food being prepared over an open fire in the center of the picture, while on the left another cook prepares *tamago-yaki* rolled egg on indirect heat.

back to the Jomon period (ca. 14,500–900 BCE). The earliest uses were in iron-making; charcoal was also used in the casting of the gilt bronze Great Buddha at Todaiji temple in Nara, said to have been completed in the year 752. The *Pillow Book* of Sei Shonagon, written around the year 1000 in the mid-Heian period, contains several mentions of charcoal, including a lament about how on cold days, the embers in the *hioke* braziers would have cooled to ash by midday. This suggests that charcoal was in use as a source of heat at least among the nobility by this time. The development of the *chanoyu* culture of tea during the sixteenth century increased the use of charcoal in daily life, but it is likely that it was not widely used in cooking until the Edo period, when the techniques for making charcoal improved.

One important innovation was the invention of white charcoal (*binchotan*), which came into use around the end of the seventeenth century. The first restaurants also started to spring up in the big cities around this time, and it is likely that demand for cooking charcoal increased in this period. Even today, *binchotan* is preferred for cooking because of its long combustion time.

## Edo-Period Cookbooks and the Development of *Yakimono*

Grilling techniques spread dramatically during the Edo period, which lasted from the early seventeenth to the mid-nineteenth century. The growth of a publishing industry meant that cookbooks were printed in substantial numbers, making it possible for the wider public to learn about techniques that had previously been the preserve of a small coterie of chefs catering to the upper classes. The opening of restaurants in cities was another factor: Competition among these businesses spurred further innovations and refinements.

The first cookbook to be published was *Ryori monogatari* (Stories of Cooking), which appeared in 1643 and is still marked by the customs of the earlier medieval period. Introduced in this book are *tai no hama-yaki* (excess catch sea bream preserved by on-site dressing and grilling) and *usugiri no makuri-yaki* (thin-cut, roll-up grill), *funa no arajio-yaki* (crucian carp, salted and grilled) and *kotori-yaki* (small birds, grilled), *eso no kinome-yaki* (lizardfish, dredged in crushed *sansho* leaves and grilled), *tofu no kiji-yaki* (tofu grilled "pheasant" style,[1] with mirin and shoyu), and *nasu no shigi-yaki* (eggplant grilled in "snipe" style[2]), as well as grilled bamboo shoots and at least two ways of roasting and grilling duck (*kamo no iri-yaki* and *hegi-yaki*).

Cookbooks continued to appear in the decades that followed, and by the mid-eighteenth century, books were being published that introduced dishes marked by a new creativity and sense of play quite different from the ceremonial cuisine served at formal banquets (known as *shikisho ryori*) that had been the focus of earlier books. The recipes in these books provided inspiration for chefs in the first commercial restaurants, and also had an influence on menus at weddings and other important feasts beyond urban areas. Chefs developed and perfected numerous variations on the different types of *yakimono* and established the foundations of the *yakimono* dishes we know today.

*Yakimono* dishes in this period can be broadly divided into two categories: those that were grilled over a direct flame using charcoal or other source of heat, and those that were cooked using indirect cooking methods, usually with a little oil in a plate, pot, or other cooking vessel. Dishes grilled directly over a fire (*jikabi-yaki*) were normally named either for the utensils used (*kushi-yaki* for skewers, *ami-yaki* for a metal grid) or for the seasonings: *shio-yaki* (salt), *tsuke-yaki* (marinade), *miso-yaki*, and so on. The basic methods used were to baste the ingredients with seasoning during grilling, or to immerse them in a marinade beforehand.

The names for different dishes cooked by indirect heat (*kansetsu-yaki*) also had names that drew on the utensils used during the cooking process: *ishi-yaki* (stone), *horaku-yaki* (a shallow earthenware roasting pan), *sugiita-yaki* (cedar board), *kai-yaki* (seashell), *suki-yaki* (iron plate), *tsubo-yaki* (pot), *denpo-yaki* (*denpo* or small pot or earthenware dish similar to a *horaku*), and so on (see p. 26). Again, seasonings were added either before or during cooking. Condiments could also be added at the table.

The ingredients used in *yakimono* were quite diverse, and included chicken, fish, vegetables and tubers, and tofu. In addition to chicken, a wide variety of other poultry was used, such as goose and duck, while *yakimono* made from crane, swan, and other wildfowl sometimes appeared at banquets for the upper classes.

The following is a brief survey of some of the types of *yakimono* dishes found in cookery books from the eighteenth century onward, both those grilled directly over an open flame and those cooked via indirect heat.

## Grilling over Direct Heat in Mid- to Late-Edo-Period Cookbooks

### ▪ *Shio-yaki*

*Arajio-yaki* is a style of *yakimono* in which white fish such as horse mackerel (*aji*), crucian carp (*funa*), or sweetfish (*ayu*) is seasoned with refined, high-purity salt before and during grilling. For *tai no shio-yaki*, the fish is seasoned with salt after being washed, then rested and rinsed in fresh water and seasoned with roasted sea salt (*yakishio*) before being grilled at a distance away from the flame. For *ayu no shio-yaki*, the cookery books suggest preparing *tade-su* sauce (a condiment made from *tade*, or *Persicaria hydropiper*/water pepper) and note that finishing with a second grilling just before serving helps to bring out the flavors of the fish.

### ▪ *Tsuke-yaki*

Various types of ingredients and condiments were used for *tsuke-yaki*. In *irotsuke-yaki*, a condiment of shoyu and sake would be applied to ingredients such as fish, tofu, or matsutake mushrooms before grilling. For *ika no tsuke-yaki* (squid) the books suggest that any dressing may be used, including combinations of ingredients such as *sansho-shoyu* (Japanese pepper and shoyu), hot peppers, black pepper, and *kinome*. For *yakitori*, cuts of chicken were skewered and lightly salted, basted with a mixture of shoyu and sake once the meat was well done, then finished with a final application of *tare* and served before the sauce had time to dry. By adding spices and flavorings to basic condiments in this way, cooks were able to produce a wide variety of flavors. As well as shoyu, there were also *yakimono* that used miso-based condiments, as well as *kasu-zuke*, in which the fish or meat was marinated in sake lees.

*Toryu ryori kondate-sho* (Contemporary Cooking Menus; author unknown, mid-eighteenth century). The section on preparing fish and poultry dishes shows people using a simple grill to cook food over a charcoal fire, and contains instructions on grilling saltwater and freshwater fish. "Saltwater fish should be grilled flesh side first; river fish skin side first."

### ■ Kaba-yaki

*Kaba-yaki* is a kind of *tsuke-yaki* that was chiefly used for eel (*unagi*). From an early period, Edo and Osaka seem to have had slightly different versions of this dish, in terms of both the seasonings and implements used. In Edo, the eel was sliced open and the head, tail, and spine removed before being skewered horizontally with two or three bamboo skewers and grilled while the chef basted the pieces with a mixture of shoyu, mirin, and sake. In Kyoto and Osaka, the same dish was prepared by removing the spine but leaving the head and tail intact, and then threading the eel horizontally across three to five bamboo skewers and grilling while basting with a mixture of shoyu to which a clear sake called *morohaku-zake* was added (this would have been similar to modern sake; in earlier times, sake was also made from unpolished brown rice). The head and tail were then removed, the meat taken off the skewers, and the eel cut into appropriately sized pieces for serving. These entries show that substantial regional differences existed from an early stage in terms of both the seasonings and utensils used in grilling.

### ■ Dengaku

Like *kaba-yaki*, *dengaku* was a popular and easily made light dish served in food stalls and *izakaya*. It was made not only with tofu and *kon'nyaku*, but also with various kinds of fish and shellfish. The cookbook *Tofu hyakuchin* (One Hundred Fine Tofu Dishes, 1782), which was one of the first to present recipes arranged by ingredients and at least partly for entertainment as well as practical purposes, contained a number of recipes for different variations on tofu *dengaku*. In addition to a basic *dengaku* in which tofu is coated with shoyu and grilled once before miso is added and the tofu grilled again, other variations include *uni dengaku*, in which the tofu is coated with sea urchin soaked in sake before grilling; *kiji-yaki dengaku* ("pheasant" *dengaku*), in which the cooked tofu was re-grilled after being basted with a mixture of *nikaeshi* shoyu (shoyu reheated with sugar, mirin, and sake) and grated yuzu peel; and *asaji dengaku*, in which *ume-bishio* (sweetened pickled plum paste) and poppy seeds were added to the tofu before grilling.

There were also variations using other ingredients. These included *hamachi no dengaku*, in which yellowtail was cut into chunks, mounted on short skewers, basted with sesame oil, and grilled until well done on both sides, then seasoned with Japanese-pepper-flavored *sansho miso* or hot-pepper-flavored *togarashi miso*, and *ika no dengaku*, in which squid was scored with a knife, skewered and grilled well, then basted once with shoyu, followed by a further application of *sansho miso*, *togarashi miso*, *kinome miso* (*sansho* leaf miso) or similar. These dishes seem to have used shoyu to provide an initial flavoring, which was then rounded out by basting with a miso-based condiment after grilling.

From the middle of the eighteenth century, *mitate* or "substitute" dishes became popular. In these, ingredients were presented in such a way as to resemble other things. In *onigara-yaki*, for example, crustaceans like Ise lobster (*Ise ebi*) or tiger prawn (*kuruma-ebi*) were seasoned with *sansho* and shoyu and then grilled in their shells, with the shells supposed to look like samurai armor. For *ro-yaki* ("wax" grill), the shrimp were removed from their shells and placed sideways on two skewers on a cutting board, then salted. A well-mixed dressing of egg, flour, and shoyu

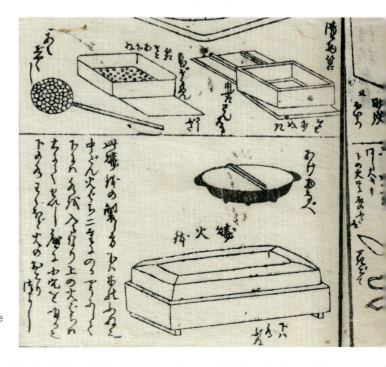

From *Ryori haya shinan* (Quick Guide to Cooking), volume 4, by Daigo Sanjin (1804). The picture at bottom left explains the use of a *yaki-hibachi* (grilling brazier). The *hibachi* has three levels, with water in the middle level.

INTRODUCING *YAKIMONO* 25

was applied to the shrimp meat five or six times before it was grilled at a distance from the flame. The name came from a perceived resemblance of the glossiness of the egg coating to wax. The same preparation was also applied to sea bream (*tai*) and trout (*masu*). *Dozo-yaki* was named for a resemblance to the earthen walls of traditional storehouses. The dish was made by coating fish with *sansho miso* or a similar miso-based condiment before grilling.

## Indirect Methods of Cooking in Mid- and Late-Edo-Period Cookbooks

### ■ *Horaku-yaki*

This style of dish, named for a shallow earthenware dish called a *horaku* or *horoku*, is found in many recipe books. One example calls for the chef to cut thick chunks of duck meat, then heat a *horaku* over a charcoal fire. When hot, a little sesame oil was added and the meat arranged in the dish. Once the meat started to change color, it would be eaten dipped in shoyu or hot-pepper-flavored *togarashi miso* diluted with sake. In another recipe, fish was arranged in a *horaku* over a bed of salt, and another *horaku* used as a lid. The dish was then heated by charcoal both from above and below, similar to roasting in an oven (*tenpi-yaki*).

### ■ *Ishi-yaki*

The name originally referred to a method of cooking in which vegetables, fish, and other ingredients were cooked by placing them on hot stones. Later, the name came to be used for dishes in which a relatively large amount of oil was heated in a pot and used to cook tofu, which was then eaten with grated daikon radish and shoyu. By the late Edo period, "ishiyaki" as a method had been forgotten, but the name seems to have remained.

### ■ *Denpo-yaki*

In this style of cooking, a bed of julienned long onions is laid in a shallow earthenware dish (*kawarake*), which is then heated over a fire. Thin sashimi-like strips of fish such as bonito and tuna were then placed on top of the onions and grilled. When they started to brown, a seasoned dashi would be poured over the whole. This was a dish similar to *horaku-yaki*.

### ■ *Suki-yaki*

The name for this type of *yakimono* comes from using a wide metal plow blade (*karasuki*) as a hot plate. The metal was oiled and then used to heat the ingredients. Different grilling styles were used for fish and poultry. For *hamachi no suki-yaki*, yellowtail would be cleaned and filleted, and the metal plate heated over a fire and oiled. The fillets would be arranged on the surface and cooked. The instructions include a warning not to overheat the fish. The dish was cooked at the table. For seasonings, the cookery books suggest grated daikon, shoyu, and hot pepper (*togarashi*), as well as yuzu- or wasabi-flavored shoyu. Probably the fish would have been dipped in condiments set out on the table. Despite the similarity of the name, the dish was probably more like teppanyaki than today's beef sukiyaki. For poultry *suki-yaki*, the books describe marinating goose or duck meat in *tamari* ("rich") shoyu, then cooking it on a metal plate over a fire.

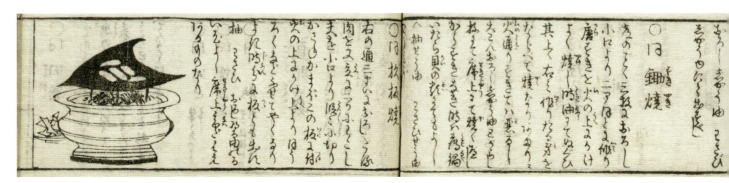

The first volume of *Shiroto-bocho* describes dishes such as *suki-yaki* (plow-blade grill) and *sugiita-yaki*. The picture on the left shows a *suki-yaki* plate being heated over a charcoal fire. The text contains step-by-step instructions on heating the plate, adding oil, and grilling fillets of fish, as well as advice not to overcook the food and other tips.

### ■ Shiogama-yaki

In *Ryori chinmi-shu* (Anthology of Rare Culinary Delicacies, 1764), one recipe calls for the chef to scale a sea bream (*tai*), then remove the gills and internal organs through the gill opening (*tsubo-nuki*, see p. 204). The fish is then placed in a large pot, dredged well in salt, and steamed before shoyu is added. The book notes that this recipe is similar to the quick way to preserve sea bream after a bumper haul called *hama-yaki* ("shore grill") mentioned above. The *Ryori haya shinan* (Quick Guide to Cooking, volume 4, 1804) explains *hama-yaki* as follows: Place the washed and scaled sea bream on a generous bed of salt spread on the earthen floor (*doma*), then cover with a roof tile (*kawara*), surround with tiles on all sides, and place plenty of embers on top of the tile in order to steam the fish. As this example shows, different recipe books often suggested different methods of preparation even for dishes with the same name.

### ■ Other types of *yakimono*

*Tori no iri-yaki* involved marinating chicken meat either in a mixture of dashi and *tamari*, or in a marinade of sake, shoyu, and *tamari*, and then cooking it in a pot. There are also descriptions in which the meat was arranged in a pot and the *tare* poured over the meat, which was then cooked over a flame. For *sugiita-yaki* and *sugi-yaki*, yellowtail (*hamachi*) was dressed and diced into small pieces that were then heaped on a wooden *kamaboko* board. This was then covered with a *horaku* or similar shallow dish and cooked over a fire. Once done, the dish was brought to the table together with the board. Regarding seasonings, the recipes frequently mention yuzu, wasabi, grated daikon, and shoyu in association with dishes meant to stand out in the menu, so it is likely that these dishes, like *hamachi no suki-yaki*, were normally seasoned at the table.

This brief survey offers a few examples of *yakimono* dishes as they appeared in early cookbooks, most of them published during the eighteenth and nineteenth centuries. But how common were these *yakimono* dishes in people's daily lives at that time?

One source we have are records of the meals served in the Edo residence of Sanada Yukihiro, a former daimyo lord. These show that in the year 1800–1801, *shio-yaki* dishes were the kind of *yakimono* served most frequently.

Sea bream (*tai*), whiting (*kisu*), silver croaker (*ishimochi*), saury pike (*kamasu*), stone flounder (*ishigarei*), flounder (*karei*), red snapper (*kodai*), and horse mackerel (*aji*) are some examples of fish served in this style. *Tade-su* was served with the horse mackerel and flounder.

The records show that an impressive variety of *yakimono* dishes were served, including *ishigarei no tsuke-yaki* and a variety of *yakimono* in which condiments and flavorings were added after cooking, such as steamed snapper (*kodai*) with sugar-sweetened miso, steamed *kisu* flavored with sesame salt, and miso-marinated dishes of sea bass and salmon, as well as *kai-yaki*, *hama-yaki dai*, and *gyoden* (fish grilled *dengaku*-style after coating with miso), suggesting that a range of grilling styles and a variety of ingredients had become well established in the daily lives of at least the upper classes by the late Edo period.

Publications listing rankings of popular daily foods and dishes also give us an idea of the kinds of things that ordinary people were eating at the time. These sources show that numerous *yakimono* dishes were available, using inventive techniques to produce tasty meals from more affordable ingredients, including *nasu no shigi-yaki* (eggplant), *tofu no dengaku* (tofu), *maguro no kiji-yaki* (tuna), *iwashi no shio-yaki* (sardine), *shiba-ebi no karairi* (shrimp), and *surume no tsuke-yaki* (squid).

During the Edo period, chefs had already developed a variety of creative techniques for grilling. Although the building blocks for most dishes were seasonings with salt, shoyu, and miso, cooks could add mirin to create a sweeter basting sauce or marinade, or add *sansho*, wasabi, hot pepper, black pepper, and *kinome* (*sansho* leaves) to produce quite diverse and complex tastes, both for dishes grilled directly over an open flame and those cooked in pots and other utensils. It is fair to say that these Edo-period cooks established the foundations for the range of *yakimono* dishes we enjoy in Japanese cuisine today.

---

Notes

1. *Kiji-yaki*: Originally pheasant marinated in shoyu and mirin before grilling, the term came to be used for fish or tofu coated with shoyu and grilled from the Edo period onward.
2. *Shigi-yaki*: Originally meant grilled snipe itself, but in the development of *shojin ryori* vegetarian cuisine, it came to apply to the eggplant dish of today.

Chapter 2

# The Basics of Grilling

How is heat transferred to food during cooking, and what changes take place inside the ingredients as they are exposed to heat? The main methods used in *yakimono* are grilling over direct heat, indirect heat, and cooking in an oven. Each approach involves different types of heat transfer. Different heat sources—charcoal, gas, electricity, and so on—also impart their own characteristics to the food.

This chapter looks at the science of heat, and the various ways in which heat is transferred to food during cooking. We also introduce basic information relating to *yakimono*, including the qualities of different fish and how the flesh changes as a result of heating, as well as important considerations of hygiene to bear in mind when preparing *yakimono* dishes.

# Types and Methods

Grilling skewered fish using direct heat (*jikabi-yaki*) over a bed of charcoal is a method of cooking that was established in Japan at an early stage. Various other methods were devised over the course of history, making use of the implements available in each period, such as cooking with indirect heat using a *horaku* pan or similar vessel, and *shiogama-yaki*, in which ingredients were wrapped in an outer layer of salt or a mixture of salt and egg whites. Today, ingredients can be grilled in electric or clay/stone ovens, and other appliances. This section takes a brief look at the different types of heat transfer involved in grilling and the characteristics of each method.

## Heat Transfer

The photo on the opposite page shows a piece of skewered mackerel (*saba*) being grilled over glowing charcoal. In cooking over direct heat, high-temperature electromagnetic waves (radiant heat) emitted by the burning charcoal come into contact with and are absorbed by the much cooler surface of the fish. Heat is converted into energy and the fish is cooked. This is known as radiant heat transfer. When charcoal is heated, it produces combustion gases. The surrounding air, which includes these combustion gases, is heated by conduction as it comes into contact with the burning charcoal. As its density falls, the air rises, bringing it into contact with the fish and transferring heat. This is convection heat transfer. Furthermore, the metal skewers that hold the fish in place also play a role. As the skewers are heated by radiation and convection, some of this heat is transferred to the fish. This is known as conduction heat transfer. Food is therefore cooked by three different types of heat transfer from the heat source.

The section that follows explains these three types of heat transfer. This is basic information for considering how heat is transferred to food during the cooking process.

*Radiation*: In radiation heat transfer, heat moves through the air as electromagnetic waves, radiating from a substance at high temperature to one at low temperature. Physical bodies (in this case, the heat source) emit electromagnetic waves of various wavelengths. Heat radiation involves waves with wavelengths that range from the visible light spectrum to the infrared. When food ingredients or other objects come into contact with electromagnetic waves in this range, their temperature rises.

The amount of energy ($E$; W/m$^2$) emitted by heat radiation can be calculated using the following equation.

$$E = \varepsilon \sigma T^4$$

In this equation, $\sigma$ stands for the Stefan–Boltzmann constant, expressed as $\sigma = 5.67 \times 10^{-8}$ W/(m$^2$•K$^4$), while $\varepsilon$ is emissivity, which measures how effectively a material emits energy as heat radiation. This varies according to the material and the condition of the surface. $T$ is absolute temperature measured on the Kelvin scale (K). Since an object emits energy proportional to the fourth power of its absolute temperature ($T^4$), the amount of energy emitted by objects of the same material changes dramatically depending on temperature.

Absolute temperature is found by adding 459.67 to the temperature in Fahrenheit and dividing by 1.8. For example, if the surface temperature of the heat source increases from 1100°F (593°C/866.48K) to 1600°F (871°C/1144.26K), the amount of energy emitted is estimated to be about three times that of the heat source.

Emissivity ranges between 0 and 1. A theoretical body that acts as a perfect emitter across all wavelengths, emitting a maximum amount of energy, has an emissivity value of 1, and is called a black body. In reality, all substances have emissivity less than 1, but charcoal has been shown to have a value quite close to 1. This is why charcoal emits more energy than other means of heating (such as an electric heater), even at the same temperature.

*Conduction*: In conduction heat transfer, heat moves from high-temperature areas to low-temperature areas within an object. The speed at which this occurs is determined

**Radiant heat transfer**
Electromagnetic waves (radiation) emitted by the hot charcoal strike the surface of the cooler fish, where they are absorbed and turned into energy, cooking the fish.

by the temperature difference (temperature gradient) and the thermal conductivity of the substance. The greater the difference in heat, the faster transference takes place. Thermal conductivity is a physical property that varies according to the temperature and composition of the substance/object. Water and most foods have low thermal conductivity, around 1 percent to 0.1 percent of the thermal conductivity of metals. It is therefore difficult for heat to be conveyed through conduction. Conduction heat transfer takes place when energy from the heat source strikes the surface of the food. The temperature rises, and heat is carried into the cooler core of the food via conduction.

*Convection*: Convection heat transfer happens through the movement of a fluid (liquid or gas). When a solid (the object to be heated) is placed inside a high-temperature fluid, the layer of fluid adjacent to the solid has the same temperature as the surface of the solid, while the fluid a little distance away is at a high temperature. The speed of heat transfer is determined by the difference in temperature between the fluid and the surface of the solid, as well as by the heat transfer coefficient. This differs from the thermal conductivity specific to particular substances in the conduction example above, since it varies according to the movement of the fluid. As the temperature of a fluid rises, its density usually reduces, and this difference in density causes thermal flux. This is called natural convection, as opposed to "forced convection," when a fluid is made to move, for example by use of a fan. Forced convection is stronger than natural convection, and liquids have a higher heat transfer coefficient than gases.

## Direct heat

Radiant heat transfer using charcoal has long been the most common method of direct-heat cooking in Japan. Alternative heat sources are increasingly common today, but for grilling, setups that use radiant heat are still the most widely used. Experimental data confirm that in a process like that shown in the photograph, where food is cooked on skewers over charcoal, around 80 percent of the heat is transmitted through radiant heat transfer. If the food is placed vertically on skewers around the charcoal, rather than horizontally on top of it, the influence of convection is reduced and the proportion of heat transferred by radiation increases even further. If the food is placed on a metal grill, conduction via the heated metal also comes into play. In cooking food, chefs will constantly keep an eye on the intensity of the heat source and adjust the distance between the source and the food.

In Japanese cuisine, many dishes call for ingredients to be skewered and cooked directly over heat. Examples include *shio-yaki* using various kinds of fish, teriyaki, and *kaba-yaki*. Cooking food on skewers over direct heat, rather than on a grill or other intermediary implement, reflects aesthetic preference in Japanese food culture. Avoiding the telltale traces of a grill surface, it allows for a more attractive finish of the cooked ingredient. Another characteristic is that ingredients are normally cut thin. This means that cooking time is generally short, even when the food is cooked through, as is the custom.

One exception is cooking over a straw-fueled fire (*wara-yaki*)—the method used, for example, in preparing seared bonito (*katsuo no tataki*). This method allows the flame to come into direct contact with the fish, and in this case the heat transfer is not primarily through radiant heat. The aim is to sear the outside of the fish rapidly—and also to impart some of the aromas of the straw used as protective wrapping. The fish is then allowed to cool, which prevents the heat from penetrating fully into the fish.

## Indirect heat

One indirect method of cooking utilizes an earthenware pan (such as a *horaku*) or metal vessel. The utensil is heated by conduction. When food comes into contact with the hot surface, the surface temperature of the food rises, and heat is transferred to the core of the food.

The cooking pan or plate is often prepared to prevent food from sticking: by sprinkling with salt in the case of a ceramic plate or pot, and by using oil in the case of a metal plate. During cooking, oils and juices seep out of the food and are heated along with the fish or meat. Chefs adjust the heat source to control the temperature of the cooking plate, and the heat retention and temperature stability of the plate or other cooking utensil vary according to the material and other qualities of the material used (thermal conductivity, specific heat, and thickness).

## Oven heat

Food can also be cooked by heating an enclosed space and placing the food inside this space, as in an oven. The food is then cooked by convection from the heated air,

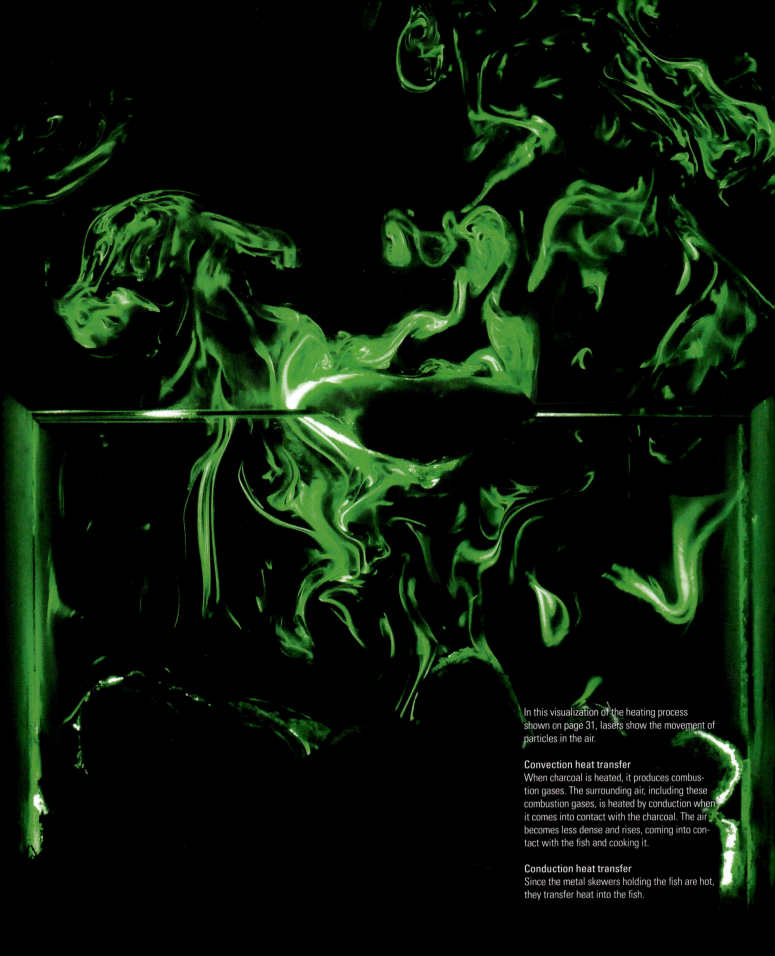

In this visualization of the heating process shown on page 31, lasers show the movement of particles in the air.

**Convection heat transfer**
When charcoal is heated, it produces combustion gases. The surrounding air, including these combustion gases, is heated by conduction when it comes into contact with the charcoal. The air becomes less dense and rises, coming into contact with the fish and cooking it.

**Conduction heat transfer**
Since the metal skewers holding the fish are hot, they transfer heat into the fish.

by radiation coming from the heating elements or other heat source, and by conduction from the pan or similar container.

There are two main types of commercial ovens: deck ovens, which use mostly radiant heat, and convection ovens, which as the name suggests rely mostly on convection heat. Brick or clay/stone ovens are similar to deck ovens, but have no door at the front. Deck ovens normally have a heat source at the top and bottom of the oven space, allowing temperatures to be set separately. The bottom of the chamber is heated to a high temperature; food is heated when it comes into contact with this surface, and heat is transferred to the core of the food via conduction. This method is most suitable when the temperature underneath the food needs to be controlled.

In a convection oven, hot air moves through the oven and makes it possible to cook the food evenly all over. Food can be placed in pans on multiple shelves, so that numerous dishes can be cooked at the same time.

The oven door is generally closed during cooking. High heat builds up inside the oven, making it easy to maintain a stable temperature. As moisture seeps out of the food, humidity inside the oven rises, creating the conditions of steam cooking.

## Heat Sources for Cooking

### Wood charcoal

Charcoal is made primarily from wood and bamboo. Wood-derived charcoal is divided into two types: "white" (*shirozumi*) and "black" (*kurozumi*). The two types are made in essentially the same way until the final stage, when the firing process is ended in different ways. This results in charcoal with quite distinct characteristics in terms of kindling and combustion temperature, how good the charcoal is at maintaining high heat, and heat intensity. White charcoal is made from various species of oak (primarily *kashi* and *nara*), while black charcoal uses mainly sawtooth oak (*kunugi*), pine (*matsu*) and *nara*. White charcoal contains fewer volatile constituents than black charcoal, and more carbon.

All charcoal is made up primarily of carbon, which reacts with oxygen in the air and burns through flameless combustion. In a wood-burning fire, heat transforms the organic matter inside the wood, producing volatile gases. These combust, igniting flames, and the flames burn the wood. By contrast, in a charcoal fire, most of the organic matter in the wood has already been burned off, and the proportion of non-carbon impurities is extremely low. Therefore, when the charcoal is ignited, flameless combustion reaction occurs on the surface of charcoal where carbon reacts with the surrounding gases. Flameless burning is slower than a flaming fire, and this makes it possible to keep the fire alive for a long time.

When charcoal burns and glows red, the surface temperature is between 900–1500°F (480–800°C). In the case of direct-heat cooking, food is mostly heated by radiation through infrared waves emitted from the surface of the charcoal. White charcoal has a higher ignition point than black charcoal and is harder to ignite, but once lit, continues to burn at high heat for a long time. The embers can easily be stimulated by fanning, and can rise to nearly 1832°F (1000°C). These are the reasons why *binchotan*—white charcoal produced from the wood of the *ubame-gashi* oak (*Quercus phillyreoides*)—is popularly used in restaurants. Black charcoal is often used for tea gatherings (*chanoyu*) and for various purposes of daily life. In addition, owing to irregularities in the shape of the original wood, the temperature may not be even in all parts of the heat source. To avoid unevenness in the cooking, food is cooked at high heat at a certain distance from the heat source. This is captured in the traditional rule-of-thumb that food should be grilled using "high heat, distant heat."

Cooking with wood differs from cooking with charcoal because the heat source contains organic matter. It is important to ascertain the impact that the combustion gases will have on the food and choose the wood accordingly.

### Gas

In a gas range, gas burns by mixing with air inside the burner (primary air), and also takes in air above and around the flame (secondary air). The hottest spot, just above the blue area of the flame, reaches temperatures of 3000–3300°F (1650–1800°C). Despite the extremely high temperatures of burning gas, only a small amount of radiant heat is emitted by the flames and very little radiant

A ceramic plate infrared burner

34   THE BASICS OF GRILLING

heat transfer is obtained by this method. For this reason, gas is generally not used for direct-heat cooking. Instead, food is placed on a metal plate or pan over the burner and cooked by conduction. Infrared burners, which use gas to heat a ceramic or skillet or griddle, are one type of cooking device often used in restaurants to produce radiant heat using gas.

## Electricity

Electric ranges are the most common way of cooking with electricity. Food is cooked by electromagnetic waves emitted from the heater surface, which is heated by electrical resistance.

# Infrared Waves in Radiant Heat Transfer

The amount of energy generated depends on the temperature and emissivity of the heat source. The wavelengths of the electromagnetic waves emitted by the heat source (mostly infrared) also have an influence. Infrared waves are electromagnetic waves with wavelengths between 0.78 micrometer and 1 millimeter: longer than the red of visible light, and shorter than electrical radio waves. This is normally divided into near infrared (shorter wavelengths) and far infrared (longer wavelengths). The division between the two differs according to field. In culinary contexts, radiation with wavelengths of 3 micrometers or more is generally regarded as "far infrared" (as per the definition of the Japan Far Infrared Rays Association).

The moisture contained in food absorbs waves in the far infrared range. Cooking with a heat source that emits waves in the far infrared range therefore ensures that these waves are efficiently converted to heat on the surface of the food. The surface temperature rises rapidly, ensuring a darker browning. Grilling time is short and the food is cooked to doneness more quickly, while preserving succulence. The faster the rise in surface temperature, the faster the core will be cooked, since heat is transferred from the surface to the core via conduction. With near infrared waves, less heat is absorbed on the surface. The waves penetrate several millimeters below the surface before they are converted into heat. Achieving the desired browning effect on the surface of the food is more difficult when cooking with a heat source that produces mostly near infrared waves, because the surface temperature rises more slowly. Use of a near infrared heat source also encourages evaporation from the surface, producing a thicker crust on the surface of food.

## Electric cooker infrared waves

Various types of electric heaters are used for cooking. Traditional sheathed heaters, in which the nichrome wires that emit the heat are covered with a metal shield, or bright halogen heaters, have low emissivity in the far infrared range. In contrast, ceramic heaters, quartz tube heaters, and graphite heaters—sometimes known as far infrared heaters—have high emissivity in the far infrared range.

## Charcoal-produced infrared rays

Charcoal emits a particularly high proportion of waves in the far infrared range. Research has shown that it has an emissivity of close to 1 in the overall infrared range,

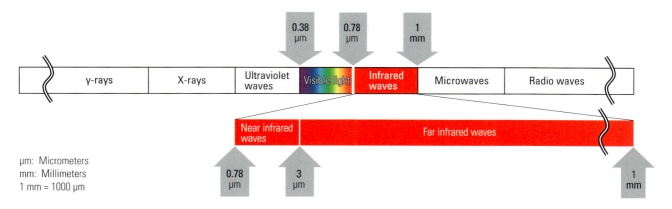

**Infrared Wavelength Range**

encompassing near to far infrared wavelengths. This means that charcoal emits more energy and transfers heat more efficiently compared to other materials at the same surface temperature.

## Replicating the Effects of Charcoal with Alternative Heat Sources

In direct-heat cooking, it has long been held that the best results can be obtained by using charcoal and cooking over "high heat, distant heat." Cooking with charcoal remains the method of choice today for *yakimono* made with fish as well as grilled eel (*unagi no kaba-yaki*) and grilled chicken (*yakitori*) in Japanese restaurants. But is it possible to obtain the same results using heat sources other than charcoal?

We ran an experiment to compare the condition of charcoal-grilled chicken breast with chicken breast cooked using two other forms of radiant heat: the first an electric ceramic heater with high far-infrared emissivity and the second a wire mesh fish grill with a high far-infrared emissivity ceramic coating heated on a gas range. We adjusted for distance from the infrared-emitting surface and the intensity of the gas range, respectively, so that the heat flux (amount of thermal energy transferred per unit area) would be equal to that of the charcoal. As a result, we were able to achieve roughly the same surface temperature, coloring, and moisture content as the chicken cooked over charcoal. However, a sensory evaluation acknowledged a noticeable difference in the surface scent (aroma) of the cooked chicken samples. An aroma analysis using gas chromatography mass spectrometry showed that the chicken cooked over charcoal contains a higher proportion of pyrazines and pyrroles, which contribute to rich aromas, compared to the chicken cooked using radiant heat from a wire fish grill with a surface coating. It was speculated that differences in the combustion gases of each heat source might be part of the explanation. To test this hypothesis, the combustion gases were analyzed, and it was found that charcoal fire contained less oxygen and higher levels of carbon monoxide, carbon dioxide, and hydrogen than gas fire.

This suggests that although it is possible to get more or less the same effects with regard to browning and moisture content, it is difficult to obtain the aromas characteristic of cooking over charcoal by using gas- or electricity-generated radiant heat. The original wood used to make the charcoal, classically the *ubame-gashi* oak from Wakayama prefecture used in good-quality white charcoal, is a precious natural resource, and it is important to devise methods that take full advantage of the unique characteristics of charcoal grilling using this fuel (see also pp. 96–105).

---

### References

Ishiguro Hatsuki, Abe Kanako, Tatsuguchi Naoko, Lihua Jiang, Kubota Kikue, and Shibukawa Shoko. "Characteristics of Broiling over Charcoal (Part 2) Flavor of Food Broiled over Charcoal" (in Japanese). *Nihon Kasei Gakkai shi* 56:2 (2005), pp. 95–103.

Sugiyama Kuniko, Miyazaki Yasuko, and Shibukawa Shoko. "Effects of Spectral Distribution on Radiative Heating of Food" (in Japanese). *Nihon Kasei Gakkai shi* 44:11 (1993), pp. 923–28.

Sugiyama Kuniko and Shibukawa Shoko. "Penetration of Infrared Radiation Energy into Model Foods" (in Japanese). *Nihon Kasei Gakkai shi* 53:4 (2002), pp. 323–29.

Tatsuguchi Naoko, Abe Kanako, Sugiyama Kuniko, and Shibukawa Shoko. "Characteristics of Broiling over Charcoal (Part 1) Comparison of Heat Transfer Characteristics under Constant Heat Flux from Different Heat Sources" (in Japanese). *Nihon Kasei Gakkai shi* 55:9 (2004), pp. 707–14.

# How Fish Changes Under the Effects of Heat

Since ancient times, people in Japan have made abundant use of the many species of fish that live in the seas surrounding the islands. Although vegetables and meat are also prepared by grilling, fish has always been the mainstay of *yakimono* dishes. In this section, we consider the different qualities of fish flesh and how it changes under the effects of heat.

## Different Uses for Different Fish

The flesh of fish varies considerably, from some kinds that have little or no characteristic quality to others that have very distinctive qualities. For example, red tilefish (*aka amadai*) caught in the Sea of Japan normally has no particularly distinctive or strong flavor and is regarded as suitable for use in a wide variety of recipes. The flesh does not become tough when cooked, and divides easily along the lines of the fibers. Yellowtail (*buri*) tends to be fatty and have a distinctive flavor. The fat in this species is concentrated in the belly, so that the dorsal fillet (*semi*) contains little fat and tends to dry out easily when cooked. This fish is generally grilled by the *teriyaki* or other method that masks the fishy smell. Different species of fish live in different areas of the sea and at different depths; they have naturally evolved to adapt to their various habitats, differences that are reflected in the character of the flesh and the amounts of fat they typically carry.

At the same time, individual specimens of the same species can vary considerably in flavor and other qualities, both as a result of environmental factors such as water temperature and availability of food—and whether the fish is caught before or after spawning—and because of the impact of transportation and handling after being caught. For example, sea bass (*suzuki*) caught in European waters often has a tender and fatty quality similar to Japanese *sawara* mackerel. It is easily cut with a knife and fork, absorbs sauce readily, and in general offers a texture quite different from that of Japanese sea bass. As this suggests, when cooking fish, it is important to consider not just the species, but the characteristics of the specimen at hand, when deciding how best to prepare and cook the fish.

## Toughness, Consistency, and Collagen

Is there any connection between the texture of a fish when raw and the consistency of the same fish when cooked? One study investigated this question by comparing five species of fish both raw and after heating to 158°F (70°C), to examine the relationship between the amount of collagen and texture of the flesh. The five species studied were marbled flounder (*makogarei*), rockfish/thornyhead (*kichiji*), flying fish (*tobiuo*), bonito (*katsuo*), and Japanese horse mackerel (*maaji*). The comparison showed that, when raw, the species ranked from toughest to least tough, as follows: *makogarei*, *kichiji*, *tobiuo*, *katsuo*, *maaji*. However, when the fish were cooked, this order was reversed. Fish that are tough when raw become tender when cooked, while species that are tender when raw tend to become tougher when exposed to heat.

When the amount of collagen in the fish was measured, it was found that species that were relatively tough when raw (*makogarei*, *kichiji*) had higher total amounts of collagen, while species that were tender when raw (*katsuo*, *maaji*) contained smaller amounts. The analysis also showed that the percentage of soluble collagen at 68°F (20°C) was higher for species with soft flesh and lower for species with firmer flesh.

However, other studies have shown that the total amount of collagen and the amount of soluble collagen at 158°F (70°C) does not have a major impact on the toughness of fish when cooked. This suggests that while connective tissue made up of collagen and other substances has an impact on the texture of fish when raw, other factors are more important in determining the mouthfeel and consistency of cooked fish, including types of proteins and the volume of fat in the fish.

Therefore, although there is a tendency for collagen-rich species (such as flounder/*hirame*) to be tough when raw and softer when cooked, and for species low in collagen (such as bonito/*katsuo*) to be soft when raw and tougher when cooked, it is important to consider other factors besides collagen when deciding how best to prepare a fish.

## Choosing a Cooking Method

In previous times, when preparing fish that spoiled quickly, it was common practice to marinate the fish in *yuan-ji* or a similar marinade to impart the aroma of shoyu to the fish before grilling. For example, butterfish (*managatsuo*) was known to spoil quickly. The fish was only sold in the winter months, and was normally marinated in *yuan-ji* before grilling. One of the main reasons for this practice of using the flavors and aromas of shoyu and miso was to minimize any unpleasant fishy or "off" smells as the fish lost freshness.

Today, of course, modern refrigeration and freezing and the development of a cooled logistics and transportation network (the so-called cold chain) make fresh fish easy to obtain year-round more or less anywhere in Japan. Butterfish, for example, can now be served as sashimi or as *shio-yaki* (i.e., without marinating). While specific techniques and cooking methods have been handed down in modern Japanese *yakimono* cuisine for specific species of fish, dishes have also been created that freely combine fish and cooking techniques, and these innovations have been made possible by the development of techniques for keeping ingredients fresh.

THE BASICS OF GRILLING   39

# Hygiene in Preparing and Cooking *Yakimono*

The causes of food poisoning are diverse, including bacteria, viruses, chemicals, parasites, and natural toxins. Heat kills most microbes, and there is a tendency to assume that there is no risk as long as food is properly heated. In fact, the conditions required to kill microbes vary considerably depending on the type; furthermore, many chemicals and natural toxins are not broken down or rendered inactive by heat alone. In order to accurately determine the hygienic condition of the ingredients to be used and plan suitable cooking methods, here we introduce definitions and classifications of some of the most important causes of food poisoning, and discuss steps that can be taken to prevent them.

Amendments to Japanese law now require restaurants and other premises serving food to adopt international standards on hazard analysis and critical control points (HACCP). While improvements are being made in risk management regarding food poisoning, this section describes the steps that should be practiced throughout the procurement and food preparation processes.

## What is food poisoning?

Food poisoning is an illness caused by toxins and other chemicals produced by harmful microbes. These can enter the body directly in food or drink, via contaminated containers, packaging, and cooking equipment, or through food handling, or other physical contact. Common acute gastrointestinal symptoms include vomiting, stomach pain, and diarrhea. Depending on the causative substance, more serious symptoms may result, including loss of consciousness and difficulty breathing.

Restaurants are implicated in around 50 percent of all cases of food poisoning. It is essential that everyone who handles food understands the toxic substances, main causes, and sources of infection that can lead to food poisoning, and the measures that must be taken to avoid them. Since chefs working in the *yakiba* handle food that is in a state generally requiring heating before it can be eaten safely, we have included a page at the back of the book that covers the particular risks involved in preparing *yakimono* and the steps that must be taken to minimize them. (See "Causes and Prevention of Food Poisoning," p. 210.)

## Principles for a safe and healthy kitchen

The three principles for a safe and healthy kitchen are: safe handling of food, keeping harmful microbes at bay, and effective cleaning and disinfecting. Since noroviruses and other infections can multiply in the guts of an infected person and spread among kitchen staff, it is also vital to take measures to prevent microbes from being brought into spaces where food is handled.

Three types of measures are essential. These relate to personal hygiene, food hygiene, and kitchen hygiene, as shown in the figure on the opposite page. Most microbes can be killed by heating food to a core temperature of 167°F (75°C) for at least 1 minute. After heating, the food must be kept at an appropriate temperature to prevent any microbes from multiplying, and kitchen workers must disinfect all surfaces and utensils thoroughly and wash their hands regularly to prevent passing on germs that might spread contamination.

## Temperature control in food hygiene and changes in proteins

In Japan, the recommendation is to heat meat and fish to a core temperature of 167°F (75°C) for at least 1 minute to kill bacteria and parasites. This temperature will eradicate enterohemorrhagic *E. coli*. On the other hand, animal proteins start to undergo important changes at temperatures substantially lower than this. Muscle fibers in fish start to coagulate at around 120°F (50°C) and those in meat at around 140°F (60°C; see figure at bottom right). A chef may decide to preserve the consistency and mouthfeel of the uncooked ingredients by not heating the food to 167°F (75°C). In this case, it is absolutely vital to observe strict standards of hygiene throughout the supply process and in the kitchen.

It is believed that the antibacterial effects of heating to 167°F (75°C) for 1 minute can also be obtained by heating to 158°F (70°C) for 3 minutes, to 156°F (69°C) for 4 minutes, to 154°F (68°C) for 5 minutes, to 153°F (67°C) for 8 minutes, to 151°F (66°C) for 11 minutes, or to 149°F (65°C) for 15 minutes.

## The Principles of Preventing Food Poisoning: Personal Hygiene, Food Hygiene, Kitchen Hygiene

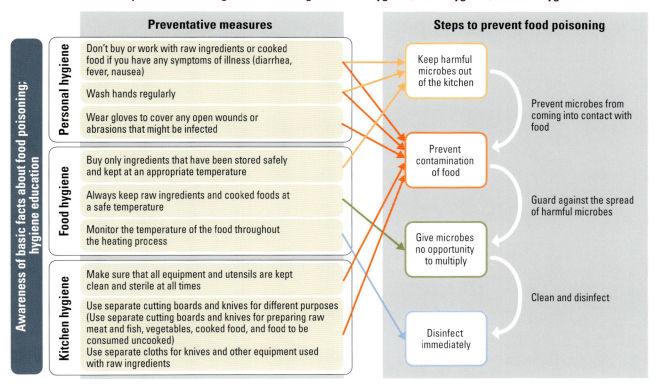

## Temperatures Needed to Kill Microbes, and Changes in Proteins

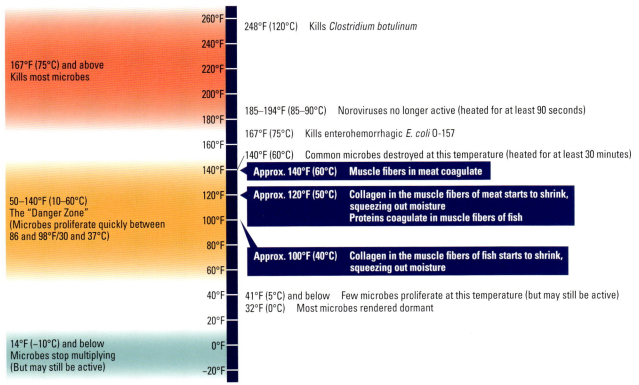

THE BASICS OF GRILLING  41

Chapter 3

# Basic Types of *Yakimono*

This chapter introduces a number of typical *yakimono* dishes with practical recipes. As well as using detailed measurements and photographs to illustrate the processes that chefs use to prepare each dish, it also includes scientific explanations of what is happening during cooking. This book divides *yakimono* into four categories: *yuan-yaki*, *shio-yaki*, *tare-yaki*, and *furishio-yaki* (see also p. 15).

### Yuan-yaki

# Yuan Style Butterfish

*Managatsuo no Yuan-yaki*

Butterfish (*managatsuo*) is found in warm and tropical waters in the East China Sea, the Indian Ocean, and the Western Pacific. In Japan, the fish is in season from early to mid-summer, when its fat reserves offer a rich flavor.

In this recipe, the fish is salted before it is immersed in a *yuan-ji* marinade. This not only makes the finished fish more succulent, but also imparts the flavors and aromas of the shoyu contained in the marinade. Care should be taken when grilling, since marinating increases the risk of charring and burning.

SAMPLE CUT: Width: 6.3 cm (2½ in.)
Length: 20.5 cm (8⅛ in.)
Thickness: 2.5 cm (1 in.)
WEIGHT: 80.0 g (2.8 oz.)

*Serves 3*

3 portions butterfish (*managatsuo*)
Salt, as needed
Mirin, as needed

*Yuan-ji* marinade

 360 ml (12.2 fl. oz.) de-alcoholized sake
 90 ml (3 fl. oz.) mirin
 36 ml (2½ Tbsp.) *koikuchi* shoyu
 18 ml (1¼ Tbsp.) *usukuchi* shoyu
 15 g (0.5 oz.) ripe yellow yuzu (*kiyuzu*), sliced into thin rounds

Mix to combine (no heating required)

Garnishes

 yuzu zest, as needed
 3 slices syrup-simmered yuzu rind (*amigasa-yuzu*; see p. 194)

**1** Clean and fillet a butterfish in the *sanmai-oroshi* style and place a cleaned fillet with the tail to the left, skin side down.

**2** Holding the knife diagonally to the fish, slice the fillet into portions. The skin side will be served face up (and grilled first).

**3** Sprinkle the salt (0.5% by weight) on both sides of the fillet and let stand for 2 hours.

**4** Transfer the fish to the marinade and leave for 8 hours.

**5** Pat each portion dry and thread on three skewers, folding both ends over using the double-tuck (*ryozuma-ori*) technique (see p. 202).

**6** Grill as shown on the following page.

**7** Transfer to a serving dish and sprinkle with yuzu zest. Garnish with the *amigasa-yuzu*.

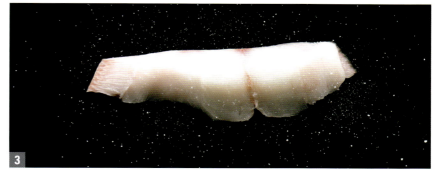

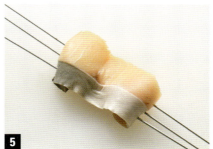

For this recipe, the fish is first salted and left for two hours, then immersed in a *yuan-ji* marinade for eight hours. This has two purposes: It allows the flavors of the marinade to be absorbed thoroughly, and also allows the fish to be grilled without becoming dry. As the salt seeps into the fish, it dissolves salt-soluble proteins and breaks down muscle cell membranes. This allows the marinade to penetrate deep into the flesh. The marinade contains sugar from the mirin as well as salt from the shoyu, so the moisture retention of the muscle fibers is higher than would be the case if salt alone were used in the preparation. Since moisture retention remains high even after exposure to heat, the muscle fibers do not fall apart when the fish is cooked.

The photographs show how the color of the shoyu in the marinade has spread evenly through the fish that was salted and then marinated. The piece that was salted and then marinated in salt water with the same salinity as the *yuan-ji* marinade has taken on a shiny luster; this shows that the cell membranes of the muscle fibers have broken down and the salt-soluble proteins in the flesh have dissolved. The *yuan-ji* marinade produces the same effect, though this is less perceptible because of the color of the marinade. The surface of the piece that was marinated without being salted first has darkened, but since the large pigmentation molecules in the shoyu are not absorbed uniformly by the fish, the color is uneven, as seen in the photograph.

BASIC TYPES OF *YAKIMONO*   45

46 BASIC TYPES OF YAKIMONO

# Effects of Salting before Immersion in the *Yuan-ji* Marinade

If the fish is cooked without being salted or marinated, thin strands of muscle fiber remain attached when the flesh is cut apart, as shown in the photograph. These make the fish seem stringy when eaten. Salting and then marinating the fish causes the muscle fibers to gelatinize and hold together with uniform consistency, so that the fish breaks cleanly when divided with chopsticks. This shows how salting helps retain moisture. The same effect is obtained in the example where the salted fish is immersed in a salt water solution with the same salinity as the *yuan-ji* marinade. If the fish is immersed in the marinade only, without preliminary salting, the marinade does not penetrate into the center of the flesh, and thin strands of muscle fiber cling to each other, as seen in the photograph.

BASIC TYPES OF *YAKIMONO*  47

### Yuan-yaki
# Grilled Salmon in Miso Marinade
*Masu no Miso Yuan-yaki*

Like other salmonid species, *masu* salmon or *masu* trout (*sakura-masu*) are anadromous: Born in rivers, they spend much of their life at sea before returning to rivers to spawn. (Japan is also home to a landlocked subspecies known as *yamame*, which spends its entire life cycle in the freshwaters of lakes and rivers.) The name *sakura-masu* comes from the fact that the spawning runs coincide with the cherry blossom season. The fish is widely eaten from winter into spring, before the last of the cold weather comes to an end.

In this recipe, the fish is marinated in a white miso *yuan-ji* marinade long enough to penetrate the fish completely. It is then grilled over charcoal at a distance from the heat to avoid scorching.

SAMPLE CUT: Width: 5.1 cm (2 in.)
Length: 14.2 cm (5⅝ in.)
Thickness: 1.3 cm (½ in.)
WEIGHT: 55.0 g (1.9 oz.)

### Serves 5

5 portions salmon (*sakura-masu*)

Mirin, as needed

Miso *yuan-ji* marinade

- 1 kg (35.3 oz.) unstrained white miso (*shirotsubu miso*)
- 1400 ml (47.3 fl. oz.) de-alcoholized sake
- 800 ml (27.1 fl. oz.) mirin
- 300 ml (10.1 fl. oz.) *koikuchi* shoyu
- 300 ml (10.1 fl. oz.) *usukuchi* shoyu
- Green or yellow yuzu, sliced into thin rounds. Approx. 3 slices per 100 ml (3.4 fl. oz.) of marinade

Mix to combine (no heating required)

Serving side of fish after skewering

Reverse side

**1** Clean and fillet a *sakura-masu* salmon in the *sanmai-oroshi* style. Remove the skin and lay the fillet flesh side up on the work surface.

**2** Holding the knife diagonally to the fish, cut the fillet into portions. The skin side has an unappealing appearance once the skin has been removed, so the flesh side should be served face up.

**3** Immerse the fish in the marinade and allow to soak, refrigerated, for two days.

**4** Remove the fish from the marinade. Pat each portion dry and thread onto two skewers using the wave-skewering (*uneri-gushi*) technique (see pp. 200–201), from the belly to the dorsal side.

**5** Grill as shown on the following page.

**6** Transfer to a large dish and arrange the salmon in layers toward the center of the dish. The topmost portion should be placed flesh side up to present an attractive appearance.

---

To allow the flavor of the miso *yuan-ji* to fully penetrate the flesh, the fish must be marinated for a long time. However, if the marinade is too salty, it will make the fish too salty. For this reason, in this recipe the fillets are marinated for two days in a marinade with around 4 percent salinity. The salt, alcohol, and sugar in the marinade increase moisture retention. In addition, the proteolytic enzymes in the miso break down proteins over time, giving the finished dish a soft texture and strong umami flavors. The marinated portions scorch easily, so it is important to heat the fish slowly and gently by grilling as far away from the heat source as possible.

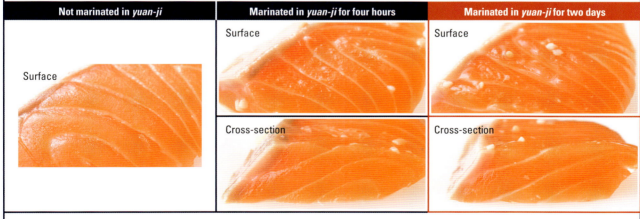

As miso consists of various particles dispersed in a substance in a colloidal state, it is slow to penetrate deep into the fish even after extended marinating. Compared to the photographs taken after four hours, the ones taken after marinating for two days show a greater luster on both the surface and the cross-section of the fish.

BASIC TYPES OF *YAKIMONO*

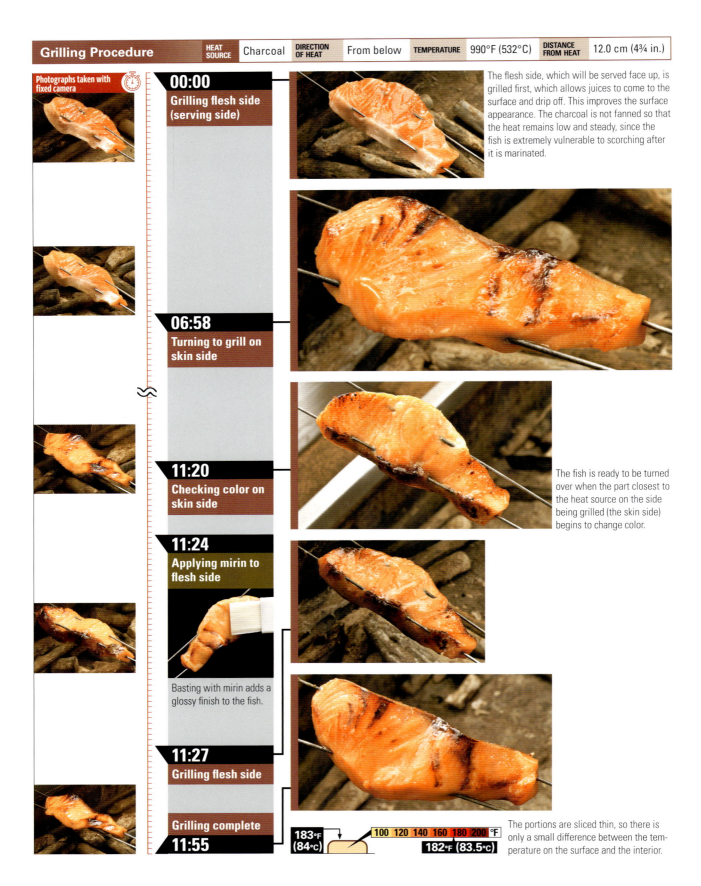

50  BASIC TYPES OF YAKIMONO

# Effects of Different Marinating Times

After cooking, white patches appear on the surface of the fish that was not marinated. This is caused by seepage of protein-containing juices during the grilling process; these proteins congeal on the surface of the flesh. In the photograph showing the flesh broken apart after cooking, thin strands of muscle fibers remain, making the fish stringy and tough when consumed.

After four hours of marinating, the *yuan-ji* marinade has still not been fully absorbed into the center of the flesh, and thin strands of fibers remain after cooking. After two days in the marinade, the muscle fibers have become salt-soluble proteins and reached a nearly uniform state, so that the cooked fish breaks cleanly when it is divided with chopsticks. This shows that the fish has good moisture retention.

Heating causes the fish to release protein-containing juices that form white spots on the surface.

BASIC TYPES OF *YAKIMONO*　51

### Yuan-yaki

# Grilled Marinated Barracuda
*Kamasu no Tsuke-yaki*

The barracuda (*kamasu*) belongs to *Sphyraenidae*, a genus with many known varieties. The one most commonly consumed in Japan is *aka-kamasu* ("red" *kamasu*, or *Sphyraena pinguis*). This species, found in the coastal waters of southern Japan as well as in the South China Sea, Africa, Australia, Polynesia, and Hawaiʻi, feeds on small fish and crustaceans. Barracuda has delicate white flesh that is light in flavor, and is in season twice a year, in spring and autumn. It is particularly prized in the autumn months, when it has built up reserves of fat.

Barracuda flesh is thin and soft. This means that it readily absorbs the *yuan-ji* marinade and that heat penetrates easily during cooking. These qualities require a shorter marinating time and the double-tuck skewering technique to protect the thinnest parts of the fillets from direct heat.

SAMPLE CUT: Width: 5.7 cm (2¼ in.)
Length: 23.0 cm (9 in.)
Thickness: 1.0 cm (⅜ in.)
WEIGHT: 82.7 g (2.9 oz.)

*Serves 3*

3 portions barracuda (*kamasu*)
Salt, as needed

Marinade and basting sauce
| 450 ml (15.2 fl. oz.) *koikuchi* shoyu
| 450 ml (15.2 fl. oz.) sake
| 270 ml (9.1 fl. oz.) de-alcoholized mirin

Mix to combine (no heating required)

1. Clean and fillet barracuda in the *sanmai-oroshi* style. Lay the fillets on the work surface flesh side down. Sprinkle the skin side with salt (2% by weight) and let stand for 10 minutes.
2. Place the fillets so that the head is to the left and the skin side is up. Cut shallow incisions into the skin at 2-mm (1/16 in.) intervals. The skin side will be served face up.
3. Transfer the fillets to the marinade and let stand for 15 minutes.

4. Remove the fillets from the marinade, pat dry, and thread each fillet onto two skewers, curling both head and tail ends toward the center in the double-tuck (*ryozuma-ori*) technique (see p. 202).

5. **Grill as shown on the following pages.**
6. Arrange the grilled fish on a serving dish.

In this recipe, allowing salt to penetrate the skin first and then marinating for a short time in a marinade with approximately 6 percent salt makes it easier for the fish to absorb the flavors of the shoyu and other seasonings. The double-tuck skewering technique makes the grilled portion thicker and less likely to overheat. To avoid scorching and ensure that the heat reaches the center, the fish is grilled slowly at a substantial distance from the heat.

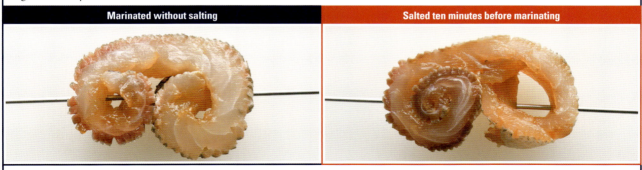

| Marinated without salting | Salted ten minutes before marinating |

The fillet that was salted before marinating has a glossy appearance, and the color of the shoyu in the marinade has penetrated evenly to the center of the fish.

BASIC TYPES OF *YAKIMONO*

54 BASIC TYPES OF YAKIMONO

The color of the skin side (left) and flesh side just before they are basted for the second time. This should be timed so that the outside of the fillet takes on color without scorching.

The color when the grilling is complete. The skin looks crisp and juices bubble from the incisions made in the skin before cooking.

## Effects of Salting before Marinating

In the fillet that was marinated without being salted first, thin muscle fibers still remain, as can be seen in the photograph showing the fish broken apart after grilling. This makes the final product stringy. If the fish is salted before being placed in the marinade, the muscle fibers gelatinize and the flesh "melts," taking on an almost perfectly even appearance, so that it breaks easily when separated with chopsticks. This shows that the flesh is still moist and has not dried out.

BASIC TYPES OF *YAKIMONO* 55

### Yuan-yaki
# Miso-Marinated Grilled Beltfish
*Tachiuo no Misozuke-yaki*

Silver beltfish or largehead hairtail (*tachiuo*; *Trichiurus lepturus*) is a widely distributed species whose range stretches from Japanese waters to the Atlantic, Australia, and Africa. The flesh has a delicate flavor balanced by a subtle fatty oiliness. As well as being used in thin-cut sashimi, the fish is grilled in a variety of ways, including teriyaki and *shio-yaki*, and is used in simmered dishes.

*Misozuke-yaki*, a method of cooking that has been used since ancient times, is distinguished by its use of a marinade based on miso, which contains live yeasts. This recipe calls for white miso from Kyoto, thinned slightly with liquid seasonings. Because the marinade scorches extremely easily, the fish should be grilled over low heat.

SAMPLE CUT: Width: 8.4 cm (3¼ in.)
Length: 11.3 cm (4½ in.)
Thickness: 1.2 cm (½ in.)
WEIGHT: 69.0 g (2.4 oz.)

*Serves 3*

3 portions silver beltfish (*tachiuo*)
Sake, as needed
Mirin, as needed

Miso marinade
- 1 kg (35.3 oz.) unstrained white miso (*shirotsubu miso*)
- 300 ml (10.1 fl. oz.) seasoning liquid (below)
- 150 ml (5.1 fl. oz.) de-alcoholized sake
- 12.5 g (0.4 oz.) sugar

Seasoning liquid
- 360 ml (12.2 fl. oz.) de-alcoholized sake
- 90 ml (3 fl. oz.) mirin
- 36 ml (2½ Tbsp.) *koikuchi* shoyu
- 18 ml (1¼ Tbsp.) *usukuchi* shoyu

Mix to combine (no heating required)

Garnishes
- *Shimeji* mushrooms, simmered *tosa-ni* style (*shimeji no tosa-ni*; see p. 194)
- 1 chrysanthemum leaf

**1** Clean and fillet silver beltfish in the *sanmai-oroshi* style and cut into portions. Sprinkle salt (0.5% by weight) on both sides of the fish and let stand for 2 hours. (The quantity of salt used is relatively small because of the saltiness of the miso marinade.)

**2** Transfer the fish to the miso marinade and allow to soak, refrigerated, for 8 hours.

**3** Remove the fish from the miso marinade and rinse off any remaining marinade with a mixture of equal parts water and sake.

**4** Score the skin to make the fish easier to eat.

The skin is scored on the dorsal and belly sides separately, taking care not to cut too deeply into the flesh on the dorsal side.

**5** The flesh side will be served face up. Thread each portion onto three skewers using the single-tuck (*katazuma-ori*) technique (see p. 202). Because the portions are narrow, skewer in the head-to-tail direction for a pleasing shape.

**6** Grill as shown on the following pages.

**7** Transfer the fish to a serving dish and serve with the chrysanthemum leaf and *shimeji* mushrooms at the front of the dish.

---

The miso marinade contains miso, sake, mirin, shoyu, and sugar. Miso contains salt, glutamic acid, and other umami compounds, as well as proteolytic enzymes (enzymes that break down proteins). The main characteristic of this recipe compared to a *yuan-ji* marinade is the presence of proteolytic enzymes from the miso. Both the sugar and the proteolytic enzymes have large molecules, so they are not easily absorbed into the flesh. Salting the fish before marinating breaks down the cell membranes of the muscle cells and makes it easier for the sugars and enzymes to reach the center of the fish.

| Cross-section of flesh marinated without salting | Cross-section of flesh marinated after salting |
|---|---|

These photographs show clearly the greater transparency in the fillet that was salted before marinating, compared to the fillet that was marinated without being salted first. The salt allows the sugar and proteolytic enzymes in the miso marinade to be absorbed by the fish, breaking down the proteins in the muscle fibers so that the flesh is softer and more transparent.

BASIC TYPES OF *YAKIMONO*   57

58　BASIC TYPES OF *YAKIMONO*

Finish by grilling just long enough to dry out the mirin.

The color on the flesh side at the end of cooking. Application of mirin gives the fish a glossy finish.

## Effects of Salting before Immersion in the Miso Marinade

Salting the fish before marinating in the miso makes it easier for the salts and proteolytic enzymes in the miso to penetrate the fish fully and break down the proteins in the muscle fibers. In addition, the salt in the shoyu works to dissolve salt-soluble proteins; the moisture-retaining effect of the mirin and sugar and the effect of the proteolytic enzymes in the miso are all active within the fish. As a result, the muscle fibers still retain moisture when they dissolve, and the proteins in the muscle fibers still retain moisture even after grilling, contributing to a soft and smooth mouthfeel and texture when eaten. The flesh on the fish that was salted before marinating breaks apart smoothly and easily when separated with chopsticks. The fish should be served hot, since it can become tough when it cools.

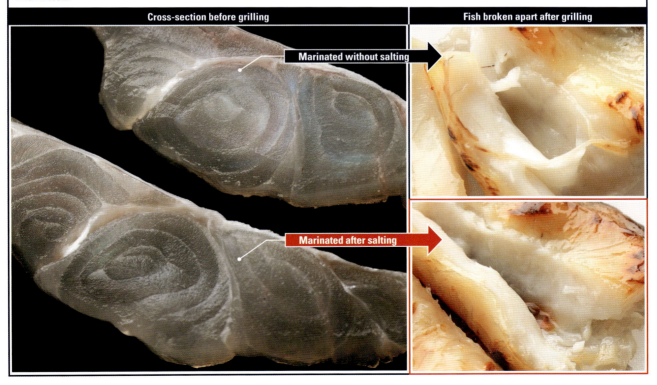

BASIC TYPES OF *YAKIMONO* 59

## Shio-yaki

# Salted and Grilled Tilefish
*Guji no Shio-yaki*

Tilefish (*amadai*) lives mostly on the continental shelf of the Indian and Pacific Oceans and the East China Sea. In Japan, the species is found in areas from central Honshu southward. A white fish with a delicious flavor, tilefish—also known affectionately as *guji*, particularly in the Kansai area—is one of the most sought-after and cherished fish in Japanese cuisine. The flesh has a characteristic sweetness and a mild flavor, with a high moisture content, and its scales are soft enough to be eaten.

In this recipe, the fish is first generously salted and left for an hour. It is then grilled slowly at a distance from the heat source, which allows the heat to penetrate the skin and scales. Partway through grilling, the skin is removed, scales and all, and deep-fried as the rest of the fish finishes cooking. One of the pleasures of this dish is the contrast between the textures of the thick, juicy flesh and the crispy skin.

SAMPLE CUT: Width: 5.2 cm (2 in.)
Length: 12.3 cm (4⅞ in.)
Thickness: 2.3 cm (⅞ in.)
WEIGHT: 75.0 g (2.6 oz.)

Portion after salting

*Serves 1*

1 portion tilefish (*amadai*)
Taihaku (untoasted) sesame oil, as needed
Salt, as needed
Sake, as needed

Garnishes
  2-cm (¾ in.) piece pickled turnip, cut "chrysanthemum" style (*kikka-kabura*; see p. 194)
  *Umeboshi* paste, as needed
  1 chrysanthemum leaf

**1** Without descaling, fillet the tilefish into two (*nimai-oroshi*) using the butterfly-cut (*sebiraki*) technique. Remove the spine and central bones and select one fillet. Sprinkle the salt (3% by weight) on both sides of the fillet, salting more heavily where the flesh is thicker, and more lightly where it is thin. Let stand for 1 hour at room temperature.

**2** Pat the fillet dry and place skin side down with the head facing left. Cut a portion, setting the knife vertically to the flesh. (Cutting vertically makes it easier to remove the skin and scales.) The fish will be served skin side up.

**3** Insert the knife between the flesh and skin on the belly side and separate approximately 3 cm (1⅛ in.) of skin from the flesh. Cut off the piece of skin.

**4** Thread the fish onto three skewers, folding the skinless flesh over using the single-tuck (*katazuma-ori*) technique (see p. 202). In inserting the skewers, gather the flesh from the belly to the dorsal side so as to give the piece a rounded shape.

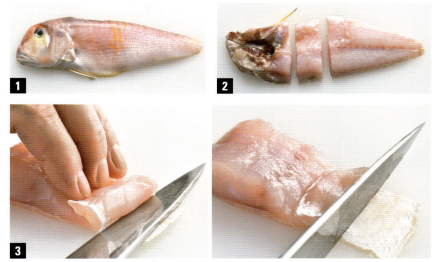

Cutting the skin from the belly side. The belly flesh will be tucked over when the fish is threaded on skewers.

Belly skin removed

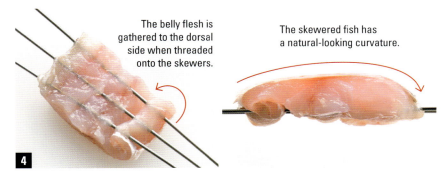

The belly flesh is gathered to the dorsal side when threaded onto the skewers.

The skewered fish has a natural-looking curvature.

**5** Grill as shown on the following pages.

**6** Transfer the grilled fish to a serving dish, skin side up, and top with the fried skin. Place the *kikka-kabura* on the chrysanthemum leaf and top with a dot of *umeboshi* paste. Serve the fish with the garnish in front.

> Tilefish is unusual in that its skin can be eaten with the scales still on. Removing the skin partway through the grilling process and deep-frying it removes the moisture from the scales and induces the Maillard reaction, imparting rich aromas and a crunchy texture. One of the attractive qualities of tilefish is its moist, soft flesh. The fish is salted for an hour before grilling to minimize loss of juiciness.

BASIC TYPES OF *YAKIMONO*   61

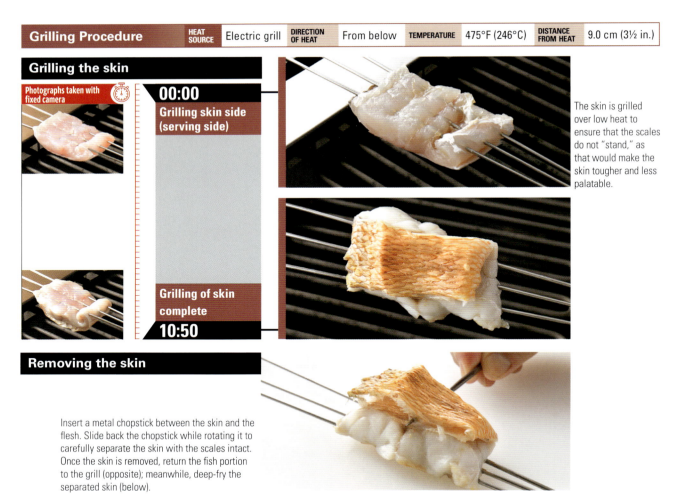

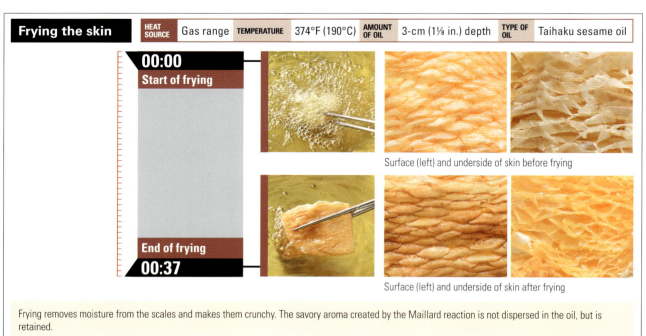

62  BASIC TYPES OF *YAKIMONO*

## Cooking the flesh

| HEAT SOURCE | Electric grill | DIRECTION OF HEAT | From below | TEMPERATURE | 639°F (337°C) | DISTANCE FROM HEAT | 9.0 cm (3½ in.) |

**11:58** Grilling flesh side

The flesh side is grilled over a stronger heat.

**17:01** Checking color on flesh side / Spritzing flesh side with sake

Spritzing the flesh side with sake helps a thin film to form on the surface, improving flavor. Fatty fish may produce enough oil during the cooking process to form this thin film on its own, in which case spritzing may be omitted.

**17:04** Grilling flesh side

**17:55** Checking color on flesh side / Spritzing skin side with sake

A thin film forms on the surface, and a faint color has started to appear.

After the flesh side is grilled, spritz sake onto the skin side. This is to remove any smell on the skin side.

**18:10** Grilling skin side

**Grilling complete 18:37**

The skin side is done when it starts to take on a very slight coloring.

### Comparison of Color (Skin Side)

Well-grilled fillet

✕

Over-grilled fillet

### Comparison of Color (Flesh Side)

Well-grilled fillet

✕

Over-grilled fillet

The benefits of proper salting will be limited if the fish is over-grilled. Since it is not possible to see the interior of the fish while grilling, a decision on "doneness" must be made based on the surface coloring. Salting means that relatively little juice will be produced; therefore, although the surface will not scorch easily, if the fish is over-grilled, as shown in the photograph here, it will be dry and unappetizing at the center.

BASIC TYPES OF *YAKIMONO*  63

# Grilled Tilefish Flavored with Sake
*Guji no Saka-yaki*

Tilefish (*amadai/guji*) is characterized by the soft, moist texture of its flesh. In *guji no saka-yaki*, the fish is salted and then left for one or two days so that the salt can be absorbed completely. The fish is then grilled slowly at a distance from the heat source, and is spritzed with sake partway through the long cooking process. Grilling the fish in this way produces a complex flavor in which the sweetness of the succulent flesh and the rich aromas of the skin combine with hints of dried food (*himono*) flavors.

SAMPLE CUT: Width: 5.2 cm (2 in.)
Length: 10.5 cm (4⅛ in.)
Thickness: 1.7 cm (⅝ in.)
WEIGHT: 74.0 g (2.6 oz.)

### Serves 1

1 portion tilefish (*amadai*)
Salt, as needed
Sake, as needed

**3**

1. Clean and fillet a tilefish in the *sanmai-oroshi* style. Sprinkle salt (1.3% by weight) on one fillet and allow it to penetrate for one or two days, refrigerated. Salt thicker or oilier flesh more heavily.

2. Pat the fillet dry. Set the knife vertically to the fish and cut a portion of the desired size. The skin side will be served face up.

3. Thread the fish onto two skewers with the flat-skewering (*hira-gushi*) technique (see p. 198). (Somewhat thicker skewers should be used, since tilefish has soft but heavy flesh.)

4. Grill as shown on the following pages.

5. Transfer the grilled tilefish to a serving dish.

---

To preserve the juicy, tender texture characteristic of tilefish, salt is allowed to penetrate the fish fully, dissolving the salt-soluble proteins and increasing moisture retention. Grilling slowly over distant heat, as if drying the fish, induces a weak Maillard reaction, imparting a concentrated flavor similar to that of dried foods (*himono*). Spritzing with sake during the slow cooking process lowers the temperature and replaces lost moisture while allowing the heat to penetrate the interior of the fish. It also prevents an excessive Maillard reaction on the surface.

| Not salted | Salt has penetrated fully |
|---|---|

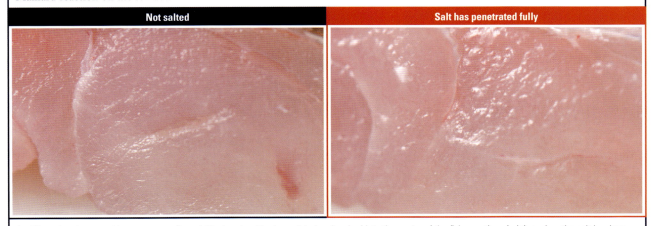

As this recipe aims to achieve an unusually moist texture by allowing salt to be absorbed into the center of the fish over time, judging when the salt has been sufficiently absorbed is an important part of getting this recipe right. The salt should be allowed to penetrate until the fish looks as shown in the photograph: The muscle fibers take on a sheen, and the flesh becomes thick and plump to the touch.

BASIC TYPES OF *YAKIMONO* 65

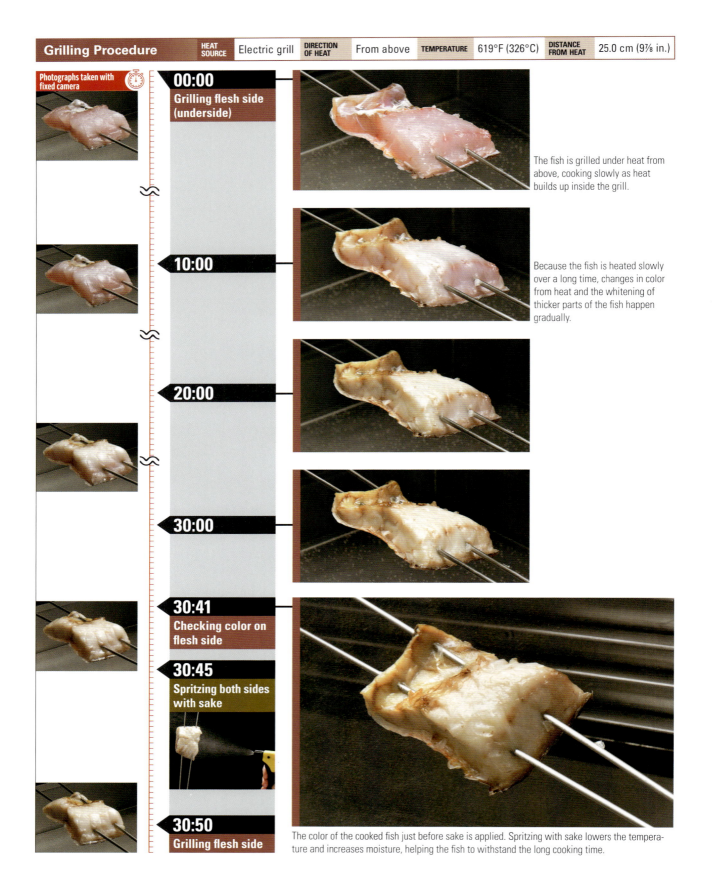

66  BASIC TYPES OF *YAKIMONO*

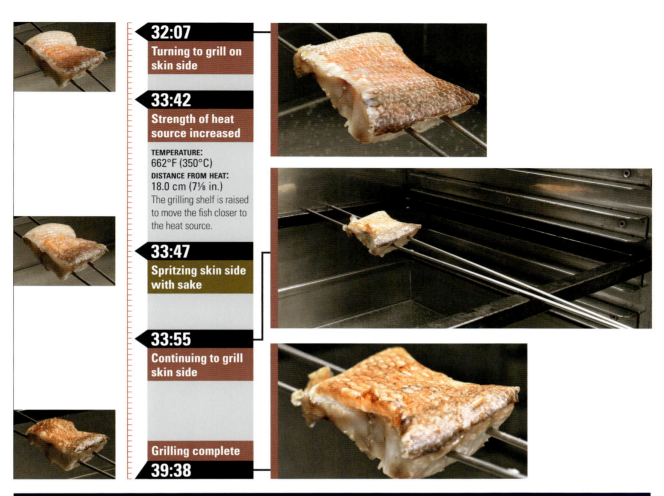

**32:07** Turning to grill on skin side

**33:42** Strength of heat source increased

TEMPERATURE:
662°F (350°C)
DISTANCE FROM HEAT:
18.0 cm (7⅛ in.)
The grilling shelf is raised to move the fish closer to the heat source.

**33:47** Spritzing skin side with sake

**33:55** Continuing to grill skin side

Grilling complete
**39:38**

## Difference in End Result Due to Salt Penetration

Allowing the tilefish to absorb the salt over one to two days to give it a moist, tender texture and then grilling the fish slowly produces results that can only be achieved by this method of cooking. Fish that is not salted retains its moisture but is stringy, and the flesh is too soft, as shown in the photographs on the upper row below. Allowing salt to penetrate fully eliminates the stringiness and imparts a firm but moist texture.

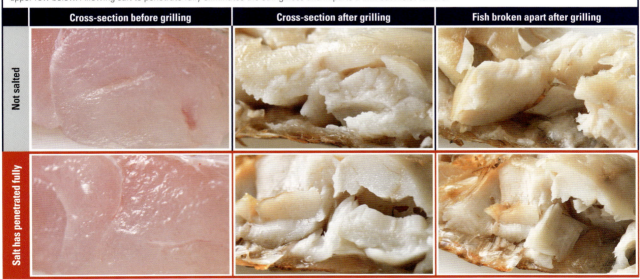

|  | Cross-section before grilling | Cross-section after grilling | Fish broken apart after grilling |
|---|---|---|---|
| Not salted | | | |
| Salt has penetrated fully | | | |

BASIC TYPES OF *YAKIMONO*  67

### Shio-yaki
# Overnight-Dried Whiting
*Kisu no Ichiya-boshi*

Japanese whiting (*kisu, Sillago japonica*) lives in sandy coastal areas of the Sea of Japan, the East China Sea, and the South China Sea, feeding on the small creatures that burrow into the sand. The flesh is characterized by a light, delicate flavor low in fat, and has been esteemed in Japan since ancient times. Historical records show that the fish was presented at court in the eighth century, during the Nara period. *Ichiya-boshi* (overnight drying), also known as *kaza-boshi*, or "wind-drying," is a method of drying in which fish are left out at night in a well-ventilated place. It therefore differs from *tenpi-boshi* (daytime drying), in which fish are exposed to sunlight. More moisture remains in the fish with this method, producing a dried fish less prone to lipid oxidization.

To prevent the fish from becoming too dry when cooked, the whiting is immersed in salt water before drying, and the moisture is given a boost by spritzing with sake before grilling. The fish is grilled carefully to bring out the distinctive rich aroma of overnight-dried fish and to preserve the texture so that the fish breaks cleanly when divided with chopsticks.

BASIC TYPES OF *YAKIMONO*    69

Fillet before drying  |  Fillet after drying for approximately two hours

**SAMPLE CUT:** Length: 12.5 cm (4⅞ in.)
Width: 3.5 cm (1⅜ in.)
Thickness: 0.7 cm (¼ in.)
**WEIGHT:** 16.0 g (0.6 oz.)

### Serves 3

3 portions Japanese whiting (*kisu*)
Salt, as needed
Sake, as needed

Garnishes

    Early harvested lotus root with crushed edamame beans (*shin-renkon no zunda-ae*; see p. 194), as needed
    Vinegar-pickled Moriguchi radish (*Moriguchi daikon no su-zuke*; see p. 195), as needed
    2 *matsuba* (pine needles)
    2 green maple leaves
    1 chrysanthemum leaf

1. Clean and fillet in the *sanmai-oroshi* style. Place the fillets in salt water (3% salinity) and leave for 1 hour.
2. Pat dry and skewer through tail end of the fillet. Leave to dry for 2 hours at night in a well-ventilated place. (If this is not possible, place between dehydrating sheets for an hour to adjust the dryness.)
3. Before grilling, spritz sake over the fish. Because dried fish is very low in moisture, the temperature rises rapidly during grilling, making the flesh susceptible to scorching. Boosting the moisture content lowers the temperature and prevents scorching.
4. Grill as shown on the following page.
5. Place the chrysanthemum leaf on a serving dish and arrange the whiting on top of the leaf. Cut the Moriguchi radish into pieces and skewer them on the pine needles for a garnish, accompanied by the lotus root with edamame. Decorate with green maple leaves.

Dried fish has a distinctively rich flavor and texture. Fish with thin flesh will dry more quickly, so it is necessary to adjust the drying time accordingly. The fish is immersed in salt water before drying; this ensures that it will retain moisture when grilled and that salt penetrates the flesh evenly. Spritzing with sake boosts moisture on the surface before grilling.

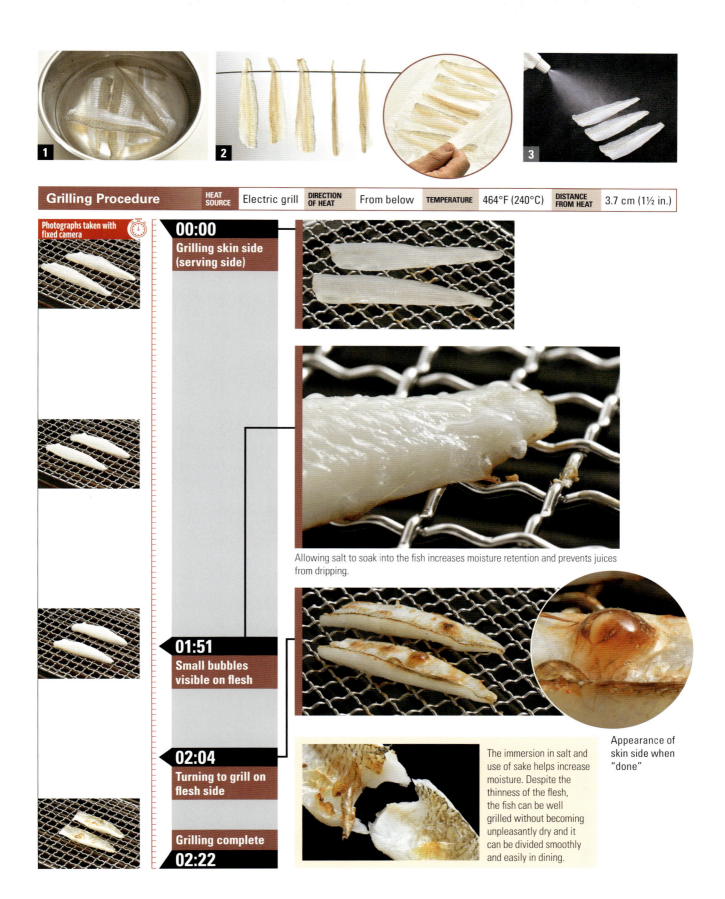

BASIC TYPES OF YAKIMONO 71

**Tare-yaki**

# Grilled Yellowtail
*Buri no Tare-yaki*

In the seas adjacent to Japan, yellowtail (*buri*) is a migratory fish that moves north during the spring and summer in pursuit of the horse mackerel (*aji*) and mackerel (*saba*) that make up the bulk of its diet, and returns south during autumn and winter. The species inhabits wide areas of temperate and tropical seas. It is considered "in season" during the winter months, when it has built up large fat reserves. The species is known by different names at different stages of its life cycle. Because of this association with growth and development, it is regarded as auspicious and is one of the foods traditionally served at New Year. Now farmed and available year-round, yellowtail is one of the most important species of fish consumed in Japan.

In this recipe, the fish is marinated in a strongly flavored *tare* sauce before grilling to impart a salty-sweet flavor to the flesh before cooking. Basting the fish with the sauce during grilling keeps the surface temperature from rising too high, allowing it to cook without scorching.

SAMPLE CUT: Width: 10.3 cm (4 in.)
Length: 14.5 cm (5¾ in.)
Thickness: 1.8 cm (¾ in.)
WEIGHT: 117.0 g (4.1 oz.)

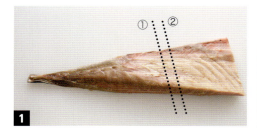

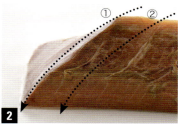

*Serves 3*

3 portions yellowtail (*buri*)

Marinade and basting sauce
- 2 L (67.6 fl. oz.) mirin
- 1.5 L (50.7 fl. oz.) sake
- 1 L (33.8 fl. oz.) *koikuchi* shoyu
- 150 ml (5.1 fl. oz.) *tamari* shoyu
- 150 g (5.3 oz.) *mizuame* syrup
- Spine, central bones, and belly bones of yellowtail, grilled

Boil all ingredients until reduced to about 1.5 liters (50.7 fl. oz.).

Garnishes
- Three 2-cm (¾ in.) pieces pickled turnip, cut "chrysanthemum" style (*kikka-kabura*; see p. 195)
- *Umeboshi* paste, as needed
- *Sansho* pepper powder, as needed
- 3 chrysanthemum leaves
- 6 persimmon leaves

**1** Clean and fillet a yellowtail in the *sanmai-oroshi* style. Take a block of the belly flesh and place it on the work surface with the tail to the left, skin side down.

**2** Cutting along lines as shown by the numbers ① and ② in the photographs above, slice three portions about 1.8-cm (¾ in.) thick, avoiding the parts near the collar and the tail. In order to make the portion appear plump, start cutting with the knife held flat and slowly lift to a vertical position, slicing in an arc. Yellowtail skin does not have an appealing appearance, so the fish is served flesh side up.

**3** Place in the marinade and leave for 5 minutes. As the marinade is concentrated, the fish will take on the color shown in the photograph despite the short marinating time.

**4** Pat dry, then fold up the belly side and thread on three skewers using the single-tuck (*katazuma-ori*) technique (see p. 202). The portion is large, so should be shaped in a slight wave with the skewering.

**5** Grill as shown on the following pages.

**6** Place the persimmon leaves on a serving dish and arrange the yellowtail on top. Garnish with the chrysanthemum leaf and *kikka-kabura*. Pour the remaining sauce over and sprinkle with *sansho* pepper powder to finish.

---

One of the characteristics of fatty fish like yellowtail is that the marinade is not easily absorbed deeply into the flesh. On the positive side, the fish can be well grilled without becoming unpleasantly dry. In the brief immersion in a concentrated marinade, the salt dehydrates muscle cells on the surface of the fish and allows the marinade to soak in. This breaks down the muscle fiber proteins on the surface. In cooking, the amino acids in the juices that seep from the fish, the amino acids from the shoyu, and the glucose from the mirin become concentrated, and a strong Maillard reaction occurs, producing an appetizing aroma.

| Not marinated | Marinated for five minutes |
|---|---|
|  |  |

The concentration of the marinade should be adjusted so that a color similar to that shown in the photograph is achieved after five minutes of marinating.

BASIC TYPES OF *YAKIMONO* 73

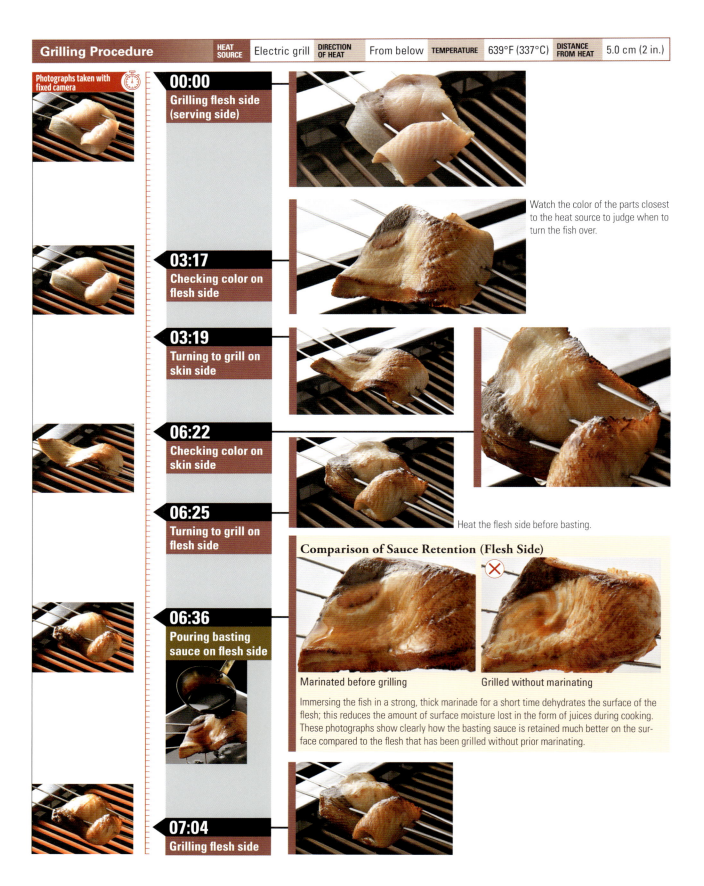

74　BASIC TYPES OF YAKIMONO

### Tare-yaki
# Grilled Eel on Rice
*Una-ju*

Most of the eel eaten in Japan belongs to a species known as the Japanese eel, or "Nihon unagi" (*Anguilla japonica*). In recent years, farmed eel has come to play an increasingly important role in the market, partly from concerns over sustainability. Eel is eaten year-round throughout the country, but is particularly associated with the hottest months of the year, because of its reputation as an excellent source of nutrition and energy during the exhausting heat of the Japanese summer. This recipe introduces a style popular in the Kanto region, in which the eel is divided down the middle using the butterfly cut and steamed before being cooked to completion over charcoal. The steamed eel is repeatedly basted with a sweet *tare* sauce and grilled so that the flesh is soft and tender and the skin savory and aromatic; it is then served over warm rice in a *jubako* lacquered box.

**SAMPLE CUT:** Width: 14.3 cm (5⅝ in.) (head and tail end laid side by side)
Length: 18.0 cm (7⅛ in.) (head end); 21.5 cm (8½ in.) (tail end)
Thickness: 1.0 cm (⅜ in., including skin thickness of 1 mm/1/24 in.)
**WEIGHT:** 168.0 g (5.9 oz.)

### Serves 1

**1 eel (*unagi*)**

***Ki-dare* sauce, as needed**

*Ki-dare* is prepared by mixing equal amounts *koikuchi* shoyu and mirin, adding sugar to adjust the sweetness, and then bringing to a boil.

***Tsuke-dare* immersion sauce, as needed**

*Tsuke-dare* is made by repeatedly immersing steamed eel in *ki-dare* sauce during the main grilling process, imparting the oils and umami flavors of the eel to the sauce. The sauce is never used up in its entirety, but is instead topped up with fresh *ki-dare* on a regular basis, creating a unique sauce that contributes to the hallmark flavor of each individual eel restaurant.

***Kake-dare* basting sauce, as needed**

*Kake-dare*, a mixture of *ki-dare* and *tsuke-dare*, is used as a sauce over the rice.

**300 g (10.6 oz.) rice**

Because of the sweetness in the *kake-dare* basting sauce, varieties of rice with high sugar content should be avoided. The rice should be cooked to be on the dry side (rather than sticky), so that it soaks up the sauce poured over it.

**1** Clean the eel and fillet using the butterfly cut (*sebiraki*). Cut the fillet crosswise, making the flesh on the tail end somewhat longer. Arrange the pieces with the head end to the left and the skin side down. Thread onto four skewers from the left, with the head end to the front and the tail end away from you.

**2** Grill as shown on the following pages.

**3** Serve the rice into a *jubako* lacquered box, drizzle the *kake-dare* sauce over the rice, and serve the eel on top.

## Skewering

Skewer through the layer of muscle above the skin and the collagen layer. Care should be taken to avoid making perforations or creating irregularities in the surface of the flesh or skin. When the eel is very fresh, the flesh can be tight, which will cause it to bunch toward the skewers. If this happens, hold down the flesh with one hand and rotate the skewer while shaping the flesh as desired (rotating the skewer also prevents the meat from sticking to the skewer when cooked). The leftmost skewer, which goes through the thickest part of the flesh, is called the *oya-gushi* (head skewer). When picking up or otherwise manipulating the eel, hold it by the *oya-gushi*.

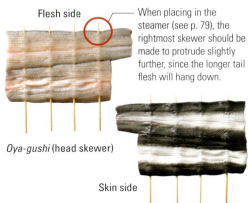

A bamboo *unagi* skewer. Eel skewers have sharper tips than ordinary skewers.

Flesh side

When placing in the steamer (see p. 79), the rightmost skewer should be made to protrude slightly further, since the longer tail flesh will hang down.

*Oya-gushi* (head skewer)

Skin side

## Skewering Checklist

The thickness of the flesh will vary in different parts of the fillet. Pass the skewers through the middle.

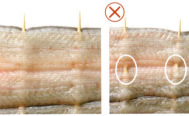
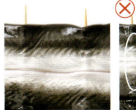

Even in thin parts, care should be taken not to perforate the surface. If the skewer breaks the surface, the flesh will fall apart when the skewer is removed after grilling.

If the outline of the skewers is clearly discernible on the skin side, this means they are too close to the skin. This will cause the flesh to peel away when the eel is grilled.

*Wearing a thimble-like protector on the finger holding the flesh can help to avoid injury when handling the sharp skewers used with eel.

As river fish, eels have a distinctive odor caused by a substance called piperidine. But when the eel is dipped in sauce and heated, the resulting reaction produces the distinctive and pleasant "kaba-yaki" aroma. This differs from the teriyaki aroma produced by the Maillard reaction of shoyu and mirin. Eels have many small bones, and are also rich in collagen. Slow grilling of the eel turns the collagen to gelatin, giving it a soft texture. The method used for preliminary heating before the main grilling differs by region: In the Kansai region, the eel is grilled slowly over open coals, while in the Kanto region, it is cooked with a combination of preliminary grilling and steaming.

BASIC TYPES OF *YAKIMONO*  77

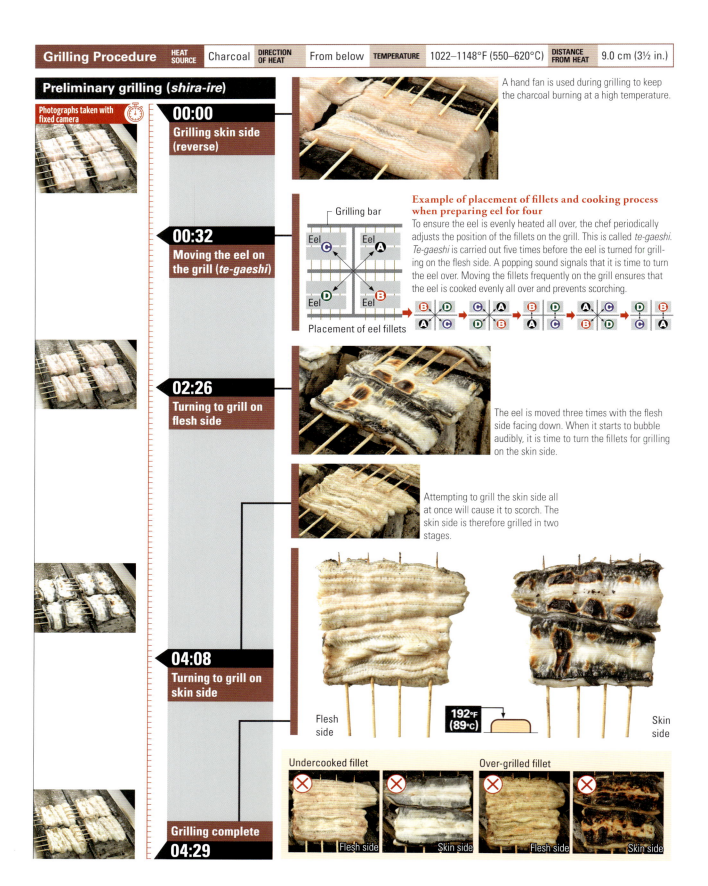

## Steaming — Steam for 13 minutes

**HEAT SOURCE:** Steamer **TEMPERATURE:** 212°F (100°C)

Bring water to a boil and stand the skewers vertically in the steamer with the sharp points facing down. This ensures that both flesh and skin sides of the eel are exposed equally to the steam.

Appearance of eel after steaming

Flesh side | Skin side

Cross-section

These photographs show clearly that plenty of collagen remains in the spaces between the skin and flesh and between the muscles in the flesh.

## Main grilling
Grill the eel, dipping repeatedly in the *tare* sauce (grill on the flesh side only)

**HEAT SOURCE:** Charcoal **TEMPERATURE:** 1022–1148°F (550–620°C)

**00:00** — Dipping eel in *tare* sauce, grilling flesh side
Allow excess *tare* sauce to drip off.

**00:28** — Moving the eel on the grill (*te-gaeshi*)
Eel is moved on the grill twice before being dipped in *tare* sauce for the second time.

**01:45** — Dipping eel in *tare* sauce, grilling flesh side

**02:38** — Dipping eel in *tare* sauce, grilling flesh side

Flesh side | 176°F (80°C) | Skin side

Appearance of over-grilled eel
❌ Flesh side | ❌ Skin side

**Grilling complete 03:21**

### Notes on the *tare* sauce
Repeatedly immersing steamed eel in a *tare* sauce made of shoyu and mirin imparts to the sauce the oxides and amino acids contained in the oils from the eel. Differences in the blend of shoyu and mirin, the provenance of the eel, steaming time, and whether the grilled head is immersed in the sauce all contribute to the distinctive flavor that makes each restaurant's eel unique.

The surface temperature on the flesh side rose to 277°F (136°C) during grilling, then fell to 187°F (86°C) when the eel was immersed in the *tare* sauce. As well as imparting the flavors of the sauce, immersion also serves to lower the temperature and prevent scorching.

BASIC TYPES OF *YAKIMONO*

**Tare-yaki**

# Grilled Quail
*Uzura no Tsuke-yaki*

Quail were domesticated early in history in many parts of the world and have been raised for food since ancient times. In Japan, where they have long been bred for their tasty eggs, they appear in cookery books for ordinary households from the seventeenth century. Japanese quail typically weigh 100 to 150 grams (3.5 to 5.3 oz.), making them smaller than the variety found in France and other countries, and their meat has a light, delicate flavor.

For grilled quail, the meat is dipped in and basted with *tare* sauce during cooking. For this recipe, it is marinated for a fairly long time to achieve a juicy texture and mouthfeel, thanks to the effect of the salt in improving moisture retention. The heating process is short, and the skin is basted with sauce at the end to bring out the appetizing aromas.

SAMPLE CUT: Length: 13.3 cm (5¼ in.)
Width: 20.5 cm (8⅛ in.)
Thickness: 2.0 cm (¾ in.)
WEIGHT: 146.0 g (5.1 oz.)

### Serves 2

1 quail

Marinade and basting sauce
- 100 ml (3.4 fl. oz.) *koikuchi* shoyu
- 100 ml (3.4 fl. oz.) mirin
- 100 ml (3.4 fl. oz.) sake

Garnishes
- Syrup-simmered yuzu rind (*amigasa-yuzu*; see p. 195), as needed
- *Sansho* pepper powder, as needed

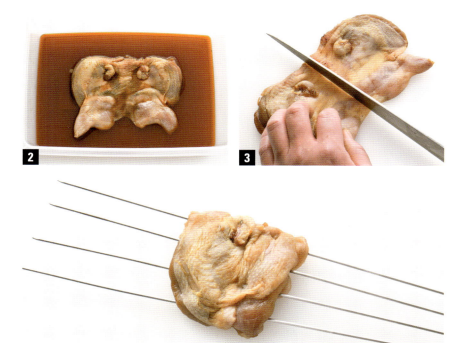

1. Carve the quail using the butterfly-cut technique to lay it flat, then remove head, thigh bones, and legs.
2. Place in marinade and leave for 20 minutes.
3. With the skin side up, cut the quail into two equal pieces down the middle. The dish may be served either skin or flesh side face up.
4. Thread the meat onto four skewers using the flat-skewering (*hira-gushi*) technique (see p. 198), piercing the meat on the flesh side.
5. Grill as shown on the following pages.
6. Cut the quail into large bite-sized pieces and transfer to a serving dish, placing one piece skin side up and the other flesh side up. Sprinkle with *sansho* pepper powder and garnish with the *amigasa-yuzu*.

Because Japanese quail have thin, lean meat, they are easily overcooked. Using a marinade with a high salt content and plenty of sugar from the mirin encourages the gelatinization of salt-soluble proteins and ensures moisture retention during cooking.

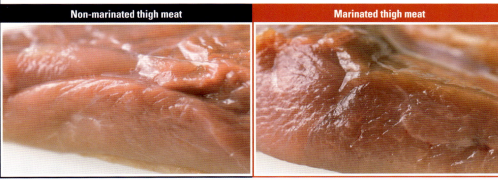

The concentration of the marinade should be adjusted so that a color similar to the photograph is achieved after marinating for five minutes.

BASIC TYPES OF *YAKIMONO*

82  BASIC TYPES OF *YAKIMONO*

## Differences in Appearance of Marinated and Non-marinated Quail (Thigh Meat) after Cooking

Poultry and wildfowl have thicker muscle fibers than fish. On the photographs showing the meat after cooking, muscle fibers can still be discerned in the thigh meat that was marinated. The photograph shows clearly that moisture still remains in the spaces between the fibers. On the unmarinated meat, by contrast, the muscle fibers are tightly packed together, and little or no moisture remains.

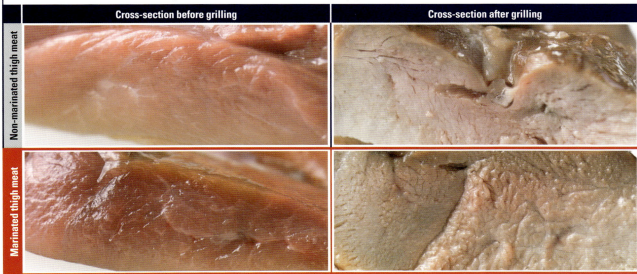

BASIC TYPES OF *YAKIMONO*    83

### Furishio-yaki

# Grilled Sweetfish

*Ayu no Shio-yaki* (Electric grill)

Sweetfish (*ayu*), a freshwater species that inhabits rivers in various parts of Japan, is beloved as one of the essential treats of summer. Sweetfish is an anadromous migratory species; the fry hatch in the autumn and migrate downriver to the sea as they grow before returning to the river, where they die after spawning the following autumn. Because of this life cycle, they are sometimes known as "one-year fish" (*nengyo*). The fish feed on the moss that grows on stones in riverbeds, and this diet imparts a crisp, refreshing aroma to the flesh and viscera; thus, they are sometimes known as "fragrant" or "perfumed" fish (*kogyo*). The fish are usually wild-caught, but in recent years progress has been made with the quality of farmed sweetfish as well.

The traditional way of cooking *ayu no shio-yaki* was to grill the fish in a way that avoided scorching the skin, so that the succulent flesh and the oily viscera could be enjoyed. The head and tail were removed and the fish was served with *tade-su*, a condiment made from *tade* water pepper. Today, the preferred method allows the small fish to be eaten in their entirety. In the following recipe, the surface of the fish is grilled over high heat to cook away the subcutaneous lipids fully. The salt sprinkled over the flesh allows them to be eaten from head to tail and grill to a flavorful, aromatic finish.

BASIC TYPES OF *YAKIMONO*

SAMPLE: Width: 4.0 cm (1⅝ in.)
Length: 19.8 cm (7¾ in.)
Thickness: 2.5 cm (1 in.)
WEIGHT: 68.0 g (2.4 oz.)

*Serves 5*

5 sweetfish (*ayu*)
Salt, as needed

Garnishes

5 boiled *satoimo* taro (*kinu-katsugi*; see p. 195)
Green maple leaves, as needed
1 *sasa* bamboo leaf

## Skewering technique: *odori-gushi*

**1** The upper side (*uwami*—the top side of the fish when viewed with head to the left) will be served face up. The first skewer should be inserted through the eye on the opposite (right/lower) side.

**2** Push the skewer so that it emerges between the dorsal fin and the pectoral fin on the lower side, then insert the skewer again to emerge in front of the tail, to produce the "dancing" or swimming effect (*odori-gushi*; see photograph at right). The skewer is made to pass through the belly in line with the spine to avoid damaging the gall bladder, which is prized for its sharp tang. To finish the skewering, insert the skewer below the spine, so that the tail rises and curves back on itself, and push the skewer to emerge just behind the anal fin. Care should be taken that the skewer does not pierce the skin or protrude anywhere on the *uwami* side that will be served face up.

**3** Taking a generous amount of salt in your fingers, rub salt into the dorsal fin, tail fin, and pectoral fin, pinching between the fingers so that the fins are coated with a layer of salt (*kesho-jio*). Salting in this way makes the fins stand out from the body of the fish so that they do not scorch.

**4** Insert a skewer crosswise to prevent the sweetfish from shifting on the grill. Keep a gap between them so that they are not touching.

**5** Apply salt all over, sprinkling more over the heads and the belly, where the flesh is thicker (see p. 86).

**6** Grill as shown on pages 87–89.

**7** Scatter green maple leaves on a serving dish and arrange the fish on top of each other to create a pleasing impression. Place the *sasa* leaf at the front of the dish and garnish with the *kinu-katsugi satoimo* taro.

---

Sweetfish is grilled with the tail higher than the head so that the oils collect toward the head of the fish. This cooks the head in the high-temperature oils and makes it crisp. The collagen in the cranial bones breaks down and loses its hardness, making for a pleasantly crunchy texture when eaten. The oil that seeps to the surface, once thought to be liver oil, is actually visceral fat stored around the organs.

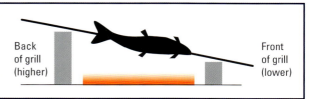

BASIC TYPES OF *YAKIMONO*

| Grilling Procedure | HEAT SOURCE | Electric grill | DIRECTION OF HEAT | From below | TEMPERATURE | 961°F (516°C) | DISTANCE FROM HEAT | 8.5 cm (3⅜ in.) | HEIGHT DIFFERENCE BETWEEN GRILLING BARS | 3.5 cm (1⅜ in.) (higher at far side) |
|---|---|---|---|---|---|---|---|---|---|---|

**Photographs taken with fixed camera**

### 00:00
**PRELIMINARY GRILLING**

Grilling upper side (the *uwami*, which will be served face up)

The back bar of the grill should be set 3.5 cm (1⅜ in.) higher than the front; the skewered sweetfish are placed with their heads on the lower front bar. Adjust the distance to move the heads closer to the heat source and the tails farther away. Place the skewered sweetfish in the middle between the front and back bars and grill the entire upper side of the fish.

### 01:14
**Turning to grill on lower side**

**Widening the mouth to open the gills**

Use a skewer or similar tool to stretch the mouth and open the gills. As well as creating a uniform appearance, this also makes it easier for heat to penetrate into the head.

### 02:04
**MAIN GRILLING**

**Grilling upper side**

Place the tails on the back bar. Since the flesh is thinner in the tail, and heat penetrates more quickly, care should be taken to avoid scorching, bursting of the flesh, or breaking of the skin. Heat until the entire upper side of the fish takes on a golden-brown color.

BASIC TYPES OF *YAKIMONO*

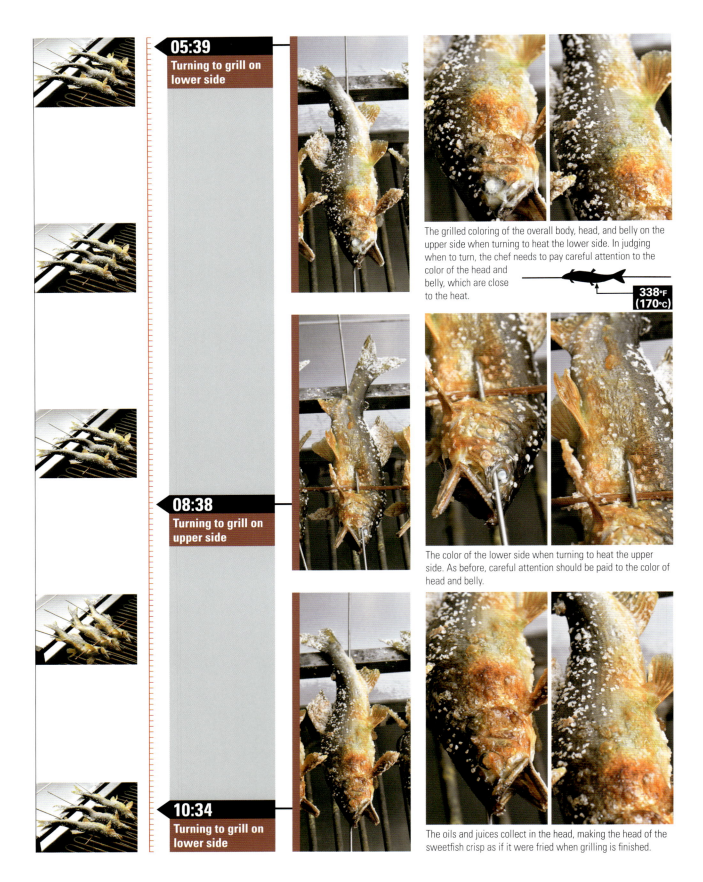

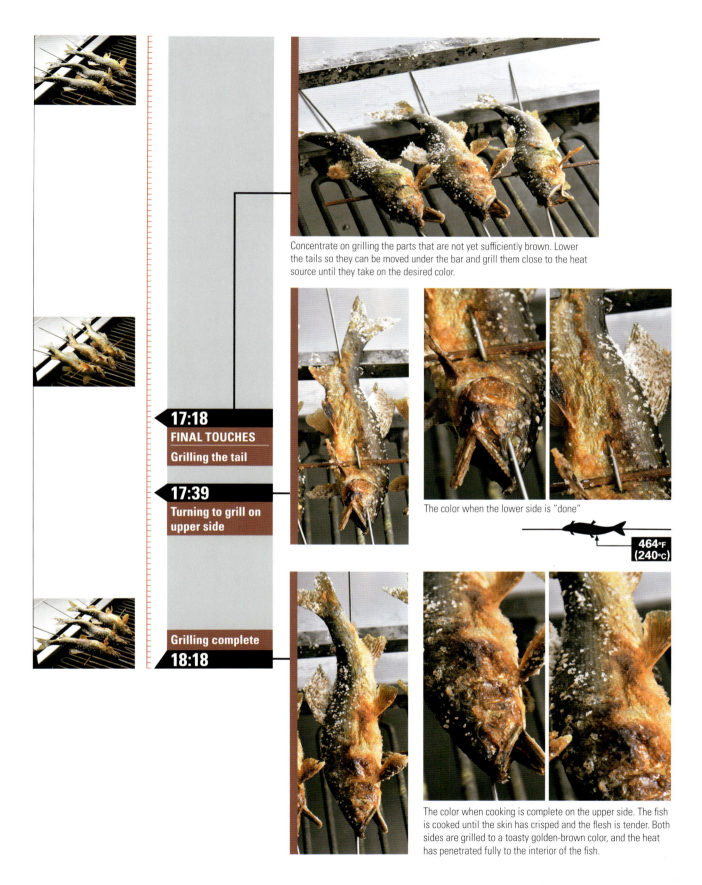

Concentrate on grilling the parts that are not yet sufficiently brown. Lower the tails so they can be moved under the bar and grill them close to the heat source until they take on the desired color.

**17:18**
**FINAL TOUCHES**
**Grilling the tail**

**17:39**
**Turning to grill on upper side**

The color when the lower side is "done"

**464°F (240°C)**

**Grilling complete**
**18:18**

The color when cooking is complete on the upper side. The fish is cooked until the skin has crisped and the flesh is tender. Both sides are grilled to a toasty golden-brown color, and the heat has penetrated fully to the interior of the fish.

BASIC TYPES OF *YAKIMONO* 89

*Furishio-yaki*

# Grilled Sweetfish
*Ayu no Shio-yaki* (Charcoal grill)

This recipe for *ayu no shio-yaki* uses stacked charcoal. This approach makes it possible to enjoy the whole fish from the head to tail, including the skin and viscera, which are noted for their subtle herbal aroma.

# Eating *Ayu* Whole: An Experiment in Different Ways of Arranging Charcoal

Two different ways of arranging charcoal to prepare a charcoal bed: laying the charcoal flat (top), and stacking the charcoal (bottom) to concentrate powerful heat on the head and belly of the fish. This side view of the two approaches makes it easy to see how the stacked method brings the charcoal closer to the cooking surface.

The entire life cycle of sweetfish (*ayu*) lasts just one year; it is not a species that grows from year to year. The sweetfish caught and consumed in the rivers in and around Kyoto are small and have relatively soft bones, which makes them suitable for being consumed whole. Nevertheless, various steps need to be taken to present the fish at its best and ensure that they can be enjoyed bones and all.

When grilled by the conventional method, the head of the fish remains tough, and the skin lacks an appetizing crunchiness. The heat penetrates only weakly to the viscera, so they retain an unpleasant bitterness, and the bones remain hard and chewy. These are aspects to address if the flavors of the whole fish are to be enjoyed at their best.

Chefs set themselves the aim of achieving the perfect grilled sweetfish: the head crisp and aromatic; the skin golden and crispy, with a nice crunch and a delicate aroma; soft flesh; and a brisk and pleasant bitterness in the viscera, with the bones soft enough to be eaten whole.

The first step taken toward achieving this was to adjust the height of the grilling bars. To grill the head to a crisp without overcooking the flesh, the bar was lowered on the head side by 1 to 2 centimeters (⅜ to ¾ in.), bringing the head closer to the heat source than the tail. When the head is placed lower than the rest of the fish, the visceral lipids released as juices during grilling trickle down the skin toward the head. The head cooks in these oils until done to a crisp, achieving a crunchy, aromatic finish. This method of grilling makes it possible to enjoy the head as well as the rest of the fish.

But further improvements were still needed to achieve the ideal crunchiness in the skin.

## From a Flat Bed of Charcoal to Stacked Piles

The next focus was the way the charcoal was arranged. Since charcoal produces a powerful heat, it is normal to lay it flat; even today, many chefs grill over a bed of charcoal in which the pieces are laid flat and straight next to one another. But to achieve the perfect grilled sweetfish—one that could be eaten whole—chefs deliberately bucked tradition by heaping the charcoal in piles instead.

Constant fanning of the charcoal helps to maintain a steady high temperature and also prevents the oily smoke produced by fats from the sweetfish from surrounding the fish.

Stacking the charcoal concentrates the power of the heat; it is normally avoided because this stronger heat can easily scorch parts of the food close to the heat source. But with sweetfish, the more powerful heat obtained by stacking the charcoal makes it possible to grill parts like the head and belly in a short time. In fact, when we tried grilling over stacked charcoal, we were able to confirm that all the oils and lipids were burned off the surface, leaving a dry skin that was crisp and crunchy. Also, the shorter heating time meant that less moisture and tenderness was lost from the flesh. The grilled fish offered the perfect combination of crispy skin on the outside and flesh that was still tender and juicy on the inside.

Another important point is the regular use of a hand-

BASIC TYPES OF *YAKIMONO*

held fan throughout grilling. This keeps the charcoal at a high temperature and prevents smoke from surrounding the fish. When oils drip into the fire they produce gouts of oily smoke. If this comes into contact with the fish, it can char the outside black, and the smoky odor impairs the pleasant natural aromas of the sweetfish. To avoid this, and to achieve the aromas and golden hue that are the major attractions of *ayu no shio-yaki*, fanning is essential. The grilling is "done" when the fish no longer drips juices or oils, and when the skin presents an attractive gold color all along the length of the fish.

### The Science behind the Flavors

What is happening to the fish during the grilling process?

Burning charcoal produces far infrared radiation, which penetrates only 1 to 2 millimeters (1/24 to 1/16 in.) below the surface (see p. 35). Heating over charcoal therefore makes it possible to heat the skin to a high temperature, and to cook the flesh through conduction heat from the skin. Since the high-temperature far infrared radiation does not cook the flesh directly, the interior of the flesh does not reach excessive temperatures.

It is known that the two different approaches to arranging the charcoal (i.e., whether the charcoal is laid flat or stacked) makes a dramatic difference to the core temperature during grilling. When laid flat, the maximum temperature of the charcoal is around 1022°F (550°C), but when it is heaped, the temperature reaches over 1112°F (600°C). This result means that the two methods have different cooking times. In both cases, the fish is turned when the surface temperature reaches around 284°F (140°C). But we found that the amount of time required to reach that temperature differed substantially: around fourteen minutes when the charcoal was laid flat, compared to just ten minutes or so when the charcoal was stacked.

The core temperature inside the fish during the final grilling also varied: With flat charcoal, the cooking time was longer, and the temperature remained at 212°F (100°C) or higher for more than ten minutes. With stacked charcoal, the heating time was shorter, and the temperature remained around 175–195°F (80–90°C). This difference in core temperature affects the tenderness of the flesh. The flesh was found to be up to 1.4 times softer at the end of the cooking process when stacked charcoal is used compared to grilling over a flat bed of charcoal.

The fish is grilled until the skin is dry and crisp, and it has a pleasant aroma when done. This is presumably because the juices that seep out onto the surface of the skin evaporate more or less immediately, ensuring that the skin remains dry. The high temperature also encourages the Maillard reaction, producing rich, appetizing aromas.

Whether the charcoal is stacked or laid flat seemed to make no discernible difference in the dryness of the skin. Nevertheless, in the fish grilled with stacked charcoal, the crunchiness of the skin was dramatically more noticeable when biting into the fish. There are two hypotheses that might explain this.

One is that the two methods result in a subtle difference in the thickness of the skin. Grilling at the high temperatures made possible by stacking the charcoal burns off the oils completely, so that only a thin layer of dry skin remains; cooking over a flat bed of charcoal, by contrast, means that some oils remain in the skin at the end of the grilling process.

The other possible explanation has to do with the tenderness of the flesh. When the flesh is softer, the sen-

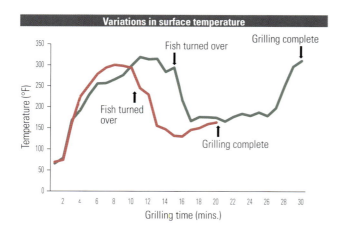

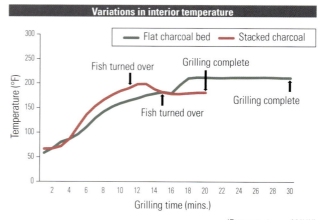

(Data courtesy of NHK)

sation of crispness of the skin when bitten into is accentuated. It is possible that in the case of sweetfish cooked over stacked charcoal, the contrast between the dry, thin skin and the soft flesh underneath makes the "crunch" of the skin more noticeable.

To summarize: Grilling over stacked charcoal produces higher temperatures compared to grilling over a flat bed of charcoal, so that the skin becomes crisp and aromatic—and since the cooking time is reduced, the flesh inside the fish is not overcooked. Further, even though the grilling time is shorter than when cooking over a flat bed of charcoal, the fish still reaches temperatures hot enough for the visceral lipids to melt and the collagen in the central bones to dissolve.

From this, it is fair to conclude that grilling over stacked charcoal is an approach well suited to the aim of grilling sweetfish so that the fish can be enjoyed from head to tail—bones and all.

SAMPLE: Width: 3.5 cm (1⅜ in.)
Length: 17.2 cm (6¾ in.)
Thickness: 2.2 cm (⅞ in.)
WEIGHT: 59.0 g (2.1 oz.)

### Serves 5

5 sweetfish (*ayu*)
Salt, as needed

Garnish

Vinegar-pickled *myoga* (*su-zuke myoga*; see p. 195), as needed

1. As the upper (left) side of the fish (*uwami*) is served face up, the first skewer should be inserted through the eye on the opposite side.

2. Push the skewer so that it emerges
4. between the dorsal fin and the pectoral fin, then insert the skewer again to emerge in front of the tail. This creates the "dancing" or swimming effect (*odori-gushi*; see photograph at right). The skewer is made to pass through the belly in line with the spine in order to avoid damaging the gall bladder, which is prized for its sharp tang. To finish the skewering, insert the skewer below the spine so that the tail rises and curves back on itself, and push the skewer to emerge just behind the anal fin. Care should be taken that the skewer does not pierce the skin or protrude anywhere on the *uwami* side that will be served face up.

5. Insert a crosswise skewer between the fish to prevent them from shifting on the grill. Keep a sufficient gap between the fish so that they do not touch at all.

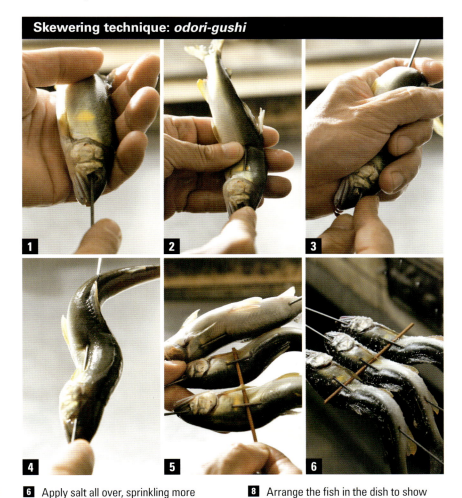

6. Apply salt all over, sprinkling more heavily over the heads and the belly where the meat is thicker.

7. Grill as shown on the following pages.

8. Arrange the fish in the dish to show their shapes to best advantage, overlapping them one at a time, and garnish with the *su-zuke myoga*.

Stack the charcoal to maintain a high temperature. Set the sweetfish over the charcoal with the heads 1 to 2 cm (⅜ to ¾ in.) lower than the tails, so that the head and belly of the fish are closer to the heat. Once oils start to drip, use a fan to prevent the taint of the smoke (produced when oils drip onto the charcoal) from adhering to the fish. Avoid overcooking, but the viscera should be heated to the point where they are denatured, and the central bones heated until the collagen dissolves.

| Grilling Procedure | HEAT SOURCE | Charcoal (stacked) | DIRECTION OF HEAT | From below | TEMPERATURE | 1310°F (710°C) | DISTANCE FROM HEAT | 5.0 cm (2 in.) | HEIGHT DIFFERENCE BETWEEN GRILLING BARS | 2.0 cm (¾ in.) (higher at far side) |
|---|---|---|---|---|---|---|---|---|---|---|

## 00:00 Grilling lower side

The chef uses a fan to keep the charcoal around 1110–1300°F (600–700°C). Such high temperatures ensure that the oils beneath the skin are fully cooked.

## 01:03 Turning to grill on upper side

When turning the fish over to grill on the upper side, press the tails against the far metal grilling bar to create a "wave" shape with the tails bent back.

With the fish in this position, the charcoal is stacked so as to concentrate the power of the heat on the head and belly.

## 04:02 Juices start to drip

The juices contain visceral fats. Setting the bar at the front (head side) lower allows the juices to gather around the head, which is cooked to a crisp. At this point in the demonstration, the surface temperature at the head was 482°F (250°C), while the surface temperature at the belly was 212°F (100°C).

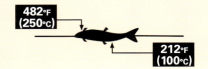

Cooking at high temperature to grill the head to a crisp.

94  BASIC TYPES OF *YAKIMONO*

**18:17**
**Turning to grill on lower side**

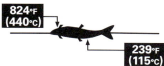

**30:41**
**Turning to grill on upper side**

Finally, the upper side (which will be served face up) is heated again to achieve the desired coloring and slightly plump consistency.

At the end of the grilling process, all the fatty oils on the inside of the skin have been cooked off. This increases the crunchiness of the skin and brings out the contrast with the soft succulence of the flesh.

**31:26**
**Checking color on upper side**

**Grilling complete**
**31:41**

The final color of the head, belly, and tail at the end of the grilling process

Note: Grilling time is different from the process explained on page 92 because different weights of fish were used.

BASIC TYPES OF *YAKIMONO*   95

# Kishu Binchotan: Charcoal Production in Harmony with the Forests

One of the characteristics of *yakimono* in Japanese cuisine is the widespread use of charcoal for grilling. With its long history of using charcoal, ways of achieving a sustainable cycle of production and coexistence with forests were established at an early stage in Japan. This section provides a history of such charcoal production, focusing on the famous Kishu Binchotan charcoal from Wakayama prefecture, and traces the history and production methods that have developed over the years in partnership with the forests of this lush, unspoiled part of the archipelago.

Charcoal has been used since ancient times in many parts of the world, often for smelting iron. The production of charcoal for industrial uses often involved cutting down trees on a large scale, indelibly associating charcoal with deforestation in many people's minds. Charcoal production causes the destruction of forests when source trees are felled indiscriminately without concern for how long it will take the forest to recover. Japan has not been immune to this: There was a serious risk that timber resources might be irreplaceably depleted when the use of charcoal became more widespread during the Edo period (1603–1868). Out of that experience, however, the practice of selective logging was born, making it possible to produce charcoal in a way that would allow the trees and forests to grow back. More will be said about this practice below.

This sustainable approach to charcoal production was established in the Edo period and has been handed down ever since, for more than 200 years. The status of charcoal as a renewable source of energy is one of the unique characteristics of its production and use in Japan.

Most of the charcoal used for grilling in Japanese restaurants today is white charcoal (*shirozumi*). The best-known type of white charcoal is *binchotan* (*tan* means "charcoal"). Kishu Binchotan from Wakayama has a particularly long history and is well known for its excellence. Kishu Binchotan is a premium white charcoal made from *ubame-gashi* and other species of evergreen oak. The word *binchotan* is said to derive from the first syllables of the name of Bitchuya Chozaemon, a merchant from Tanabe in Kishu province (now central Wakayama prefecture), who sold charcoal made from *ubame-gashi* during the Genroku era (1688–1704) of the Edo period. Today, the term refers to white charcoal produced within Wakayama prefecture, from *ubame-gashi* and certain other oak species, made using traditional charcoal-making methods, which are registered as an intangible cultural asset of the prefecture. *Ubame-gashi* (*Quercus phillyreoides*) is a broad-leafed evergreen that belongs to the *Quercus* (oak) genus of the

Jutting out into the Pacific Ocean from central Honshu, the Kii peninsula is the largest in Japan. Dense forests cover much of the peninsula, which is dominated by the Kii mountain range. *Ubame-gashi* oaks are distributed widely throughout the region, particularly in coastal areas.

96  BASIC TYPES OF *YAKIMONO*

After refining, the charcoal is slowly raked out of the kiln door and buried in *subai* (a mixture of clay-like earth and ash) for an entire day to smother the fire. The ash blocks off the flow of air and stops the combustion process in the charcoal. The color of the white ash is what gives *shirozumi* charcoal its name.

beech (*Fagaceae*) family. In Japan, it can be found in warm coastal regions and rocky areas, as well as inland. The tree grows slowly, so that the grain of the wood is dense and the wood itself extremely hard, with a specific gravity so high that it sinks in water. These qualities make the wood ideal for white charcoal.

Charcoal-making in Japan can be traced back to ancient times. Evidence of primitive charcoal fire deposits has been excavated from sites dated to the prehistoric Jomon period (ca. 14,000–300 BCE). This would have been a simple kind of charcoal produced by burning wood until it carbonized. Over time, the technology was gradually refined, producing *nikozumi* (a soft type of charcoal), *arazumi* (hard, rough charcoal), *irizumi* (see below), and finally white charcoal, or *shirozumi*.

*Nikozumi* was close to the primitive charcoal found at Jomon sites. Its method of production was already in existence by the third century, when forging iron tools became established in the archipelago during the Yayoi period. It was a soft charcoal with a low carbonization rate, but it ignited

The axe (*nata*) used for felling *ubame-gashi* (left) and the Kishu billhook (*yoki*) used for preparing the timber.

98   BASIC TYPES OF *YAKIMONO*

A charcoal kiln in the mountains. During refining, workers tend the kiln through the night, constantly making small adjustments to the interior temperature.

Timber ready for use after the wood preparation process, during which workers make sure that the wood is straight and evenly sized.

easily and had a high combustion temperature, making it suitable for metalsmithing.

From the Nara period (710–794), charcoal came to be used in the homes of the aristocracy for heating and cooking. There was a need for good-quality charcoal that would continue to burn for a long time and was less likely to cause fires if bits of the charcoal "popped" and flew out of the fireplace. The charcoal produced to meet these needs was *arazumi*. The name (which literally means "rough charcoal") referred to charcoal that was somewhat harder than the soft *nikozumi*. Even at this early stage, the two types of charcoal were used in quite different settings: *nikozumi* for forging and metalworking, and the harder *arazumi* as a premium heating fuel for the nobility. This use of charcoal both for industrial and domestic purposes was another of the characteristics of Japanese charcoal.

From the early Heian period (794–1185), the demand for good-quality charcoal for household heating and similar uses increased, leading to the development of *irizumi*. This is produced by subjecting *arazumi* or *nikozumi*

BASIC TYPES OF *YAKIMONO* 99

to a secondary combustion process, or by refining it at high temperatures at the end of the carbonization process to increase the extent of carbonization. This is the basic prototype of the method used to produce white charcoal; further refinements eventually led to the invention of *shirozumi*. In fact, the word *shirozumi* entered widespread use during the Edo period, suggesting that the techniques for producing this type of charcoal had become established by this time.

While charcoal was used for domestic heating in centuries past, this kind of use in a domestic setting is no longer common today. Today it is chiefly used for grilling and for *chanoyu* tea gatherings. White charcoal is most commonly used by professional chefs, while black charcoal (*kurozumi*) is favored for *chanoyu*.

The combustion temperature of white charcoal is generally 930–1100°F (500–600°C), but it is easy to increase the heat by fanning the charcoal. With a steady flow of air, it is possible to cook food at temperatures close to 1830°F (1000°C), and to maintain a steady, strong heat for long periods of time. Since white charcoal is produced by combustion at high temperatures, it contains very few impurities and is almost pure carbon. In addition to producing very little flame or smoke, it is odorless. Thanks to these characteristics, white charcoal has been widely used for culinary purposes in Japan—and for grilling in particular.

The color is not the only difference between white and black charcoal. Black charcoal (*kurozumi*) was perfected between the Muromachi period (1336–1573) and the Edo period for use in serving tea at *chanoyu* tea gatherings. The main wood used is *kunugi* (sawtooth oak, *Quercus acutissima*), which has a beautifully patterned grain, so that even the ash left in the brazier is said to impart an aesthetically pleasing impression. The process of making black charcoal is mostly the same as for white charcoal, apart from a major difference in the way the combustion process is brought to an end. When making black charcoal, the doors and other openings to the kiln are closed when carbonization is complete, shutting off the flow of air and extinguishing the fire. For white charcoal, the kiln door is opened when carbonization is coming to an end, allowing air in. This is the start of the refinement process, which continues until almost all the non-carbon impurities have been burned off. This process, called *nerashi*, is a crucial part of the production process for white charcoal. As a result of these differences, black charcoal is relatively soft and produces a sound like a clay pot when struck. It has a low ignition temperature making it easier to light and burns well at high temperatures for a short period of time. White charcoal is much harder and gives a ringing metallic sound when struck. Its high ignition temperature can make it hard to light, but once lit, white charcoal will continue to burn for a long time and give out steady, consistent heat.

Binchotan charcoal in production. This photograph shows the charcoal being removed from the kiln after refining. The photograph on page 97 shows charcoal that has been removed from the kiln in this way. The name *binchotan* is sometimes used as a catchall term for hard charcoal in general, but officially charcoal must satisfy certain conditions to use this appellation. True *binchotan* refers only to white charcoal made from carbonized wood from *ubame-gashi* or other species of evergreen oak, with a fixed carbon content of at least 90 percent, calorific value of at least 6800 kilocalories, ash content of 5 percent or less, moisture content no more than 10 percent, and a refinement/purity score of between 0 and 2. This score (*seirendo*) is obtained by measuring electrical resistance with a kind of ohmmeter known in the industry as a purity meter (*seiren-kei*). Since carbon conducts electricity, when an electric current is passed through the charcoal, electrical resistance will be inversely proportional to the extent to which carbonization has taken place (i.e., the higher the carbon purity, the lower the electrical resistance). Charcoal refined to have the appropriate level of purity is regarded as the best quality.

Many of the logs used for charcoal are twisted and bent in their natural state, and need to be straightened before they can be used.

Artisans make incisions and insert wooden wedges to straighten out awkward twists and turns in the wood.

Straightened wood at the end of the *ki-zukuri* process. Processing the wood so that all the logs have more or less the same shape makes it easier to load the kiln.

## The White Charcoal Production Process

Next, let's look at the entire process of making white charcoal, using Kishu Binchotan as our case study example. Kishu Binchotan is normally made in batches of around three tons of raw wood at a time. The process of wood preparation (*ki-zukuri*) takes three days, while unloading the charcoal and preparing the kiln for the next batch takes another day. The entire process, from setting the fire in the loaded kiln to removing the charcoal from the kiln, takes seven to ten days.

**Wood-preparation (*ki-zukuri*):** Bent and twisted logs are straightened (see photographs at left). Thick logs are split with an axe.

**Loading the kiln (*kama-zume*):** The structure of kilns varies somewhat by region, and the methods of kiln loading also differ. For Kishu Binchotan, around one or two hours after the finished charcoal is removed from the kiln, the prepared logs are layered in the kiln and work on the next batch begins, using the residual heat from the previous batch. The kiln is loaded according to the traditional method, with the logs arranged standing up; the wood at the back of the kiln is known as *hane-ki*, while the wood toward the front is called *hori-ki*.

**Raising the kiln temperature (*kuchi-daki*):** Scrub wood and kindling are burned at the kiln door to dry out the wood inside the kiln. The charcoal burners wait for the temperature in the kiln to rise and the carbonization process to begin.

**Carbonization:** Once carbonization of the wood inside the kiln begins, the kiln doors and other openings are blocked and the wood is left to carbonize. Assessing conditions inside the kiln based on the smell, amount, and color of the smoke, the charcoal burners promote carbonization while making fine adjustments by opening small openings and adjusting the size of the chimney vents. For white charcoal, the carbonization process takes around seventy hours, at a temperature of around 390°F (200°C). The smoke from the chimney taking on a blueish tinge indicates that the carbonization has entered its final stages. This is the sign to start the refining process.

**Refining (*nerashi*):** The kiln door is gradually widened to let in air, increasing the temperature inside the kiln to 1830°F (1000°C) or more. The refining process, which continues

102  BASIC TYPES OF *YAKIMONO*

for fifteen hours or longer, increases the purity of the carbon and produces a harder, purer charcoal. The distinctive characteristics of white charcoal—the high combustion temperature, long burn, and lack of smoke and flame during burning—are the result of this refining process.

**Unloading the kiln and smothering the fire (*kama-dashi/shoka*)**: After the refining process, the charcoal is slowly raked out of the kiln via the kiln door and buried in *subai*, a mixture of clay-like earth and ash, to smother the fire (see p. 98). The charcoal has around one-third of the thickness of the wood when it was loaded into the kiln and around 11 to 12 percent of its original weight.

**Selection and packaging**: After the charcoal cools, it undergoes a rigorous selection process conforming to official Kishu Binchotan standards. It is then cut to size and shipped.

On the far left is an original piece of wood. On the far right is *binchotan* charcoal made from a piece of wood roughly the same size and shape as the one shown here. After undergoing carbonization for roughly seventy hours (second from left), the charcoal is subjected to further refining, and eventually resembles the finished charcoal on the far right.

BASIC TYPES OF *YAKIMONO*

| Third year of growth | Fifteenth year | Tenth year | Fifth year | Fifth year |

Selective logging encourages new shoots to grow from a cut-back stump of *ubame-gashi* oak. This reduces the number of years required for the wood to grow to harvestable size and encourages the regeneration of the *ubame-gashi* forest.

## Coppicing and Forest Management

Production of Kishu Binchotan charcoal has long been considered part and parcel of the production and upkeep of the trees that provide the raw timber. Japanese charcoal developed as a sustainable, renewable source of energy thanks to the practice of selective woodland cutting. This method was born out of a crisis during the Edo period, when the popularity of *binchotan* caused production to increase rapidly, placing the forests at risk of depletion. The practice of selective cutting or coppicing of trees that emerged from this experience has continued to the present day.

*Ubame-gashi* oaks grow slowly: If all the new growth sprouting from a stump is cut off, it takes around forty years for the trunks to grow back to fully grown timber. However, if the trees are coppiced, with the thicker trunks best suited for use in charcoal harvested and the thinner ones left, the number of years required until timber can be harvested from the tree again can be reduced dramatically. The tree derives energy from the leaves on the parts that have been left, nourishing the growth of new branching trunks from the same stump that can grow to a size suitable for harvesting for charcoal in about fifteen years. This more than doubles the amount of timber that can be harvested, and also prevents depletion of the species that supply the wood.

If the forest is left to its own devices, competition for survival will result in a natural transition in the forest, as *ubame-gashi* oaks lose out to faster-growing trees. Charcoal production therefore requires high levels of expertise in woodland management as well as charcoal making. Variables such as sunlight, temperature, humidity, and the amount of moisture contained in the wood can all have an impact on the quality of the wood, and it is vital to adjust conditions inside the kiln according to the characteristics of the wood. It is therefore critical for charcoal burners to understand the provenance of the raw wood they use during the charcoal-making process.

By practicing coppicing in a forest, wood can be harvested on a fifteen-year cycle. This means that charcoal burners generally harvest wood from the same patch of forest three times over the course of their professional lives. Their work is part of a cycle in which the artisans coexist with the forest that provides their raw materials, and in turn help to shape, maintain, and revitalize the forest through selective logging. In order to maintain this cycle, it is vital to bear this regeneration and regrowth cycle in mind at all times. This will ensure that the precious natural resource of charcoal continues to be available for generations into the future.

When cutting timber, thin trunks are left; thicker ones are cut low down on the tree to provide plenty of sunlight and make it easier for new sprouts to grow. The thin sprouts (marked with circles) emerging from the stump will grow to become new trunks.

Chapter 4

# Yakimono Variations

*Yakimono* encompass a diversity of forms—seasonal dishes, celebratory foods served to mark special events and festivals throughout the year, and historical recipes given a contemporary twist. This chapter introduces a selection of these dishes, arranged by main ingredient. Even the same ingredients vary in texture and flavor depending on the season, and many of these recipes make the most of this diversity to offer flavors that can be enjoyed only at certain times of year. The vessels in which the food is presented and the garnishes that accompany it are also carefully contrived to evoke a specific effect at the table and heighten appreciation of the changing seasons.

The final part of this chapter covers chicken grilled *yakitori* style, probably the most popular example of more "casual" style *yakimono*, and introduces the steps involved in preparing and grilling different parts of the chicken.

### Shio-yaki

# Awayuki Grilled Sea Bream
Madai no Awayuki-yaki

*Awayuki* (light snow) is a word used to describe the ephemeral dusting of snow that sometimes falls in spring. Here, it refers to a topping of whipped egg white mixed with cherry-blossom petals that impart a subtle flavor while recalling the late snow that falls when cherry trees are in bloom. The petals of the blossoms are carefully removed, spread out, and coated with egg white. Salt is sprinkled on the sea bream (*madai*) and allowed to permeate the flesh before grilling to increase moisture retention. After the *awayuki* topping is added, grilling time is kept short to prevent the topping from losing its shape or scorching. Garnishes of grilled bamboo shoot and *kinome* further accentuate the early spring feel of the dish.

**SAMPLE CUT:** Width: 5.3 cm (2⅛ in.)
Length: 14.7 cm (5¾ in.)
Thickness: 1.7 cm (⅝ in.)
**WEIGHT:** 64.0 g (2.3 oz.)

*Serves 1*

1 portion sea bream (*madai*)
Salt, as needed

*Awayuki* ("light snow" topping)
  42 g (1.5 oz.) egg white, whipped until stiff
  8 g (0.3 oz.) *tsukune-imo* yam
  Salt-pickled cherry blossoms, as needed

Garnishes
  Grilled bamboo shoot (*yaki-takenoko*; see p. 195), as needed
  *Kinome* (*sansho* leaves), as needed

Salt-pickled cherry blossoms

1. Sprinkle salt (2% by weight) on the sea bream and leave for an hour. Thread the fish onto two skewers in the wave-skewering (*uneri-gushi*) technique. The skin side will be served face up, and will be topped with the *awayuki*.
2. Make the *awayuki*: Whisk the egg
3. whites until stiff and combine with the grated yam. The mixture should have a thick consistency.
4. Remove individual petals from the cherry blossoms and add to water so that they expand, then place on a paper towel to absorb excess moisture.
5. Stir the cherry petals into the egg-white mixture.
6. Grill as shown at right.
7. Transfer the sea bream with *awayuki* topping to a serving plate, and garnish with grilled bamboo shoot and chopped *kinome*.

### Grilling Procedure
**Grilling the flesh**

| HEAT SOURCE | DIRECTION OF HEAT | TEMPERATURE | DISTANCE FROM HEAT |
|---|---|---|---|
| Electric grill | From below | 664°F (351°C) | 8.5 cm (3⅜ in.) |

**00:00  Grilling skin side (serving side)**

**02:46  Turning to grill on flesh side**

When the skin side starts to curl, grill briefly to heat skin side.

**05:16  Grilling complete**

Color of flesh side when grilling is complete

### Adding the *awayuki* topping

Transfer a generous scoop of the *awayuki* mixture to the skin side of the fish.

**Grilling the *awayuki* topping**

| DIRECTION OF HEAT | TEMPERATURE | DISTANCE FROM HEAT |
|---|---|---|
| From above | 680°F (360°C) | 10.0 cm (3⅞ in.) |

**00:00  Grilling the *awayuki***

The topping is heated for a short time from above in order to preserve the snowlike whiteness of the egg white/yam mixture.

**00:39  Grilling complete**

Color of the *awayuki* topping when grilling is complete

YAKIMONO VARIATIONS   109

### Shio-yaki
# Salt-Crust Baked Sea Bream
*Madai no Shiogama-yaki*

*Shiogama-yaki* (literally "salt-pot grilling"), which originated in salt-producing areas close to the sea, is a style of cooking in which ingredients are encased and steamed whole in a crust of salt mixed with egg whites. In this recipe, a whole sea bream (*madai*) is descaled and the gills and internal organs removed through the gill opening (*tsubo-nuki*), then covered with a thick layer of salt and baked. Sea bream is considered auspicious; it is often served whole with the head and tail on special occasions, with diners gathering around and helping themselves. Here, the sea bream is immersed in salt water to increase water retention before cooking. Residual heat helps to cook the flesh to a moist and tender consistency.

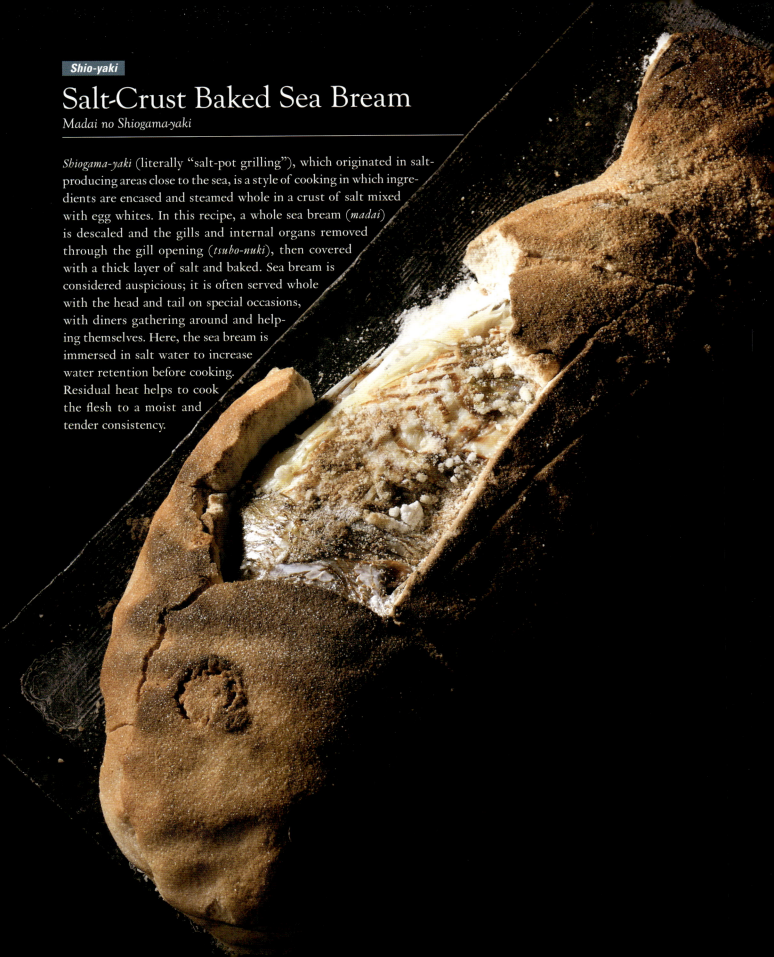

**SAMPLE:** Width: 16.0 cm (6¼ in.)
Length: 48.0 cm (18⅞ in.)
Thickness: 6.5 cm (2½ in.)
**WEIGHT:** 1.2 kg (42.3 oz.; internal organs removed)

The fish covered in a 2-cm (¾ in.) thick casing of salt.

Metal skewers are used to pierce the thickest parts of the flesh in at least three places. The skewers should penetrate to the core of the fish; pine needles are then placed in these holes. Since chlorophyll loses its green color and turns yellowish brown at 176°F (80°C), monitoring the pine needles during cooking makes it possible to ascertain how well the heat is penetrating to the core of the fish. The stronger needles of the black pine tree should be used for this purpose.

Change in color of pine needles (top: before cooking; bottom: after cooking)

*Serves 4–5*

1 sea bream (*madai*)
Salt, as needed

*Shiogama* ("salt pot" casing)
| 3 kg (6.6 lbs.) salt
| 4 egg whites

Black pine tree needles, as needed

**1** Descale the fish and remove the gills and internal organs through the gill opening (*tsubo-nuki*; see p. 204). Immerse in salt water (3% salinity) and leave for an hour.

**2** Pat with paper towel to remove excess moisture. Pierce the thickest part of the flesh with seven to eight metal skewers arranged in a circle in order to allow the flesh to cook through.

**3** Mix together the salt and egg white and spread a 2-cm (¾ in.) layer over a cooking platter. Place the sea bream on top and cover it with a 2-cm (¾ in.) layer of the salt mixture. Pat smooth and insert pine needles in at least three places in the thickest parts of the fish.

**4** Cook as shown at right.

### Cooking Procedure

| HEAT SOURCE | Brick oven | TEMPERATURE | 860°F (460°C) |

**00:00 Baking in the brick oven**

The fish is placed in the oven head first, since the temperature is highest in the inner part of the oven.

**11:10 Changing the position of the fish within the brick oven**

The fish is moved within the oven to ensure that it is evenly cooked all over. At this time, the temperature on the surface was 421°F (216°C); the core temperature was 138°F (59°C).

**18:53 Baking complete**

The fish is left to rest. Residual heat will continue to cook the fish. Around 5 minutes of residual heat should be sufficient to cook the fish to the desired finish.

**23:53 Cooking by residual heat complete**

The outside of the salt casing is well browned, but the flesh inside is done to a soft, juicy consistency.

YAKIMONO VARIATIONS   111

### Furishio-yaki
# Grilled Sea Bream Head
*Madai no Kabuto-yaki*

Sea bream (*madai*) is an essential part of any celebratory meal, prized for its superlative flavor, elegant appearance, and attractive color. *Kabuto-yaki* is a style of cooking in which half a fish head is grilled. The head is cut vertically in two—the name comes from the resemblance of the pectoral fins to the horns on a samurai helmet (the word *kabuto* means "helmet"). When sea bream is served in this style at celebrations, it is customary to use a female fish, since these generally have a more attractive shape and color.

Salting only immediately before grilling allows the juices containing amino acids to seep to the surface, where heating induces the Maillard reaction, producing rich and appetizing aromas. As the fish is not left to rest after sprinkling salt prior to grilling, the flesh tends to fall away easily. For this reason, skewers are used to hold the flesh in place.

SAMPLE CUT: Width: 15.5 cm (6⅛ in.)
Length: 21.3 cm (8⅜ in.)
Thickness: 4.2 cm (1⅝ in.)
WEIGHT: 398.0 g (14.0 oz.)

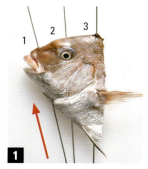
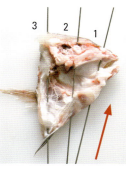

1. Insert the first skewer at the base of the gills, threading it through the cartilage in the upper mouth to emerge near the nostrils.
2. Insert the second skewer slightly above the base of the ventral fin, passing it through the space between the cartilage around the eye to emerge above the eye.
3. Insert the third skewer to pass through the flesh attached to the collar.

*Serves 1*

1 sea bream (*madai*) head, halved (the head should be from a female fish)
Salt, as needed
1 egg white (wrapped in a gauze pouch and squeezed to strain)
Sake, as needed

Garnishes
| ¼ lemon
| *Urajiro* ferns, as needed
| Pine sprigs, as needed

**1** Remove the head, leaving plenty of flesh attached, and cut vertically down the middle. Descale one half of the head, making sure all scales are removed, and insert three skewers in a radial pattern as described above.

**2** Salt both sides as needed. Salt lightly on the skin side (serving side) to enhance the appearance (*kesho-jio*), and a little more heavily for flavoring in places on the reverse side where the flesh is thicker.

**3** Brush the egg white on the surface of the fins and apply a thicker layer of salt (*kesho-jio*) to protect them.

**4** Grill as shown at right.

**5** Transfer to a serving dish, placing on a bed of *urajiro* ferns and pine sprigs, and garnish with the lemon wedges.

### Grilling Procedure
#### Grilling the flesh

| HEAT SOURCE | DIRECTION OF HEAT | TEMPERATURE | DISTANCE FROM HEAT |
|---|---|---|---|
| Electric grill | From below | 716°F (380°C) | 8.0 cm (3⅛ in.) |

**00:00 Grilling skin side (serving side)**

The skin side is grilled quickly over high heat to fix the salt to the surface.

Lifting the fin away from the heat with a skewer to avoid scorching.

**03:41 Lowering the heat**

Once the salt is fixed, the heat is reduced; the fish is grilled over lower heat (662°F/350°C) to avoid charring the surface.

**12:43 Turning to grill on flesh side**

 383°F (195°C)

**20:21 Checking color and spritzing with sake on flesh side**

Spritzing with sake during grilling gets rid of the fishy smell, which evaporates with the sake.

**20:29 Grilling flesh side**

#### Finish with browning

| DIRECTION OF HEAT | TEMPERATURE | DISTANCE FROM HEAT |
|---|---|---|
| From above | 662°F (350°C) | 7.2 cm (2⅞ in.) |

**22:07 Switching to heat from above for grilling the skin side**

Since the grilled flesh is now delicate and apt to fall apart, the chef switches to grilling from above to balance out the color on the skin side.

**22:26 Grilling complete**

284°F (140°C)

172°F (78°C)

YAKIMONO VARIATIONS  113

*Furishio-yaki*

# Kenchin Style Grilled Sea Bream
*Madai no Kenchin-yaki*

*Kenchin* is originally a tofu-based vegetarian dish in the *shojin ryori* tradition of Buddhist temple cuisine. This dish was traditionally made by folding *kenchin* into yellowback sea bream (*kodai*), but here we give the recipe a modern twist by using a fillet of sea bream to wrap the *kenchin*. Since the *kenchin* is prepared in advance, grilling over direct heat is carried out only to cook the fish. Because salt does not penetrate the flesh before grilling, moisture is easily released from the fish. For this reason, the fish is grilled over low heat to prevent excessive moisture loss.

SAMPLE CUT: Width: 4.7 cm (1⅞ in.)
Length: 10.1 cm (4 in.)
Thickness: 1.3 cm (½ in.)
WEIGHT: 47.0 g (1.7 oz.)

A portion cut open and laid flat

*Serves 3*

3 portions sea bream (*madai*)
Sake, as needed

*Kenchin*

400 g (14.1 oz.) tofu

45 g (1.6 oz.) *yama-imo* yam

Minced *kikurage* (wood ear), shiitake mushroom, carrot, burdock root (*gobo*), *mitsuba* stems, as needed

1 egg

100 ml (3.4 fl. oz.) seasoning liquid
To 200 ml (6.8 fl. oz.) of *ichiban* or *niban* dashi, add 20 ml (1 Tbsp. plus 1 tsp.) each *koikuchi* shoyu, mirin, and sake, and 10 g (1 Tbsp.) sugar.

*An* (thickened sauce)

200 ml (6.8 fl. oz.) stock from sea bream bones

20 ml (1 Tbsp. plus 1 tsp.) water

20 g (0.7 oz.) *kuzu* starch

Garnish

Simmered *shimeji* mushrooms and soused spinach (*shimeji to horenso no ohitashi*; see p. 195), as needed

1. Cut a portion open on the dorsal side where the flesh is thicker and lay flat.
2. Make the *kenchin*. Wrap the tofu in a paper towel and weight it to drain. Leave for 1 hour.
3. Heat the tofu in a frying pan, breaking up to release moisture.
4. Add the egg and mix while stir-frying.
5. Press through a sieve, transfer to a *suribachi*, add the grated *yama-imo*, and combine.
6. Stir-fry the *kikurage*, shiitake mushrooms, carrot, and burdock. Add the seasoning liquid and stir-fry for around 2 more minutes; transfer to a strainer and drain.
7. Combine the tofu mix 5 and the vegetable mix 6 and stir-fry. Finally, add the *mitsuba* and stir gently.
8. Shape the ingredients to form the *kenchin* ball; wrap the sea bream around the ball. Secure the fish with three skewers.
9. Grill as shown below.
10. Make the *an* (thickened sauce). Heat the stock of sea bream bones, add the *kuzu* starch dissolved in water, bring to a boil, and allow to thicken.
11. Pour the sauce over the grilled sea bream and *kenchin*, transfer to a serving plate, and garnish with the *shimeji* mushrooms and soused spinach.

Before draining (406 g/14.3 oz.)
After draining (231 g/8.1 oz.)

### Grilling Procedure

| HEAT SOURCE | DIRECTION OF HEAT | TEMPERATURE | DISTANCE FROM HEAT |
|---|---|---|---|
| Electric grill | From below | 649°F (343°C) | 7.5 cm (3 in.) |

**00:00 Grilling the underside**

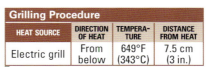

**02:08 Turning to grill the upper side (over which the thickened sauce will be poured)**

If the flesh on the grill side contracts, the *kenchin* stuffing may fall out when roll is turned, so start by grilling both sides evenly.

**03:27 Turning to grill the underside**

**08:22 Turning to grill the upper side**

**11:56 Basting upper side with sake**

Once the upper side starts to take on color, baste with sake to lower the temperature and avoid scorching.

**12:02 Grilling the upper side**

**14:37 Grilling complete**

244°F (118°C) — 100 120 140 160 180 200 °F
154°F (68°C) (Sea bream)

**Making the *an* (thickened sauce)**

YAKIMONO VARIATIONS 115

### Miscellaneous

# Sea Bream Grilled with Oil
*Madai no Abura-yaki*

*Abura-yaki* is a method of cooking in which oil is applied to ingredients as they are grilled. In this recipe, very hot oil is poured over the surface of fish, briefly exposing it to intense heat. The fish is then grilled at a high temperature with far infrared radiation from charcoal, while the excess oil is allowed to drip off, heating to bring out a savory aroma. The fish is not salted before cooking, but dehydration is limited by the quick, high-temperature searing of the surface. Grilling with oil is often used with small fish such as young sweetfish (*ayu*) and Biwa gudgeon (*moroko*), but here a thick cut of sea bream (*madai*) is used and the oil poured over it. This procedure makes it possible to enjoy a range of textures from crisp to soft produced by the different levels of heat.

SAMPLE CUT: Width: 3.8 cm (1½ in.)
Length: 7.7 cm (3 in.)
Thickness: 2.8 cm (1⅛ in.)
WEIGHT: 58.0 g (2.0 oz.)

Serves 3

3 portions sea bream (*madai*)

Taihaku (untoasted) sesame oil, as needed

(Use a thinner oil with a low coagulation point, so that excess oil will easily drain off when poured over the fish grilled over direct heat. Use fresh oil and remove from heat after the temperature rises to about 410°F (210°C). The smoke point of oil depends on the type, so it is important to keep track of the temperature of the oil and know its smoke point.)

Garnishes

2 *sudachi*

Marinated lotus root (*renkon no san-baizu-zuke*; see p. 195), as needed

3 pickled ginger shoots (*hajikami*)

1 paper mulberry leaf (*kaji no ha*)

**1** Score the block (sea bream) diagonally, cutting the skin to a depth of around 2 mm (1/16 in.), then cut into thick pieces. This will keep the flesh from curling even when the skin shrinks with the application of hot oil.

**2** Thread the fish onto two skewers using the flat-skewering (*hira-gushi*) technique. Thicker skewers should be used because of the density of sea bream flesh.

**3** Grill as shown at right.

**4** Transfer the sea bream to a serving dish, laying the fish on top of the paper mulberry leaf, and garnish with the *sudachi* slices, marinated lotus root, and pickled ginger shoots.

1

2

### Grilling Procedure
#### Cooking under hot oil

| HEAT SOURCE | Gas range | TEMPERATURE | 482°F (250°C) |
|---|---|---|---|

Heat the Taihaku sesame oil to close to the smoke point at 392°F (200°C), then pour approximately 50 ml (3 Tbsp. plus 1 tsp.) of the oil over the skin side (serving side) three times and over the flesh side twice.

Color and cross-section after pouring oil

At this stage, only the surface of the fish is cooked.

Color of cross-section when grilling is complete
The fish is cooked through to the center, but the flesh retains a slight transparency.

### Cooking over direct heat

| HEAT SOURCE | DIRECTION OF HEAT | TEMPERATURE | DISTANCE FROM HEAT |
|---|---|---|---|
| Charcoal | From below | 1161°F (627°C) | 4.0 cm (1⅝ in.) |

**00:00** Grilling flesh side (reverse)

**02:03** Turning to grill on skin side

**03:16** Grilling complete

143°F (61.7°C)   100°F (38°C)

Sea bream has little fishy smell and can be enjoyed just by sprinkling salt right before grilling, rather than applying salt in advance and allowing it to permeate. This lends itself to grilling that does not markedly increase the core temperature of the fish. Even at high temperatures, oil cools quickly when it touches the surface, and does not increase the internal temperature of the flesh much. Cooking by far infrared radiation from charcoal also heats only the external surface of the fish to high temperatures. As a result, the internal temperature increases gradually by conduction heat transfer from the surface, making for a soft texture.

YAKIMONO VARIATIONS   117

**Yuan-yaki**

# Yuan Style Sawara Mackerel
Sawara no Yuan-yaki

*Sawara* (*Scomberomorus niphonius*) is a species of mackerel especially popular in western Japan. It has traditionally been regarded as a fish that is in season in spring, since it is caught in large amounts in the Inland Sea at that time of year. In fact, it is delicious throughout the year, except during the summer spawning season. During the winter months, in particular, when the fish have built up reserves of fat and the flesh is rich in flavor, it is called "cold-weather" *sawara* (*kan-sawara*) and valued as a premium fish. In this recipe, the marinade is not allowed to penetrate deeply in order to retain the original flavor of the flesh when grilling. Cooking time is kept short, and the core of the fish is cooked by residual heat, to produce a delicate, fluffy texture.

SAMPLE CUT: Length: 4.6 cm (1¾ in.)
Width: 13.5 cm (5⅜ in.)
Thickness: 1.2 cm (½ in.)
WEIGHT: 50.0 g (1.8 oz.)

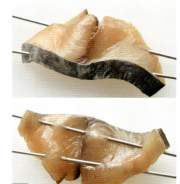

*Serves 5*

5 portions *sawara* mackerel
Salt, as needed

*Yuan-ji* marinade
- 200 ml (6.8 fl. oz.) sake
- 150 ml (5.1 fl. oz.) mirin
- 50 ml (3 Tbsp. plus 1 tsp.) *koikuchi* shoyu
- 50 ml (3 Tbsp. plus 1 tsp.) *usukuchi* shoyu
- ½ yuzu, cut into rounds

*Yubeshi shira-su* dressing, as needed
- 200 g (7.1 oz.) silken (*kinugoshi*) tofu
- ½ *yubeshi* (yuzu-flavored sweet; see Glossary)
- 9 g (1 Tbsp.) sugar
- 15 ml (1 Tbsp.) *usukuchi* shoyu
- 15 ml (1 Tbsp.) rice vinegar
- 7 g (1 Tbsp.) ground sesame
- Dash lemon juice

Boil the tofu for about 5 minutes, drain, and combine with the *yubeshi* in a blender, then add all other ingredients and combine.

1. Sprinkle salt (0.5% by weight) on the fish and let stand for 6 hours, then immerse in the *yuan-ji* marinade for 90 minutes.
2. The skin side will be served face up. Thread each portion onto two skewers in the wave-skewering (*uneri-gushi*) technique.
3. **Grill as shown at right.**
4. Transfer the fish to a serving dish and top with the *yubeshi shira-su* dressing.

## Grilling Procedure

| HEAT SOURCE | DIRECTION OF HEAT | TEMPERATURE | DISTANCE FROM HEAT |
|---|---|---|---|
| Electric grill | From below | 509°F (265°C) | 9.0 cm (3½ in.) |

00:00 **Grilling skin side (serving side)**

03:55 **Turning to grill on flesh side**

05:24 **Grilling complete**

Cooking is finished with residual heat.

126°F (52°C)

06:42 **Cooking by residual heat complete**

## Cooking by Residual Heat

After the grilling is complete, it takes around one and a half minutes for residual heat to cook the center of the fish. Take this time into account when deciding when to conclude grilling. The top and bottom photographs show how the muscle fibers change as they are cooked by residual heat.

Cross-section after 35 seconds of cooking by residual heat

Cross-section after 1 minute 28 seconds of cooking by residual heat

YAKIMONO VARIATIONS   119

# Grilled *Sawara* Mackerel with *Natane* Topping

*Sawara no Natane-yaki*

In spring, *sawara* mackerel start to gather in large numbers in the Inland Sea for the spring spawning season; thus, they are associated with the onset of mild, pleasant weather. This dish is named for the yellow rape blossoms called *natane* or *nanohana* that brighten the spring landscape. A topping of egg yolks soft-scrambled over boiling water, then mixed with green peas, is lightly grilled on top of the fish. The *sawara* is seasoned by immersing briefly in a marinade and then basting with the same sauce while grilling. The dish is garnished with the buds of the rape plant, rather than the blossoms, as the greens become bitter once the flowers open. The spring feel is heightened by scattering cherry-blossom petals across the red-lacquered serving plate.

SAMPLE CUT: Width: 5.7 cm (2¼ in.)
Length: 14.0 cm (5½ in.)
Thickness: 2.3 cm (⅞ in.)
WEIGHT: 66.0 g (2.3 oz.)

## Serves 3

3 portions *sawara* mackerel

Marinade and basting sauce
| 250 ml (8.5 fl. oz.) *koikuchi* shoyu
| 150 ml (5.1 fl. oz.) sake
| 100 ml (3.4 fl. oz.) mirin

Mix to combine, then burn off the alcohol.

*Natane* mixture
| 10 g (0.4 oz.) white miso
| 3 egg yolks
| 36 ml (2½ Tbsp.) *niban* dashi
| 50 g (1.8 oz.) peas in the pods (*usui-endo*)

Garnishes
| Soused *nanohana* (rape blossom) shoots (*nanohana no ohitashi*; see p. 196), as needed
| Cherry-blossom petals, as needed

**1** Marinade fish for 15 minutes.

**2** Pat dry and score the skin at intervals of around 3 cm (1⅛ in.) to prevent the skin from peeling off in one piece when eaten.

**3** Treating the skin side as the serving side, skewer using the flat-skewering (*hira-gushi*) technique.

**4** Mix together the *natane* ingredients. Heat in a double boiler until the egg is soft-boiled.

**5** Press the egg mixture through a sieve (mesh size of 50).

**6** Shell the peas, boil in salt water, and remove the outer skins. Lightly fold into the egg mixture.

**7** Grill as shown at right.

**8** Transfer the fish with the *natane* topping to a serving dish, garnish with the soused rape-blossom shoots, and scatter the cherry-blossom petals over all.

### Grilling Procedure
#### Grilling the flesh

| HEAT SOURCE | DIRECTION OF HEAT | TEMPERATURE | DISTANCE FROM HEAT |
|---|---|---|---|
| Electric grill | From below | 516°F (269°C) | 9.3 cm (3⅝ in.) |

**00:00** Grilling flesh side (serving side)

**06:38** Turning to grill on skin side

**11:45** Pouring basting sauce on skin side

**11:50** Grilling skin side

**13:00** Checking color on skin side

**13:05** Pouring basting sauce on flesh side

**13:12** Grilling flesh side

**14:25** Pouring basting sauce on flesh side

The sauce scorches easily. When the first application of sauce starts to dry out, add more to keep it from scorching.

**16:12** Grilling complete

Top with the *natane* mixture

### Grilling the *natane* mixture

| DIRECTION OF HEAT | From above | DISTANCE FROM HEAT | 14.5 cm (5¾ in.) |
|---|---|---|---|

**00:00** Grilling the *natane* mixture

The mixture is heated gently from above to avoid scorching.

**03:13** Grilling complete

117°F (47°C)  (*Natane* mixture)

YAKIMONO VARIATIONS    121

**Yuan-yaki**

# Sawara Mackerel Hoba-yaki
*Sawara no Hoba-yaki*

After spawning in the summer, *sawara* (known as "Japanese Spanish mackerel"; *Scomberomorus niphonius*) bulk up on rich nutrients and enter a second prime season in the autumn. For *hoba-yaki*, a rustic winter dish, the fish is cooked with miso on *hoba* leaves, which can withstand intense heat and also impart a pleasant aroma to food. In this recipe, the fish is briefly grilled over direct heat before being placed on the large leaves of the *ho* magnolia tree along with miso, ginkgo nuts, and other autumn ingredients, then steam-roasted in an earthenware *horaku* pot. The lid of the *horaku* is opened just before eating so that guests can savor the appetizing aromas that are released.

**SAMPLE CUT:** Width: 4.3 cm (1¾ in.)
Length: 6.6 cm (2⅝ in.)
Thickness: 1.4 cm (½ in.)
**WEIGHT:** 19.0 g (0.7 oz.)

*Serves 2*

4 portions *sawara* mackerel

Marinade
| 250 ml (8.5 fl. oz.) *koikuchi* shoyu
| 150 ml (5.1 fl. oz.) sake
| 100 ml (3.4 fl. oz.) mirin

Mix to combine, then burn off the alcohol.

*Hoba* miso
| 350 g (12.3 oz.) Sendai miso
| 150 g (5.3 oz.) white miso
| 180 ml (6.1 fl. oz.) sake
| 126 ml (4.3 fl. oz.) mirin
| 2 egg yolks

Whisk all ingredients together, then place over heat to thicken and reduce.

Garnishes
| 4 ginkgo nuts
| 40 g (1.4 oz.) *maitake* mushrooms

2 (dried) *hoba* leaves

Salt (for lining the *horaku*), as needed
Pine needles, as needed

**1** Marinate the fish for 15 minutes. Make incisions in the skin at approximately 3-cm (1⅛ in.) intervals to prevent the skin from peeling off in one piece when eaten. (See p. 121, step **2**.)

**2** Thread two portions consecutively onto two skewers using the flat-skewering (*hira-gushi*) technique.

**3** Grill and roast as shown at right.

**4** Use a kitchen torch to brown the surface, as shown at far right.

**5** Serve with the lid still on the *horaku* pot. Remove the lid just before eating to release the aroma of the roasted *hoba* leaves.

### Grilling Procedure
#### Grilling the flesh

| HEAT SOURCE | DIRECTION OF HEAT | TEMPERATURE | DISTANCE FROM HEAT |
|---|---|---|---|
| Electric grill | From below | 516°F (269°C) | 5.0 cm (2 in.) |

**00:00 Grilling flesh side (reverse side)**

The flesh side, which will be served face down, is grilled first. The proteins on the flesh side coagulate, ensuring that the fish retains its shape when the skin side contracts during grilling.

**02:54 Turning to grill on skin side**

**03:15 Turning to grill on flesh side**

**04:30 Checking color on flesh side**

**04:40 Turning to grill on skin side**

**07:53 Grilling complete**

The purpose here is to impart color and aroma. The flesh is not yet cooked through at this stage.

165°F (74°C)

### Arranging in the *horaku* pot

1. Spread miso on a *hoba* leaf.
2. Arrange one serving by placing two ginkgo nuts, half the *maitake* mushrooms, and one portion of the *sawara* on the miso. Top with *hoba* miso.
3. Place a second piece of fish on the first and top with *hoba* miso. Arrange another serving on the second *hoba* leaf in the same way.
4. Cover the bottom of the *horaku* with a layer of salt and sprinkle with water until moist. (The moisture in the salt will steam-roast the ingredients in the pot.) Spread the pine needles on the salt, arrange the fish on the *hoba* leaves, and cover with the lid.

### Steam-roasting in the *horaku* pot

| HEAT SOURCE | HEAT STRENGTH |
|---|---|
| Gas range | Outer-ring flame: medium<br>Inner-ring flame: high |

**00:00 Start of cooking**

**10:51 Cooking complete**

The temperature inside the *horaku* at the end of cooking was 259°F (126°C).

#### Imparting color

To finish, use a kitchen torch to brown the surface of the *hoba* miso.

YAKIMONO VARIATIONS 123

# Sea Bass Roasted in Green *Hoba* Leaves
*Suzuki no Aohoba-yaki*

Sea bass (*suzuki*) is an auspicious fish, prized since ancient times for its bright white flesh. It is known by different names throughout its life cycle. Summer is considered its peak season, and this recipe uses early season sea bass, flavored with fragrant early summer green *hoba* leaves and fresh *sansho* peppercorns. The fish is grilled until heated through, then slow-roasted wrapped in *hoba* leaves that impart their refreshing aroma when heated in the oven.

SAMPLE CUT: Width: 5.6 cm (2¼ in.)
Length: 13.0 cm (5⅛ in.)
Thickness: 2.3 cm (⅞ in.)
WEIGHT: 107.0 g (3.8 oz.)

*Serves 3*

3 portions sea bass (*suzuki*)

Marinade

360 ml (12.2 fl. oz.) de-alcoholized sake
60 ml (2 fl. oz.) *usukuchi* shoyu
60 ml (2 fl. oz.) mirin
10 g (0.4 oz.) *sansho* peppercorns (*mi-zansho*)

Mix to combine (no heating required)

Garnishes

¾ bud vinegar-pickled *myoga* (*su-zuke myoga*; see p. 196)
3 green *hoba* leaves
3 bamboo-sheath cords

**1** Clean and fillet sea bass in the *sanmai-oroshi* style and cut into portions. The flesh side will be served face up. Sprinkle salt (0.5% by weight) on the flesh side of the fish and let stand for 2 hours.

**2** Make lengthwise incisions on the flesh side, down to a depth of 3 mm (⅛ in.) before the skin. (Incisions are also made on the skin side, but if this is done before immersion in the marinade the flesh will fall apart, so at this stage incisions are made in the flesh side only.)

**3** Transfer to the marinade for 6 hours.

**4** Cut 2-mm (1/16 in.) incisions into the skin side, perpendicular to the incisions made on the flesh side. Sea bass has tough, thick skin; these incisions make the skin easier to eat and allow heat to penetrate more easily.

**5** Place two portions of fish alongside each other and thread them on five skewers crosswise from head to tail. Insert the *sansho* peppercorns from the marinade in the lengthwise incisions in the flesh.

**6** Grill and roast as shown at right.

**7** Arrange the cooked portions on a serving dish and garnish with the vinegar-pickled *myoga*.

### Grilling Procedure
**Cooking the flesh**

| HEAT SOURCE | DIRECTION OF HEAT | TEMPERATURE | DISTANCE FROM HEAT |
|---|---|---|---|
| Electric grill | From below | 774°F (412°C) | 3.8 cm (1½ in.) |

**00:00 Grilling skin side (reverse side)**

**01:50 Turning to grill on flesh side**

The skin is well browned after grilling.

**02:42 Grilling complete**

131°F (55°C)

### Wrapping in green *hoba* leaf

To prepare the green *hoba* leaves, trim the stems and use a rolling pin to flatten the hard veins near the stem on the underside of the leaf.

Place the grilled sea bass on the top side of the leaf near the stem. Wrap the leaf around the fish  and secure it with a bamboo-sheath cord.

### Cooking in oven

| HEAT SOURCE | TEMPERATURE | FAN SPEED | COOKING TIME |
|---|---|---|---|
| Steam convection oven (Hot air setting) | 338°F (170°C) | 1 (of 5) | 3 min. 35 sec. |

**00:00 Start of cooking**

**03:35 Cooking complete**

Cooking is finished when the surface of the leaves dries out.

147°F (64°C)

YAKIMONO VARIATIONS

### Tare-yaki

# Tade-Miso Grilled Sea Bass
*Suzuki no Tade-Miso-yaki*

This summer recipe enhances the fresh, clean flavor of sea bass by grilling it with a topping of *taki-miso* (cooked miso sauce) and *tade* water pepper, creating aromas and flavors similar to *dengaku*. (In *dengaku*, mild-tasting ingredients like tofu are paired with the bold flavors of *taki-miso*, which makes for rich aromas and browning when grilled.) This recipe leaves the central bones intact, and the fish is prepared so as to highlight the lean flesh that surrounds them. The surface is spritzed with sake to replenish moisture and ensure even cooking; the fish is cooked slowly so that heat penetrates to the center. Basting with *tare* sauce partway through the grilling process adds flavors and aromas and keeps the surface from overheating.

**SAMPLE CUT:** Width: 4.3 cm (1¾ in.)
Length: 9.7 cm (3⅞ in.)
Thickness: 3.5 cm (1⅜ in.)
**WEIGHT:** 75.0 g (2.6 oz.)

*Serves 1*

1 portion sea bass (*suzuki*)
Sake, as needed
Salt, as needed

*Tare* sauce (for basting)
| 180 ml (6.1 fl. oz.) sake
| 60 ml (2 fl. oz.) shoyu

Mix to combine (no heating required)

*Tade-miso*, as needed
(Salt *tade* water pepper leaves and crush in a *suribachi*; thicken with rice pressed into a paste, mix with *taki-miso*, and thin with sake. All ingredient quantities are discretional.)

*Taki-miso* (easy-to-make amount)
| 1 kg (35.3 oz.) white miso
| 900 ml (30.4 fl. oz.) Mikawa mirin
| 30 egg yolks
| Sugar, as needed

Mix to combine, then burn off the alcohol. Adjust the sweetness of the miso by adding sugar.

Garnishes
| 2 slices mustard-filled lotus root (*karashi renkon*; see p. 196)
| 5 pieces simmered wild butterbur (*yama-buki kyara-ni*; see p. 196)
| *Tade* leaves, as needed
| 1 paper mulberry leaf (*kaji no ha*)

**1** Fillet a cleaned sea bass into two pieces (*nimai-oroshi*), leaving the central bones intact. Cut a portion from the fillet with the central bones. Score the skin lengthwise to a depth of 5 mm (¼ in.) at 5-mm (¼ in.) intervals.

**2** The fish will be served skin side up. Insert skewers from the belly to the dorsal side using the flat-skewering (*hira-gushi*) technique.

**3** Spritz both sides of the fish with sake and sprinkle with salt (1% by weight).

**4** Grill as shown at right.

**5** Place the paper mulberry leaf on a serving dish, arrange the sea bass on the leaf, and scatter with *tade* leaves.

Garnish with the mustard-filled lotus root and simmered wild butterbur.

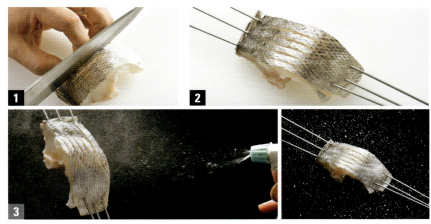

### Grilling procedure
#### Grilling the flesh

| HEAT SOURCE | DIRECTION OF HEAT | TEMPERATURE | DISTANCE FROM HEAT |
|---|---|---|---|
| Electric grill | From below | 833°F (445°C) | 8.7 cm (3⅜ in.) |

**00:00 Grilling skin side (serving side)**

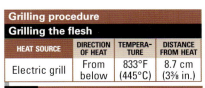

**04:54 Turning to grill on flesh side**

**06:37 Checking color on flesh side, and basting both sides with *tare* sauce**

Color on flesh side just before basting

**06:50 Grilling flesh side**

**07:08 Turning to grill on skin side**

**07:34 Checking color on skin side, applying *tade-miso* to skin side**

Color on skin side just before addition of *tade-miso*

162°F (72°C)

#### Grilling *tade-miso*

| DIRECTION OF HEAT | TEMPERATURE | DISTANCE FROM HEAT |
|---|---|---|
| From above | 833°F (445°C) | 11.0 cm (4⅜ in.) |

**00:00 Grilling *tade-miso***

The *tade-miso* is heated from above for a short time until it starts to color slightly.

187°F (86.3°C)

**01:13 Grilling complete**

YAKIMONO VARIATIONS 127

### Furishio-yaki
# Grilled Sea Bass with *Hosho* Paper
*Suzuki no Hosho-yaki*

Sea bass has a long history as a food fish, and in ancient times was cooked over an open fire. This dish is thought to originate in the practice of preparing fish by wrapping in *hosho* paper (used for official documents) to keep it clean in presenting to a ruler and placing the wrapped fish directly in the embers of the fire. In this recipe, the sea bass is infused with umami from kombu kelp before it is grilled over charcoal to impart color and aroma. The fish is then placed in a "boat" of kombu filled with delicately flavored stock, covered with *hosho* paper, and tied with red and white ceremonial *mizuhiki* cords to create a celebratory dish ideal for special occasions.

SAMPLE CUT: Width: 4.5 cm (1¾ in.)
Length: 5.0 cm (2 in.)
Thickness: 2.5 cm (1 in.)
WEIGHT: 50.0 g (1.8 oz.)

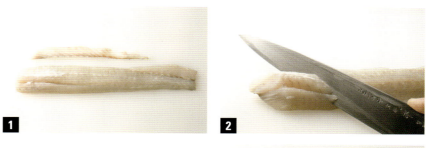

Not used | Parts used in this recipe | Not used

### Serves 3

3 portions sea bass (*suzuki*)

Salt, as needed

Three 10-cm (3⅞ in.) square pieces dried kombu

3 okra pods

*Koikuchi* shoyu, as needed

Kombu dashi, as needed

3 kombu "boats" (piece of kelp with the two ends tied together to make a vessel resembling a boat)

**1** Clean and fillet a sea bass in *sanmai-oroshi* style, removing the belly part and the bloodline bones (*chiaibone*).

**2** Cut three portions from the thickest part of the fillet.

**3** Cut two incisions to a depth of around 4 mm (⅛ in.) in the skin.

**4** Sprinkle both sides of the fish with salt (1% by weight) and let stand for 1 hour, then sandwich between two sheets of kombu and leave for 30 minutes.

**5** The fish will be served skin side up. Thread onto two skewers using the flat-skewering (*hira-gushi*) technique.

**6** Grill as shown on the following page.

**7** Place the kombu "boat" containing the sea bass on a tabletop brazier, cover with *hosho* paper, and tie with *mizuhiki* cords. Serve as the fish gently cooks over charcoal.

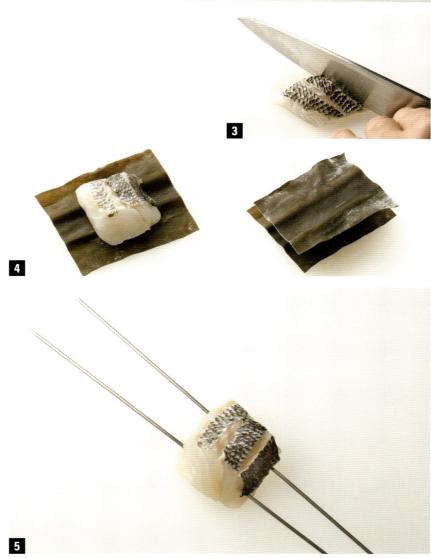

YAKIMONO VARIATIONS   129

## Grilling Procedure
### Grilling the flesh

| HEAT SOURCE | DIRECTION OF HEAT | TEMPERATURE | DISTANCE FROM HEAT |
|---|---|---|---|
| Charcoal | From below | 1400°F (760°C) | 9.0 cm (3½ in.) |

**00:00 Grilling skin side (serving side)**

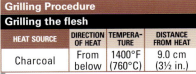

**01:53 Checking color on skin side**

At the same time as checking the color, press lightly to confirm that the skin is crisp.

**02:00 Turning to grill on flesh side**

**02:27 Checking color on flesh side**

**02:45 Spritzing on both sides with shoyu**

Apply shoyu to both skin and flesh sides.

**02:51 Grilling flesh side**

**03:18 Turning to grill on skin side**

**03:30 Grilling complete**

Do not overcook, since the fish will be heated again on the tabletop brazier. The center is still uncooked, with a core temperature of 135°F (57°C). The skin is well-grilled and crisp.

Cross-section immediately after grilling over charcoal

135°F (57°C)

### Slow heating on a tabletop brazier

Transfer the sea bass to a kombu "boat," garnish with an okra pod, and add kombu dashi to a level below the skin of the sea bass. Lay a bed of straw on the rack and place the kelp boat on top. Transfer the rack to a tabletop brazier containing a small amount of charcoal and straw for aroma. Cover the boat with *hosho* paper and secure with *mizuhiki* cords before serving. Allow the sea bass to cook slowly for around 4 minutes. The fragrant smoke from the straw will whet the diner's appetite while the heat penetrates evenly to the center of the fish.

Cross-section immediately after heating for 4 minutes on table-top brazier

138°F (59°C)

# Tilefish Grilled with *Karasumi* Powder
Guji no Karasumi-ko-yaki

*Karasumi*—salted, dried mullet roe—is an essential component of celebratory winter dishes. Particularly prized as a dish accompanying sake, it is one of the "three great delicacies"—*chinmi*—of Japanese cuisine, made by processing the ovaries of mullet. *Karasumi* powder is produced by making the most of parts trimmed off in serving *karasumi*; rather than let these parts be discarded, they are cooked, dried and ground into a fine powder. This recipe pairs *karasumi* powder with the premium fish tilefish (*amadai/guji*) for a dish that has become standard for the autumn-to-winter season. The tilefish is salted before grilling to retain moisture. The fish is topped with *karasumi* powder to enhance the umami flavors; finally, the *karasumi* powder is lightly grilled to bring out its distinctive aroma.

SAMPLE CUT: Width: 4.7 cm (1⅞ in.)
Length: 14.0 cm (5½ in.)
Thickness: 2.6 cm (1 in.)
WEIGHT: 72.0 g (2.5 oz.)

*Serves 1*

1 portion tilefish (*amadai*)

Salt, as needed

*Karasumi* powder, as needed

*Karasumi* powder

1 egg white (wrapped in a gauze pouch and squeezed to strain)

Garnishes

Soused spinach (*horenso no ohitashi*; see p. 196), as needed

4 maple leaves

**1** Without descaling, fillet the tilefish into two using the butterfly cut (*sebiraki*). Remove the spine and central bones. Sprinkle salt (1.3% by weight) on both sides of the fillet, salting more heavily where the flesh is thicker and more lightly where it is thin. Insert the knife close to the base of the ventral fin and remove the flesh (leave flesh attached to the collar so it can be used for a separate dish).

**2** Make a cut approximately 5 cm (2 in.) between the flesh and skin on the belly side of one portion and carefully slice off the skin.

**3** Roll the flesh on the belly side and thread onto three skewers using the single-tuck (*katazuma-ori*) technique. When inserting the skewers, "scoop" the flesh from the belly to the dorsal side to create a natural-looking roll.

**4** Pat the fish with a paper towel to remove excess moisture and ensure the scales will be crisp when finished.

**5** Grill as shown at right.

**6** Transfer the tilefish topped with *karasumi* powder to a serving dish, placing the crispy skin alongside. Garnish with the soused spinach and festoon with maple leaves.

**1**

**2**

**3**

### Grilling Procedure
#### Grilling the skin

| HEAT SOURCE | DIRECTION OF HEAT | TEMPERATURE | DISTANCE FROM HEAT |
|---|---|---|---|
| Electric grill | From below | 475°F (246°C) | 9.3 cm (3⅝ in.) |

**00:00** Grilling skin side (serving side)

Grill with the skin facing down to prevent fat from dripping out. Cook slowly over low heat so that the fish is fully heated, but the scales do not scorch.

**08:40** Grilling complete

Color when grilling is complete. If the fish is grilled beyond this point, the skin becomes hard to remove and the flesh is liable to fall apart.

Over-grilled scales ⊗

Using a metal chopstick, carefully remove the skin, taking care to retain its shape.

| DIRECTION OF HEAT | TEMPERATURE | DISTANCE FROM HEAT |
|---|---|---|
| From above | 639°F (337°C) | 16 cm (6¼ in.) |

Using heat from above, cook the inner side of the skin (the side that was attached to the flesh) for approximately 10 minutes.

### Grilling the flesh

| DIRECTION OF HEAT | TEMPERATURE | DISTANCE FROM HEAT |
|---|---|---|
| From below | 639°F (337°C) | 7.2 cm (2⅞ in.) |

Increase the intensity of the heat. The grilling bars are lowered to move the fish closer to the heat source.

**09:27** Grilling flesh side

**14:00** Checking color on flesh side

**14:09** Changing to heat from above and grilling skin side

The skin side, which will be brushed with egg white, is heated for a short time from above.

**14:31** Grilling complete

#### Adding the *karasumi* powder

Brush the skin side with egg white, then spread *karasumi* powder thickly and press with chopsticks so that it adheres.

#### Grilling the *karasumi* powder

| DIRECTION OF HEAT | TEMPERATURE | DISTANCE FROM HEAT |
|---|---|---|
| From above | 475°F (246°C) | 14.8 cm (5⅞ in.) |

**00:00** Grilling the *karasumi* powder

Grill using heat from above at low heat until an aroma is produced, taking care not to scorch or overcook.

**03:03** Grilling complete

136°F (58°C)

YAKIMONO VARIATIONS

# Tilefish, *Shiba-yaki* Style
*Guji no Shiba-yaki*

*Shiba-yaki* is a dish in which deep-fried potato strips resemble twigs of brushwood (*shiba*) gathered for firewood, an image capturing the feeling of autumn. In this recipe, grilled tilefish (*amadai/guji*) is served with a *shiba-yaki* topping festooned with ginkgo and maple leaf shapes made from sweet potato and *kuwai* (arrowhead bulb) slices and arranged to represent windswept autumn foliage. The *shiba* (twigs) are made with thinly sliced and julienned potatoes, soaked to remove starch and prevent scorching, and deep-fried without batter. Salt is allowed to penetrate the tilefish flesh deeply before cooking to improve moisture retention, and the fish is grilled so as to minimize moisture loss and maintain collagen.

SAMPLE CUT: Width: 4 cm (1⅝ in.)
Length: 9.2 cm (3⅝ in.)
Thickness: 1.6 cm (⅝ in.)
WEIGHT: 51.0 g (1.8 oz.)

*Serves 1*

1 fillet tilefish (*amadai*)
Salt, as needed

*Shiba-yaki* "brushwood" topping
  Potatoes, as needed
  Carrots, as needed
  Snow peas (*kinusaya*), as needed
  Egg white
  Rice oil, enough to cover the potatoes when deep-frying

Garnishes
  4 pieces deep-fried sweet potato
  3 pieces deep-fried *kuwai*
  (The sweet potato slices cut to resemble ginkgo and maple leaves and the *kuwai* slices cut into octagonal shapes should be tinted with food-coloring powder and dried, then deep-fried.)
  *Aomi* (green) radish pickled in miso (*aomi daikon no miso-zuke*; see p. 196), as needed

1. Clean and descale the tilefish using the *sukibiki* technique, fillet and cut a portion. Sprinkle salt (2% by weight) on both sides and allow to rest for 6 hours. Thread the fish onto three skewers using the *hira-gushi* technique.
2. Julienne the carrots, transfer to salt water (around 1% salinity) and bring to a boil, then drain.
3. Remove the stems, strings, and peas from the snow peas. Julienne the pods, then blanch in salt water (around 1% salinity). Remove and plunge in cold water, and transfer to a strainer.
4. Cut the potato thinly in the *katsura-muki* style, julienne, and immerse in water to remove excess starch. Drain, then deep-fry in rice oil at 338°F (170°C).
5. Whisk the egg white, but do not allow it to thicken.
6. Mix a small amount of the egg white with a loose pile of the carrot, pea, and potato "brushwood."
7. Grill as shown below.
8. Transfer the tilefish and *shiba-yaki* topping to a serving dish, garnish with *aomi* radish pickled in miso, and top with deep-fried *kuwai* octagons and sweet potato cut to resemble ginkgo and maple leaves.

### Grilling Procedure
#### Grilling the flesh

| HEAT SOURCE | DIRECTION OF HEAT | TEMPERATURE | DISTANCE FROM HEAT |
|---|---|---|---|
| Electric grill | From below | 585°F (307°C) | 9.5 cm (3¾ in.) |

**00:00 Grilling skin side (serving side)**

Initial grilling on the skin side to cook the fish around 80 percent through.

**06:09 Turning to grill on flesh side**

**06:49 Grilling complete**

180°F (82°C)

### Adding *shiba-yaki* topping on the skin side

#### Grilling the *shiba-yaki* topping

| DIRECTION OF HEAT | TEMPERATURE | DISTANCE FROM HEAT |
|---|---|---|
| From above | 585°F (307°C) | 16.5 cm (6½ in.) |

**00:00 Grilling the *shiba-yaki* topping**

Grill from above for a short time until the egg white sets.

**01:12 Grilling complete**

223°F (106°C)

YAKIMONO VARIATIONS 135

# Grilled *Kinmedai* Marinated in Sake Lees
Kinmedai no Sake-kasu-yaki

*Kinmedai* (splendid alfonsino; *Beryx splendens*, lit. "golden-eye snapper") is a widely distributed deep-sea species found in the Atlantic, Australia, and Africa as well as in seas around Japan. The flesh has a soft texture, with plenty of fat, and is used in a wide range of culinary styles, from sashimi to *yakimono* and *nimono* (simmered dishes).

Sake lees (*sake kasu*) are a byproduct of the sake-brewing process resulting from the pressing of the mash (*moromi*) to extract the sake. Since ancient times, the pleasant flavor and high nutritional value of sake lees have led to their use in a wide variety of culinary applications. In this recipe, the lees are cooked and used as a marinating bed after being slightly rehydrated with de-alcoholized sake. The fish is cooked over low heat, since the lees clinging to the fish are prone to scorching. This recipe is categorized as a *yuan-yaki* recipe in this book.

SAMPLE CUT: Width: 6.3 cm (2½ in.)
Length: 18.0 cm (7⅛ in.)
Thickness: 1.4 cm (½ in.)
WEIGHT: 60.0 g (2.1 oz.)

*Serves 3*

3 portions *kinmedai*
Salt, as needed

Sake lees bed (*kasu-doko*) for marinating
 500 g (17.6 oz.) sake lees (processed for marinating)
 200 g (7.1 oz.) sugar
 100 ml (3.4 fl. oz.) *koikuchi* shoyu
 100 ml (3.4 fl. oz.) de-alcoholized sake

Sake lees

Sake, as needed

Garnishes
 Candied walnuts (*kurumi ame-ni*; see p. 197), as needed
 Yellow yuzu zest

**1** Sprinkle salt (0.5% by weight) on the fish and let stand for 2 hours.

**2** Combine the sake lees with the other ingredients to make the marinating bed. Place the fish portions between two layers of gauze, and sandwich them between layers of the sake lees bed. Allow to stand for 8 hours.

**3** Thread each portion onto three skewers using the single-tuck (*kata-zuma-ori*) technique. Treat the skin side as the serving side.

**4** Grill as shown at right.

**5** Transfer the fish to a serving dish and garnish with the candied walnuts. Sprinkle with yellow yuzu zest.

1

3

2

**Grilling Procedure**

| HEAT SOURCE | DIRECTION OF HEAT | TEMPERATURE | DISTANCE FROM HEAT |
|---|---|---|---|
| Electric grill | From below | 658°F (348°C) | 7.3 cm (2⅞ in.) |

**00:00** Grilling skin side (serving side)

**03:05** Checking color on skin side

**03:11** Turning to grill on flesh side

**05:25** Checking color on flesh side and spritzing with sake on skin side

In addition to lowering the temperature and preventing scorching, spritzing also imparts the aroma of the sake.

**05:34** Grilling skin side

Finish by heating just enough to burn off the sake.

**07:05** Grilling complete

## Effects of Marinating in Sake Lees Bed

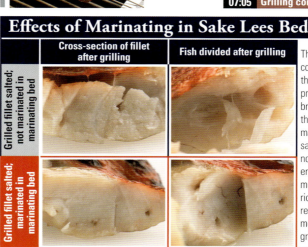

The koji mold in sake lees contains amylase enzymes that break down starch and proteolytic enzymes that break down proteins. When the fish is immersed in a marinating bed containing sake lees, sugar, and shoyu, not only do the proteolytic enzymes break down the muscle fibers, but the saccharides also help with moisture retention. This results in a more succulent finish than grilling with salt alone.

YAKIMONO VARIATIONS 137

### Yuan-yaki
# Koji Grilled Salmon
*Sake no Koji-yaki*

---

Salmon are found in a wide range of habitats in the North Pacific and Arctic, including seas around Japan, Canada, and Norway. There are many species, but in Japan, the variety most commonly used as food since ancient times is the chum salmon (*Oncorhynchus keta*), called *shirozake* (white salmon) in Japanese.

Koji, an essential ingredient in Japanese cuisine, is made by inoculating rice, barley, wheat, or soybeans with the *Aspergillus oryzae* mold and allowing it to proliferate. In this recipe, the salmon is immersed in a koji marinade and then grilled to preserve the aroma and mellow sweetness of the koji. To reduce the sweetness, one variation would be to add salt to the koji and marinate the fish in the resulting *shiokoji* before grilling.

SAMPLE CUT: Width: 6.2 cm (2½ in.)
Length: 19.5 cm (7⅝ in.)
Thickness: 1.5 cm (⅝ in.)
WEIGHT: 72.0 g (2.5 oz.)

*Serves 3*

3 portions salmon (*sake*)
Salt, as needed

Koji bed (koji *doko*) for marinating
| 1 kg (35.3 oz.) dried rice koji
| 1 L (33.8 fl. oz.) de-alcoholized sake

Dried rice koji

Garnish
| Syrup-simmered yuzu rind (*amigasa-yuzu*; see p. 197), as needed

**1** Make the koji marinade. Place the rice koji and de-alcoholized sake in a stainless steel marinating pan and mix, then cover with plastic wrap. Heat in a steam convection oven for 4 to 5 hours, then allow to cool.

**2** Sprinkle salt (1% by weight) on the salmon and let stand for 2 hours. (If making the *shiokoji* variation, reduce salt to 0.5% by weight for this step.)

**3** Place the salmon pieces in the koji marinade and leave for 8 hours.

**4** Remove the salmon from the koji marinade, brush excess koji off the

| Making the koji marinade | | | |
|---|---|---|---|
| HEAT SOURCE | TEMPERATURE | FAN SPEED | COOKING TIME |
| Steam convection oven (Steam setting) | 140°F (60°C) | 3 (of 5) | 4–5 hours |

To prevent the koji mold from becoming inactive, the temperature setting should be kept at 140°F (60°C) or lower.

surface of the fish, and thread each piece onto three skewers using the single-tuck (*katazuma-ori*) technique, treating the skin side as the serving side. A little koji may adhere to the surface of the fish; this is fine.

**5** Grill as shown at right.

**6** Transfer the salmon to a serving dish and garnish with the syrup-simmered yuzu rind.

## Grilling Procedure
### Grilling the flesh

| HEAT SOURCE | DIRECTION OF HEAT | TEMPERATURE | DISTANCE FROM HEAT |
|---|---|---|---|
| Electric grill | From below | 712°F (378°C) | 6.9 cm (2¾ in.) |

**00:00** Grilling skin side (serving side)
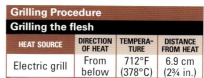

**02:38** Checking color on skin side

**02:42** Turning to grill on flesh side

**05:51** Checking color on flesh side

**05:55** Turning to grill on skin side

**06:26** Grilling complete

189°F (87°C)    162°F (72.2°C)

## Effects of Immersion in the Koji Marinade

| | Cross-section before grilling | Cross-section after grilling | Fish divided after grilling |
|---|---|---|---|
| Fish salted but not marinated in koji | | | |
| Fish salted and marinated in koji | | | |

Koji mold contains amylase enzymes that break down starch and proteolytic enzymes that break down proteins. When the koji marinade is made, the starches in the rice are broken down into sugars, while the proteins are broken down into amino acids. Because the enzymes in the koji marinade are still active, when the fish is immersed in the marinade, proteolytic enzymes break down the proteins in the muscle cells, while saccharides help with moisture retention. This results in a softer, more succulent outcome than grilling with salt alone.

YAKIMONO VARIATIONS   139

# Rikyu Style Sesame-Grilled Flounder
*Hirame no Rikyu-yaki*

Flounder (*hirame*), which is in season from autumn and winter, ranks alongside sea bream (*tai*) as one of the most commonly consumed fish in Japanese cuisine, and is widely farmed. It has muscular, firm flesh and a delicate and refined flavor. Recipes featuring sesame seeds are sometimes referred to as "rikyu" style after the sixteenth-century tea master Sen no Rikyu. He was known not only for his profound influence on the development of tea culture, but also for his fondness for dishes using sesame seeds. This dish is enjoyable for the contrasting textures and aromas of the springy flesh and crunchy sesame seeds.

SAMPLE CUT: Width: 5.4 cm (2⅛ in.)
Length: 8.2 cm (3¼ in.)
Thickness: 0.8 cm (⅜ in.)
WEIGHT: 23.0 g (0.8 oz.)

*Serves 2*

6 portions flounder (*hirame*)
Salt, as needed

Shoyu marinade for black sesame portions
| 450 ml (15.2 fl. oz.) sake
| 270 ml (9.1 fl. oz.) *koikuchi* shoyu
| 90 ml (3 fl. oz.) de-alcoholized mirin

Mix to combine (no heating required)

Miso marinade for white sesame portions
| 450 ml (15.2 fl. oz.) sake
| 270 ml (9.1 fl. oz.) *koikuchi* shoyu
| 180 g (6.3 oz.) white miso
| 90 ml (3 fl. oz.) de-alcoholized mirin

Mix to combine (no heating required)

Gold sesame seeds, as needed
Black sesame seeds, as needed
White sesame seeds, as needed
Egg white, whisked with chopsticks

Gold sesame seeds | Black sesame seeds | White sesame seeds

Garnish
| Soused butterbur (*fuki no ohitashi*; see p. 197), as needed

**1** Fillet the flounder into five pieces (*gomai-oroshi*) and remove the scales using the *sukibiki* technique. Cut portions from the dorsal fillet. Remove the *engawa* (the chewy muscle located near the base of the dorsal and anal fins), and make small, narrow incisions in the skin side (serving side).

**2** Sprinkle salt (2% by weight) on gold sesame seed portion. Immerse the portions to be used with black sesame seeds in the shoyu marinade and leave for 15 minutes. Immerse the portions to be used with white sesame seeds in the miso marinade and leave for 15 minutes.

**3** Thread each portion on two skewers using the flat-skewering (*hira-gushi*) technique.

**4** Grill as shown below and on following pages.

**5** Transfer the three different preparations of flounder to a serving dish and garnish with the soused butterbur.

Shoyu marinade | Miso marinade

## Gold sesame seed portion

### Grilling Procedure
### Grilling the flesh

| HEAT SOURCE | DIRECTION OF HEAT | TEMPERATURE | DISTANCE FROM HEAT |
|---|---|---|---|
| Electric grill | From below | 414°F (212°C) | 10.2 cm (4 in.) |

**00:00** Grilling flesh side (reverse side)

**02:10** Turning to grill on skin side

**05:06** Turning to grill on flesh side
**06:27** Turning to grill on skin side
**07:41** Checking color

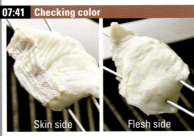

Skin side | Flesh side

Color immediately before adding the gold sesame seeds

**Applying egg white to the skin side and adding gold sesame seeds**

**Coating the fish in sesame seeds**

**00:00** Grilling flesh side

**00:41** Turning to grill on skin side

**02:17** Grilling complete

## Black and white sesame seed portions

### Grilling Procedure
#### Grilling the flesh

| HEAT SOURCE | DIRECTION OF HEAT | TEMPERATURE | DISTANCE FROM HEAT |
|---|---|---|---|
| Electric grill | From below | 414°F (212°C) | 10.2 cm (4 in.) |

**00:00  Grilling flesh side (reverse side)**

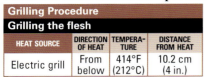

For use with white sesame seeds (miso)

For use with black sesame seeds (shoyu)

**02:10  Grilling skin side**

**03:54  Basting the portions that will be coated in black sesame seeds and white sesame seeds with their respective basting sauce, and heating on the flesh side**

Black sesame seed portion (shoyu)

White sesame seed portion (miso)

**Turning over**

Both portions should be turned twice.

**07:33  Basting the two portions with their respective sauces and heating on the flesh side**

**Turning over**

The black sesame portion is turned five times, and the white sesame portion three times, before application of egg white. For both, heat the skin side immediately before adding the egg white.

**11:02  Checking color**

Flesh side — White sesame seed portion (miso); Black sesame seed portion (shoyu)

Skin side — White sesame seed portion (miso); Black sesame seed portion (shoyu)

Color immediately before adding the sesame seeds

### Applying egg white to the skin side and coating with sesame seeds

Black sesame seeds

White sesame seeds

### Coating the fish in sesame seeds

**00:00  Grilling flesh side**

**01:25  Turning to grill on skin side**

**02:25  Grilling complete**

142  YAKIMONO VARIATIONS

The sesame plant is believed to have originated in the African savanna. It likely arrived in Japan via China; seeds have been excavated from sites from the late Jomon period (around 1200 BCE). By the Nara period (eighth century), sesame oil was being used for cooking. Favored as an important source of oil in the vegetarian style of food prepared in Buddhist temples (*shojin ryori*), sesame seeds were adopted for use in various types of cuisine. In addition to being used in ground form (*suri-goma*), whole roasted sesame seeds (*iri-goma*), and chopped sesame seeds (*kiri-goma*) are an ingredient in many types of Japanese cuisine: For example, mixed with tofu in *shira-ae* (a dish of mashed tofu and toasted sesame seeds), or combined with *kuzu* and dashi to make *goma-dofu* (sesame-based tofu). Different types of sesame seeds—gold, black, and white, based on the color of the outer hull—have their own distinctive flavors.

## Grilled Pufferfish
### *Furishio-yaki* / *Yaki-fugu*

Pufferfish (*fugu*) is a premium fish that is at its best in the winter. In addition to being grilled, it can be served in a variety of ways—as sashimi, or in a *nabe* hotpot. The flesh is lean but high in collagen, which gelatinizes when heated, creating a delightfully springy and firm texture. In this recipe, the milt and flesh, characterized by refined umami and sweetness, are salted and grilled. The *totoumi* (a gelatinous membrane layer between the flesh and the skin, which has a resilient consistency) is marinated and then grilled. Its distinctive texture is one of the attractions of this recipe.

**Central bones**
SAMPLE CUT:
Width: 3.8 cm (1½ in.)
Length: 5.0 cm (2 in.)
Thickness: 2.5 cm (1 in.)
WEIGHT: 38.0 g (1.3 oz.)

**Milt (*shirako*)**
SAMPLE CUT:
Width: 4.5 cm (1¾ in.)
Length: 6.3 cm (2½ in.)
Thickness: 2.0 cm (¾ in.)
WEIGHT: 32.0 g (1.1 oz.)

***Totoumi***
SAMPLE CUT:
Width: 5.3 cm (2⅛ in.)
Length: 5.6 cm (2¼ in.)
Thickness: 0.6 cm (¼ in.)
WEIGHT: 10.0 g (0.4 oz.)

*Serves 3*

6 portions pufferfish (*fugu*) central bones and attached flesh
3 portions milt
3 portions *totoumi*
Salt, as needed
90 ml (3 fl. oz.) sake

Marinade for *totoumi*
| 450 ml (15.2 fl. oz.) sake
| 450 ml (15.2 fl. oz.) *koikuchi* shoyu
| 270 ml (9.1 fl. oz.) de-alcoholized mirin
Mix to combine (no heating required)

Garnishes
| 2 *sudachi*
| 1 sprig nandina (*nanten*)

**1** Sprinkle the central bones (and *kama* collar if using) with salt (2% by weight), add the sake, and massage gently to allow the flavors to penetrate.

**2** Thread the central bones and the milt on skewers. Use two skewers for each, threading them in such a way as to ensure that the cut side of the central bones and the milt face the heat source. Either side may be used as the serving side.

**3** Salt the milt. (Because of the dense flavor of the milt, it is normally salted rather heavily, but chefs may adjust according to preference.)

**4** Marinate the *totoumi* for 2 to 3 minutes.

**5** Grill as shown at right.

**6** Lay the nandina in a serving dish and arrange the central bones, milt, and *totoumi* on the plate. Garnish with the *sudachi*.

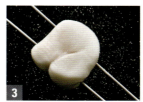

### Grilling Procedure
#### Grilling central bones and milt

| HEAT SOURCE | DIRECTION OF HEAT | TEMPERATURE | DISTANCE FROM HEAT |
|---|---|---|---|
| Electric grill | From below | 498°F (259°C) | 9.0 cm (3½ in.) |

**00:00** Start of grilling (either side may be grilled first)

**03:37** Turning to grill on reverse side

Heat until the surface becomes dry.

**06:32** Turning central bones to grill on serving side

**08:45** Turning milt to grill on serving side

**10:42** Turning central bones to grill on reverse side

**12:20** Grilling of central bones complete

**12:30** Grilling of milt complete

165°F (74°C) (Milt)

### Grilling the *totoumi*

| HEAT SOURCE | DIRECTION OF HEAT | TEMPERATURE | DISTANCE FROM HEAT |
|---|---|---|---|
| Electric grill | From below | 498°F (259°C) | 11.0 cm (4⅜ in.) |

**00:00** Grilling flesh side (reverse)

The flesh side is grilled first, because the flesh tends to curl when heated.

**02:10** Turning to grill on skin side

**03:09** Turning to grill on flesh side

**03:53** Turning to grill on skin side

**06:11** Grilling complete

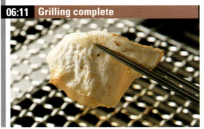

### Pufferfish Poison
Pufferfish are extremely poisonous, and consumption of the toxins is fatal in many cases. For this reason, there are strict laws in Japan regulating the species and parts that can be offered for consumption and the way they are prepared and cooked. Only licensed chefs who have obtained specialized qualifications are allowed to prepare the fish.

YAKIMONO VARIATIONS

## Grilled Pike Conger with *Tare* Sauce

Hamo no Tare-yaki

Pike conger (*hamo*) is one of the tastes of summer, coming into season just after the early summer rains have passed and enjoyed until early autumn. It is said to gain its flavor by drinking the rains of the *tsuyu*, or rainy season, which affects most of the archipelago through the early summer months. The tough, long body is filled with numerous small bones, so the *honekiri* technique is used to sever the bones and make the flesh palatable before cooking. In this recipe, the *honekiri*-prepared pike conger is "sandwiched" between sheets of kombu to imbue the fish with umami flavors before it is grilled with sauce. Pike conger is rich in collagen, and slow cooking allows the collagen to gelatinize, giving the finished fish a tender texture. The skin is grilled at high heat to make it easier to eat and to impart aroma. To prevent scorching, care should be taken to keep the sauce from dripping onto the skin during the final stages of grilling.

SAMPLE CUT: Length: 12.4 cm (4⅞ in.)
Width: 11.1 cm (4⅜ in.)
Thickness: 1.5 cm (⅝ in.)
WEIGHT: 111.0 g (3.9 oz.)

*Serves 3*

3 portions pike conger (*hamo*), with flesh scored to sever the small bones (*honekiri*)

Salt, as needed

6 pieces kombu (15 cm/5⅞ in. square sheets)

Basting sauce

| 1.8 L (60.9 fl. oz.) mirin
| 1 L (33.8 fl. oz.) *koikuchi* shoyu

Bring the mirin to a boil to burn off the alcohol and simmer for 5 minutes, then add half the *koikuchi* shoyu and simmer for 5 minutes on low heat. Add the remaining shoyu and simmer for 5 minutes more until the liquid thickens.

Garnishes

| Yam-and-egg sauce (*tamago imo*; see p. 197), as needed
| Chopped *shiso* leaf (*oba*)
| Chopped *myoga*
| White sesame seeds
| *Shichimi* spice mixture

**1** Cut the *honekiri*-prepared pike conger into pieces suitable for skewering, sprinkle with salt (0.5% by weight) and let stand for 1 hour. Sandwich each piece with the skin side down between two sheets of kombu and leave for 30 minutes more.

**2** Orient the pieces vertically on the work surface and insert four skewers along the skin, starting from the narrow end and working toward the wider side, from head to tail. The pieces will be served flesh side up. Since the skin shrinks during cooking, insert skewers horizontally above and below to prevent the flesh from curling.

**3** Grill as shown at right.

**4** Transfer the pike conger to a serving dish, garnish with the yam-and-egg sauce, and top with the *shiso* leaf, *myoga*, white sesame seeds, and *shichimi* spice mixture.

### Grilling Procedure
#### Grilling the skin

**Searing the skin side with charcoal to create char marks before cooking**

Press charcoal heated to 1400°F (760°C) against the skin to char it to achieve the Maillard effect. Remove the horizontal skewers.

#### Grilling the flesh

| HEAT SOURCE | DIRECTION OF HEAT | TEMPERATURE | DISTANCE FROM HEAT |
|---|---|---|---|
| Charcoal | From below | 1222–1400°F (661–760°C) | 8.5 cm (3⅜ in.) |

#### Pouring basting sauce on flesh side

Care should be taken to keep the *tare* sauce from making contact with the skin side so that the aroma of the charred skin is preserved.

**00:00 Grilling flesh side (serving side)**

Rotate the skewers regularly during grilling so that the flesh does not stick to the hot metal.

Pike conger is rich in collagen, and once it has been processed by the *honekiri* technique, it remains tender even when grilled at high temperatures. To protect the natural flavor of the fish, *tare* is not applied to the skin side. Care should also be taken to ensure that the flesh side does not absorb too much *tare* during grilling. Grilling concentrates the sauce on the surface of the flesh, creating a contrast between the rich flavor of the sauce and the delicate natural flavor of the pike conger.

**Checking color on flesh side**

**02:56 Basting and grilling flesh side**

As cooking progresses, frequently turn the pike conger over to prevent the heated side from scorching (in this example, the fish was turned 13 times by the 03:51 mark while regularly checking color).

**Checking color on flesh side**

**03:51 Basting and grilling flesh side**

Turn frequently, as the *tare* sauce scorches easily.

**04:34 Grilling skin side**

**04:46 Grilling complete**

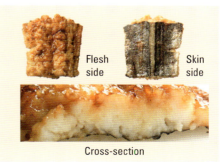

Flesh side    Skin side

Cross-section

# Grilled Conger Eel, Yawata Style
*Anago no Yawata-maki*

*Yawata-maki* is a style of cooking in which eel (*unagi*) or conger eel (*anago*) are wrapped around burdock root (*gobo*) and grilled. The name comes from Yawata, a town outside Kyoto that was once a well-known center of burdock production. The conger eel flesh is tied and knotted in the *aioi* style (see p. 205), then wrapped securely around a burdock core and grilled. During cooking, the flesh is basted repeatedly to achieve an even, glossy sheen. In this recipe, the finished rolls are served on a glass dish evoking coolness, garnished with green maple leaves and a bright orange *hozuki* fruit (*Physalis alkekengi*; Chinese lantern).

SAMPLE CUT: Width: 3.4 cm (1⅜ in.)
Length: 45.4 cm (17⅞ in.)
Thickness: 1.3 cm (½ in.)
WEIGHT: 81.0 g (2.9 oz.)
(SINGLE FILLET)

See page 205 for instructions for long-fish-wrapped burdock, Yawata style.

**1**

*Serves 3*

1 conger eel (*anago*)
½ burdock root (*gobo*)

Basting sauce
  200 ml (6.8 fl. oz.) *koikuchi* shoyu
  190 ml (6.4 fl. oz.) mirin
  40 ml (2 Tbsp. plus 2 tsp.) *tamari* shoyu
  40 ml (2 Tbsp. plus 2 tsp.) sake

Garnishes
  3 *manganji* peppers, grilled, with the stem and seeds removed
  1 *hozuki* Chinese lantern
  2 green maple leaves

**1** Place three *Yawata-maki* in a row lengthwise and mount them on five skewers arranged like the ribs of a fan.

**2** Grill as shown at right.

**3** Cut the rolls into bite-sized pieces and transfer to a serving dish. Arrange the *manganji* peppers alongside and garnish with the *hozuki* and green maple leaves.

## Grilling Procedure
### Preliminary grilling

| HEAT SOURCE | DIRECTION OF HEAT | TEMPERATURE | DISTANCE FROM HEAT |
|---|---|---|---|
| Electric grill | From below | 392°F (200°C) | 18.2 cm (7⅛ in.) |

Grilling takes place at low heat from a distance, since the skin can blister at high temperatures. The surface temperature was 145°F (63°C) before the heat was increased.

**00:00** Start of grilling (either side may be grilled first)

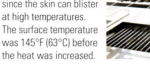

**17:16** Turning to grill on reverse side

**31:25** Adjusting rolls on skewers

Grilling is paused. Each *Yawata-maki* is turned 90 degrees and remounted on the skewers. This allows heat to reach uncooked areas of the surface.

**34:11** Grilling resumes

**42:29** Increasing heat to brown the surface
TEMPERATURE: 635°F (335°C)

**43:18** Turning to grill on reverse side

**47:02** Grilling complete

## Cutting in half and re-skewering

After preliminary grilling, the *Yawata-maki* are cut in half crosswise and remounted on skewers. Space should be left between the pieces so that the basting sauce can be applied evenly to all parts of the rolls.

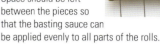

### Main grilling

| TEMPERATURE | DISTANCE FROM HEAT |
|---|---|
| 516°F (269°C) | 9.5 cm (3¾ in.) |

**00:00** Grilling serving side

**02:03** Turning to grill on reverse side

**03:10** Basting and grilling

Stand the *Yawata-maki* vertically and pour basting sauce over the burdock filling at the center. Pour sauce into one end and grill horizontally, then pour into the opposite end and grill in the same way. Repeat this process four times, re-skewering each time to alternate the side exposed to heat.

**10:27** Grilling complete

The glazed effect is produced when the surface is even. The fats in the conger eel and the viscosity from the mirin and other ingredients in the basting sauce create a thick layer with a smooth, uniform surface that takes on a glossy finish.

YAKIMONO VARIATIONS 149

**Miscellaneous**

# Grilled Sea Bream and Shrimp Roasted in a *Horaku*

Madai to Ebi no Horaku-yaki

*Horaku-yaki* is a preparation in which seafood, vegetables, and other ingredients are steam-roasted by placing them in a lidded unglazed earthenware pot called a *horaku*. In this recipe, the *horaku* is lined with black Nachiguro slate stones. Slices of sea bream, tiger prawns, matsutake mushrooms, and soft-boiled eggs are added and topped with *kuzu* leaves, then steamed. The sea bream and prawns are grilled over charcoal beforehand to impart color and aroma. The lid is lifted just before serving, dramatically releasing the delicious autumnal aromas at the table.

### Sea bream (*madai*)

SAMPLE CUT: Width: 3.2 cm (1¼ in.)
Length: 7.4 cm (2⅞ in.)
Thickness: 3.3 cm (1¼ in.)
WEIGHT: 51.4 g (1.8 oz.)

### Tiger prawn (*kuruma-ebi*)

SAMPLE: Width: 3.3 cm (1¼ in.)
Length: 20.0 cm (7⅞ in.)
Thickness: 2.7 cm (1⅛ in.)
WEIGHT: 52.8 g (1.9 oz.)

*Serves 4*

4 portions sea bream (*madai*)
4 tiger prawns (*kuruma-ebi*)
1 matsutake mushroom quartered vertically
2 eggs (immerse in cold water and cook for 7 to 8 minutes, until soft-boiled)
Salt, as needed

Black Nachiguro stones, as needed
Pine needles, as needed
5 *kuzu* leaves

**1** Thread the sea bream two portions at a time onto two skewers using the flat-skewering (*hira-gushi*) technique with the skin as the serving side. Skewer the tiger prawns individually using the wave-skewering (*uneri-gushi*) technique.

**2** Secure the tiger prawns together by skewering horizontally through the bellies. Apply a coating of salt (*kesho-jio*) to the tips of the heads, legs, and tails, and sprinkle salt on the abdomens.

**3** Grill as shown at right.

**4** Serve the *horaku* with the lid still on, removing it at the table so diners can savor the appetizing aromas that waft from the pot.

**1**

### Grilling Procedure
#### Grilling over charcoal

| HEAT SOURCE | DIRECTION OF HEAT | TEMPERATURE | DISTANCE FROM HEAT |
|---|---|---|---|
| Charcoal | From below | 1022°F (550°C) | 6.0 cm (2⅜ in.) |

**00:00  Grilling skin side of sea bream, dorsal side of tiger prawns**

The sea bream is grilled on the skin side only, and the prawns on the dorsal side only, to impart light grill marks.

**01:39  Grilling of tiger prawns complete**

**02:12  Grilling of sea bream complete**

### Transferring to *horaku*

Place a bed of washed black Nachiguro stones in the *horaku*, top with the pine needles, and add the pre-grilled sea bream and tiger prawns, as well as the matsutake mushroom (quartered) and soft-boiled eggs.

Mist the *kuzu* leaves, lay them over the ingredients, and close the lid of the *horaku*. In addition to imparting their aroma during cooking, the dampened *kuzu* leaves add moisture.

### Steam-roasting in brick oven

| HEAT SOURCE | TEMPERATURE |
|---|---|
| Brick oven | 788°F (420°C) |

**00:00  Start of cooking**

**07:00  Cooking complete**

194°F (90°C)   156°F (69°C) (Sea bream)

Cross-section of tiger prawn    Cross-section of sea bream

The flesh of the tiger prawn is tender and moist, while the sea bream flesh separates easily along the lines of the muscle fibers.

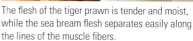

YAKIMONO VARIATIONS  151

Miscellaneous

# Grilled Lobster in the Shell
*Ise ebi no Onigara-yaki*

*Onigara-yaki* is a method of cooking lobsters or other crustaceans by splitting and grilling them in their shells, effectively using the shell as a cooking vessel. The dish is often served to mark the arrival of spring, playing on the association of driving away demons (*oni*) with the rituals of Setsubun that are held in early February. In this recipe, Ise lobster is grilled in its shell and served with a topping of sea urchin—looking festive atop a bed of green *urajiro* ferns, which are also used in traditional New Year's decorations. Care is taken not to overcook the lobster so that the flesh remains somewhat firm.

**SAMPLE:** Width: 19.0 cm (7½ in.)
Length: 5.0 cm (2 in.)
Thickness: 4.5 cm (1¾ in.)
**WEIGHT:** 285.0 g (10.1 oz.)

***Serves 2***

1 lobster (*Ise ebi*)
Sea urchin (*uni*), as needed
Salt, as needed

Garnishes
 2 *sudachi*
 *Urajiro* ferns, as needed

1. Place the lobster on a cutting board with the belly up and the tail pointing toward you. Split the lobster lengthwise, starting with the tail.
2. Turn the lobster so that the head is facing toward you, and split the rest of the lobster down the middle.
3. Sprinkle salt (to taste) on the cut faces of the two halves of the lobster. Grill immediately. (If the salt is allowed to sit for too long, the lobster may become slippery.)
4. **Grill as shown at right.**
5. Place the lobster on a bed of *urajiro* ferns arranged in a serving dish and garnish with the *sudachi*.

### Grilling Procedure

| HEAT SOURCE | DIRECTION OF HEAT | TEMPERATURE | DISTANCE FROM HEAT |
|---|---|---|---|
| Electric grill | From above | 545°F (285°C) | 14.5 cm (5¾ in.) |

**00:00 Grilling the cut surface (serving side)**

The legs will detach naturally as grilling proceeds.

**07:56 Grilling complete**

Split side

The flesh is cooked to leave some fibrous quality in the texture.

118°F (48°C)

### Remove the flesh, cut into bite-sized pieces, and add sea urchin topping

Remove the flesh from both halves of the carapace by inserting a knife at the head and tail ends. Cut the flesh into bite-sized pieces, return to the shells, and top with the sea urchin.

### Imparting color

Use a kitchen torch to add light grill marks on the surface of the sea urchin. Do not cook through, as this will reduce the creaminess and cause the flesh to toughen.

128°F (53.1°C)

Miscellaneous

# Grilled Cuttlefish, *Ro-yaki* Style
Ika no Ro-yaki

*Ro-yaki* ("wax" grilling), also known as *kimi-*(yolk) or *kogane-*(gold) *yaki*, is a style of cooking in which egg yolk imparts a brightly colored, glossy finish to grilled food. This recipe is a standard dish often used to add color to *hassun* and traditional New Year's dishes. It is made by grilling salted cuttlefish while basting the serving side of the flesh with egg yolk. Since the egg yolk changes color with the application of heat and scorches easily, additional yolk is repeatedly applied during heating to preserve the shiny, vibrant color. Brushing the cuttlefish with egg yolk also enriches the flavor. The dish is garnished with *kikka-kabura* (one of the foods traditionally served at the New Year) and sprigs of *goyo-matsu*, a five-needled species of pine with festive associations.

SAMPLE CUT: Width: 13.2 cm (5¼ in.)
Length: 14.8 cm (5⅞ in.)
Thickness: 1.0 cm (⅜ in.)
WEIGHT: 147.0 g (5.2 oz.)

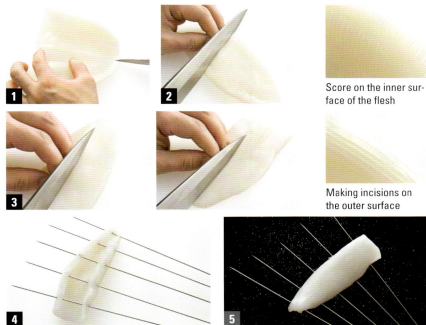

Score on the inner surface of the flesh

Making incisions on the outer surface

*Serves 3*

1 golden cuttlefish (*ko-ika*)
Salt, as needed
3 egg yolks (whisk gently)

Garnishes
　Three 2-cm (¾ in.) pieces pickled turnip, cut "chrysanthemum" style (*kikka-kabura*; see p. 197)
　3 small rings dried red chili pepper
　*Goyo-matsu* (*Pinus parviflora*, five-needle pine), as needed

1. Clean the cuttlefish and peel the surface membrane from the flesh. Place serving side down on a cutting board and cut in half lengthwise.
2. Make diagonal incisions on the inside of the flesh.
3. Make lengthwise incisions on the outside of the flesh. Do this in two stages to account for the variation in the thickness of the flesh at the base and tip. Incisions of the same depth should be made across the entire mantle. Cutting incisions into both sides makes it easier to curl the flesh.
4. Thread onto five skewers using a double-tuck technique similar to *ryozuma-ori*, curling the flesh to make a rounded shape.
5. Sprinkle salt (1% by weight) on both sides.
6. Grill as shown at right.
7. Slice the cuttlefish into bite-sized pieces and transfer to a serving dish. Top each *kikka-kabura* with a chili pepper ring and arrange alongside. Garnish with *goyo-matsu* pine sprigs.

### Grilling Procedure
#### Grilling the flesh

| HEAT SOURCE | DIRECTION OF HEAT | TEMPERATURE | DISTANCE FROM HEAT |
|---|---|---|---|
| Electric grill | From below | 635°F (335°C) | 9.3 cm (3⅝ in.) |

00:00 Grilling inner (reverse) side of flesh
02:26 Turning to grill serving side
03:34 Grilling complete

131°F (55°C)

### Brushing the serving side with egg yolk
#### Heating the egg yolk

| DIRECTION OF HEAT | TEMPERATURE | DISTANCE FROM HEAT |
|---|---|---|
| From above | 635°F (335°C) | 24.5 cm (9⅝ in.) |

00:00 Grilling serving side
Heat the egg yolk from a distance, taking care not to scorch it.

00:57 Applying additional egg yolk to the surface

01:14 Grilling serving side

02:08 Grilling complete
Color of egg yolk when grilling is complete

136°F (58°C)

YAKIMONO VARIATIONS　155

### Miscellaneous
# Clam Grilled in the Shell
*Yaki Hamaguri*

---

Clams (*hamaguri*; Meretrix lusoria) are at their best during the winter months, and are an essential part of seasonal celebrations including the New Year and Dolls' Day (Momo no Sekku) in early March. Clams are bivalves; that is, they are formed of a pair of uniquely matched shells. These perfectly matched "pairs," considered symbols of conjugal happiness, are often served at weddings to wish the new couple a long and happy life. In this recipe, the clam is cooked in the shell; the water found in the shell when it opens is discarded and the clam is grilled slowly, with sake added to the juices that seep from the flesh as it cooks. To finish, the meat is topped with *karasumi* powder and heated with a kitchen torch to add aroma and umami. It is garnished with a sprig of *kinome* for serving.

**SAMPLE WEIGHT:** 192.0 g (6.8 oz.)

*Serves 1*

1 *hamaguri* clam
Salt, as needed
Sake, as needed
*Karasumi* powder, as needed

Garnish
| 1 *kinome* sprig

**1** Place the clam in salt water (3% salinity) and leave for 5 hours to purge the sand. (This step may be omitted for pre-purged clams.)

**2** Grill as shown at right.

**3** Remove the flesh and cut it into three pieces, then return it to the shell, place on a tabletop brazier loaded with burning charcoal, and heat.

**4** Add a small amount of sake to the shell and bring briefly to a boil.

**5** Top with *karasumi* powder and use a kitchen torch to impart color. Garnish with the *kinome* sprig and serve on the brazier.

## Grilling Procedure
### Grilling the flesh

| HEAT SOURCE | DIRECTION OF HEAT | TEMPERATURE |
|---|---|---|
| Tabletop brazier | From below | Low medium |

**00:00  Start of grilling**

The shell of the clam serves as the cooking vessel. The clam is steam-baked in its shell from the start of cooking until the shell opens.

**00:43  Shell starts to open**

Heat causes the adductor muscle to separate from the shell on the side closer to the heat, leaving the meat attached to the uppermost half of the shell.

**01:08  Turning to grill opposite side**

After the shell opens, the clam is turned before it tips over, and the opposite side is heated. Discard remaining moisture.

**01:24  Grilling complete**

### Remove the top shell, cut out the meat, and divide into three pieces.

Remove the empty half of the shell by hand.  Cut the flesh from the remaining half-shell with a knife.

The flesh cut into three pieces

### Heating on the tabletop brazier

**3**

Return the flesh to the half-shell and place on the brazier for heating.

### Adding sake

The core temperature at this time was 136°F (58°C).

**4**

100 120 140 160 180 200 °F
136°F (58°C)

### Adding *karasumi* powder and heating with kitchen torch

Heating reduces the strong smell of the fatty *karasumi* powder and imparts a rich, toasted aroma.

**5**

Letting the juices from the clam mingle with the *karasumi* powder makes it possible to enjoy the flavors of the clam and the umami of the *karasumi* powder at the same time.

YAKIMONO VARIATIONS  157

### Miscellaneous
# Abalone Grilled in a Salt Crust
*Awabi no Shiogama-yaki*

In Japan, abalone (*awabi*) has long been treated as a luxury—even a sacred—food. It is in season in summer, and the *ama* divers of the Shima peninsula of Mie prefecture and the abalone they harvest are part of the cultural imagery of summer. Abalone contains extremely high amounts of collagen. In this recipe, it is cooked slowly, which gelatinizes the collagen and gives the flesh a soft texture. The abalone is stuffed with layers of sea urchin for a luxurious feast ideal for auspicious celebrations.

SAMPLE: Width: 7.6 cm (3 in.)
Length: 9.7 cm (3⅞ in.)
Thickness: 2.6 cm (1 in.)
WEIGHT: 98.0 g (3.5 oz.)

*Serves 1*

1 abalone (*awabi*)
100 g (3.5 oz.) salt-preserved wakame seaweed (rehydrated)
20 g (0.7 oz.) sea urchin (*uni*)

*Shiogama* ("salt pot" casing)
| 250 g (8.8 oz.) salt
| 10 g (0.4 oz.) egg white
| 8 ml (1½ tsp.) water

Garnishes
| Abalone liver sauce (*awabi-kimo-dare*; see p. 197), as needed
| Citrus sauce (*kankitsu-shio*; see p. 197), as needed
| *Matsuba* (pine needles), as needed

**1** Remove the abalone from its shell, taking care not to puncture the liver. Brush off any surface debris and cut away the mouth, liver, and fringe. With the side that was attached to the shell facing up, cut three deep lengthwise incisions into the oval-shaped adductor muscle.

**2** Cut the abalone in 1-cm (⅜ in.) slices across the short side of the oval. Turn over.

**3** Place a bed of rough-chopped wakame in the shell. Lay the abalone on the wakame and place the sea urchin between the abalone slices.

**4** Cover the abalone and sea urchin with wakame so that they will not come into direct contact with the salt casing.

**5** Mix the salt with the egg white and water and spread over the shell and the abalone and sea urchin to cover to a thickness of 1 cm (⅜ in.).

**6** Cook as shown at right.

**7** Remove the salt casing and the top covering of wakame. Spread pine needles on a serving dish and lay the abalone in its shell on top. Serve accompanied by two small dishes containing abalone liver sauce and citrus sauce.

**1**

**2**

Turned over

**3**

**4**

**5**

### Cooking Procedure

| HEAT SOURCE | TEMPERATURE | FAN SPEED | COOKING TIME |
|---|---|---|---|
| Steam convection oven (Setting: Hot air) | 338°F (170°C) | 3 (of 5) | 30 min. |

**00:00** Start of cooking

Turn around after 15 minutes so that the dish is cooked evenly throughout.

**30:00** Cooking complete

YAKIMONO VARIATIONS 159

# Tsubo-yaki Style Grilled Horned Turban Shell
*Sazae no Tsubo-yaki*

The horned turban shell sea snail (*sazae*) is found in reefs and shallow shoals, and is in season from spring through early summer. The flesh of this marine gastropod, which feeds on algae, is characterized by a pronounced briny tang and a gentle bitterness from the liver. Like *hamaguri* clams, *sazae* is often served around Dolls' Day in early March. *Tsubo-yaki*, a style of cooking *sazae* and similar gastropods by grilling them in their shells, is the most common way of cooking turban shell. The various parts of this sea snail contain different types of protein, which take on distinct consistencies when cooked—the adductor muscle turns soft, while the liver becomes chewy. This recipe adds the fresh, crispy texture of *mitsuba*, a fragrant herb that is one of the characteristic flavors of spring.

**SAMPLE WEIGHT:** 303.0 g (10.7 oz.)

2. Liver    Organs    Flesh

**Ingredients placed inside shell for cooking**
From top left: wakame, shiitake, *mitsuba*, *sazae* flesh, liver, cooking liquid

*Serves 1*

1 horned turban shell (*sazae*)

20 g (0.7 oz.) wakame, cut into large pieces

3 stems *mitsuba*, cut into 1-cm (⅜ in.) lengths

1 shiitake mushroom, stem removed and cut into thin slices

Cooking liquid, as needed
- 200 ml (6.8 fl. oz.) *ichiban* dashi
- 15 ml (1 Tbsp.) *koikuchi* shoyu
- 15 ml (1 Tbsp.) mirin

Garnish
- *Sudachi*

Salt, as needed

Egg white, as needed

**1** Remove the *sazae* from its shell, and discard the "lid" (operculum).

**2** Separate the flesh, liver, and internal organs (intestine and gizzard). Other than the liver, the organs are not used.

**3** Rub the flesh with salt to clean away debris and mucus, then wash in cold water.

**4** Remove the fringe (*engawa*) and mouth from the flesh, then cut flesh into small, thin slices. (The fringe and mouth are not used.) Cut the liver into 1-cm (⅜ in.) pieces.

**5** Place the wakame in the shell and top with the *sazae* liver and flesh, the shiitake, and the *mitsuba*. Add the cooking liquid.

**6** Grill as shown at right.

**7** Combine salt and egg white and mound the mixture on a serving dish. Place the turban shell securely on the bed of salt and garnish with the *sudachi*.

### Grilling Procedure

| HEAT SOURCE | DIRECTION OF HEAT | HEAT STRENGTH |
|---|---|---|
| Gas range | From below | Medium |

**00:00 Start of grilling**

Everything is cooked inside the shell, which serves as a kind of cooking vessel. In this example, the shell contains around 90 ml (3 fl. oz.) of cooking liquid.

**04:00 Topping up cooking liquid**

Around 5 ml (1 tsp.) of cooking liquid is added.

**11:10 Cooking liquid starts to bubble**

**26:07 Grilling complete**

207°F (97°C)
(Cooking liquid)

During grilling, heat softens the flesh while firming up the liver, giving it a pleasantly chewy texture. These effects occur because of changes in the proteins—but heat affects the two parts in different ways because of their distinct protein compositions.

**Miscellaneous**

# Kamo Eggplant *Dengaku*
*Kamo nasu no Dengaku*

Eggplant, at its best in Japan in the summer and autumn, has a neutral flavor and aroma, and is perfect for frying in oil. *Kamo nasu*, a variety of eggplant grown in the Kyoto countryside, is distinguished by its firm flesh and roughly round shape. *Dengaku* was originally a style of cooking in which tofu and other ingredients were coated with miso paste and then grilled. In this recipe, the eggplant is fried in oil at a high temperature, then grilled over direct heat to remove the excess oil before being topped with white and red miso. The dish offers a pleasant contrast between the delicate taste of the eggplant and the dense flavor of the miso.

**SAMPLE CUT:** Diameter: 9.7 cm (3⅞ in.)
Thickness: 3.5 cm (1⅜ in.)
**WEIGHT:** 129.0 g (4.6 oz.)

*Serves 1*

1 portion Kamo eggplant (*Kamo nasu*)
Rice oil, as needed

White miso *dengaku* paste, as needed
 1 kg (35.3 oz.) white miso
 900 ml (30.4 fl. oz.) Mikawa mirin
 30 egg yolks
 Sugar, as needed

Red miso *dengaku* paste, as needed
 1 kg (35.3 oz.) red miso
 500 ml (16.9 fl. oz.) Mikawa mirin
 30 egg yolks
 Sugar, as needed

To make both types of *dengaku* paste, mix the respective ingredients together and heat to burn off the alcohol in the mirin. Sugar may be added to taste, since the sweetness of the miso varies depending on the manufacturer.

Poppy seeds, as needed
Green yuzu, as needed

Garnishes
 3 *chamame* (edamame) pods (see p. 197)
 1 paper mulberry leaf (*kaji no ha*)

**1** Remove the stem from the eggplant and slice in half horizontally. The eggplant will be served with the wider surface facing up.

**2** Peel strips off the skin from the narrow end to the wide end in a striped pattern.

**3** Score the serving side in a crisscross pattern. This allows the heat to penetrate more easily and also makes the eggplant easier to eat.

**4** Grill as shown at right.

**5** Lay the paper mulberry leaf on a serving dish, place the eggplant on top, and garnish with boiled *chamame*.

**1**    **2**

### Cooking Procedure
#### Frying

| HEAT SOURCE | TEMPERATURE | AMOUNT OF OIL |
|---|---|---|
| Gas range | 329°F (165°C) | 2-cm (¾ in.) depth |

**00:00 Start of frying**

Place in the hot oil with the wider side (serving side) facing down.

**03:07 Turning to fry on reverse side**

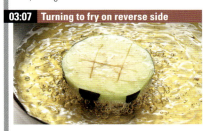

**04:36 Frying complete**

Transfer to a pan and drain excess oil.

Frying in oil causes the cells to collapse, since the pectin in the cell walls dissolves at temperatures of 194°F (90°C) or higher. The anthocyanin pigment that gives the eggplant its distinctive purple color is soluble in water. Frying in oil dries the surface and forms a barrier that prevents the water-soluble pigment from leaching away, while also helping to preserve moisture inside the eggplant flesh.

**Cross-section after removal from oil**

Keeping frying time short avoids overcooking; the eggplant is removed from the oil while still juicy on the inside.

196°F (91°C)

**3**

### Grilling in electric grill

| HEAT SOURCE | DIRECTION OF HEAT | TEMPERATURE | DISTANCE FROM HEAT |
|---|---|---|---|
| Electric grill | From above | 752°F (400°C) | 15.0 cm (5⅞ in.) |

**00:00 Grilling serving side**

**01:49 Turning to grill on reverse side**

**03:12 Grilling complete**

#### Applying the *dengaku* sauce

Remove excess oil and spread equal amounts of red and white miso *dengaku* sauce on the serving side.

Garnish the red miso sauce with poppy seeds and the white miso sauce with green yuzu zest.

### Grilling the *dengaku* sauce

**00:00 Grilling the *dengaku* sauce**

**02:12 Grilling complete**

YAKIMONO VARIATIONS   163

*Tare-yaki*

# Pan-Grilled Mallard Breast

*Magamo no Kuwa-yaki*

*Kuwa-yaki* is said to derive from the practice in olden times of using *kuwa* (a hoe or spade) or other farming implement as a hot plate for cooking wildfowl and vegetables. Duck is one of the most widely consumed waterfowl, and wild mallard, a migratory species that returns from Siberia to winter in Japan, is familiar as one of the flavors of the colder months. The breast muscle is more developed in wild birds than in *aigamo* (a cross between mallard and domestic duck), and the meat has a rich flavor that farmed poultry lacks. In this recipe, the skin and flesh are seared in a pan in the *kuwa-yaki* tradition and then immediately cooled to avoid further cooking by residual heat. The meat is sliced thinly and then flash-braised in a rich sauce to preserve the tenderness of the meat.

SAMPLE CUT: Width: 8.7 cm (3⅜ in.)
Length: 21.0 cm (8¼ in.)
Thickness: 2.9 cm (1⅛ in.)
WEIGHT: 299.0 g (10.5 oz.)

**1**

### Serves 5

1 portion mallard (*magamo*) breast

Braising sauce
| 160 ml (5.4 fl. oz.) mirin
| 60 ml (2 fl. oz.) *koikuchi* shoyu
| 40 ml (2 Tbsp. plus 2 tsp.) sake

*Kuzu* starch, as needed
15 ml (1 Tbsp.) vegetable oil

Garnishes
| 1 Kujo long onion (*Kujo negi*), sliced thinly on the diagonal
| 100 g (3.5 oz.) grated daikon radish
| 15 ml (1 Tbsp.) wholegrain mustard
| *Sansho* pepper powder, as needed

**1** Place the mallard breast skin side up on a cutting board and pierce the skin evenly with metal skewers. (This allows fat to render out during cooking.)

**2** Cook as shown at right.

**3** Transfer the meat to a serving dish and sprinkle with powdered *sansho* pepper. Serve with the sliced long onion together with grated daikon mixed with wholegrain mustard.

YAKIMONO VARIATIONS 165

**Miscellaneous**

# Roast Duck Breast
*Kamo Rosu*

Duck that is a cross between wild mallard and domesticated duck (known as *aigamo* in Japan) is noted for its lack of gaminess and widely consumed in many countries. In this recipe, *aigamo* duck breast is prepared by searing to brown the skin while heating the fat underneath and allowing it to render out. The meat is immersed in marinade and steamed, then allowed to slowly cook in the residual heat. After cooking is complete, the meat is returned to the marinade and left overnight to allow the flavors to penetrate slowly and thoroughly. The finished dish is garnished with a refreshing vegetable salad and egg and vinegar dressing.

SAMPLE CUT: Width: 11.0 cm (4⅜ in.)
Length: 28.0 cm (11 in.)
Thickness: 4.0 cm (1⅝ in.)
WEIGHT: 512.0 g (18.1 oz.)

**1**

### Serves 2

1 portion duck (*aigamo*) breast

Marinade
| 800 ml (27.1 fl. oz.) de-alcoholized sake
| 200 ml (6.8 fl. oz.) *koikuchi shoyu*
| 200 ml (6.8 fl. oz.) de-alcoholized mirin

Garnishes
| Egg and vinegar dressing (*kimi-zu*; see p. 197), as needed
| Broccoli sprouts and red cabbage sprouts, chopped and mixed, as needed
| Asparagus tips, as needed (blanch the tips in salt water, then plunge into ice water)
| 2 thin slices red radish
| Prepared *karashi* mustard, as needed
| 1 lettuce leaf

**1** Place the duck breast on a cutting board, skin side up, and use metal skewers to pierce the skin evenly all over. (This allows fat to render during cooking.)

**2** Cook as shown at right.

**3** Transfer the duck to the serving dish and garnish with the salad of asparagus and sprouts on a leaf of lettuce, along with egg and vinegar dressing, radish, and prepared mustard.

## Grilling Procedure
### Imparting color

| HEAT SOURCE | Frying pan | TEMPERATURE | 518°F (270°C) |

**00:00 Searing skin side**

Sear to render the fat and allow it to escape.

**03:34 Turning to sear on flesh side**

Sear the skin side to brown, but sear the flesh side for just 10 seconds.

**03:43 Searing complete**

Cross-section when searing is complete

The duck is immersed briefly in boiling water to rinse off the excess fat.

Place the duck in a pan, pour the heated marinade over, cover with paper towel to ensure the marinade is thoroughly absorbed. Cover pan with plastic wrap.

## Steaming

| HEAT SOURCE | TEMPERATURE | FAN SPEED | COOKING TIME |
|---|---|---|---|
| Steam convection oven (Steam setting) | 212°F (100°C) | 3 (of 5) | 9 min. |

**00:00 Start of cooking**

**09:00 Cooking complete**

Finish cooking, remove from the pan and allow to rest for 45 minutes, during which time the residual heat will continue to cook the meat.

Cross-section when cooking is complete

126°F (52°C)

Cross-section after cooking through with residual heat

### Immersing in marinade and leaving overnight

Once the marinade has cooled, return the duck breast to the liquid and leave overnight to absorb the flavor.

Cross-section after marinating overnight

YAKIMONO VARIATIONS 167

# Beef Tenderloin in Miso *Yuan-ji* Marinade
*Gyuniku no Miso Yuan-yaki*

Marinating a thick-cut beef fillet in a miso *yuan-ji* marinade for an extended time allows the flavor and aromas to penetrate deeply into the meat, subduing the assertive beefiness of the meat to make it less prominent. The beef is cooked evenly and completely at a low temperature in a steam convection oven; the surface is then grilled at a high temperature directly over charcoal. This not only imparts rich aromas but also eliminates excess fattiness, giving the dish a typically Japanese finish.

SAMPLE CUT: Width: 7.1 cm (2¾ in.)
Length: 7.4 cm (2⅞ in.)
Thickness: 3.3 cm (1¼ in.)
WEIGHT: 155.0 g (5.5 oz.)

Cross-section after marinating

*Serves 3*

3 beef tenderloin steaks

Miso *yuan-ji* marinade

| 1 kg (35.3 oz.) ground white miso (*shiro surimiso*)
| 180 ml (6.1 fl. oz.) *koikuchi* shoyu
| 180 ml (6.1 fl. oz.) sake
| 285 ml (9.6 fl. oz.) mirin
| 1 yellow yuzu, sliced into thin rounds

Mix to combine (no heating required)

Garnishes

| 3 *manganji* peppers (stems and seeds removed)
| *Karashi* mustard, as needed

**1** Use beef tenderloin that can safely be eaten raw; it should be sliced against the grain.

**2** Immerse in the marinade for 12 hours.

**3** Thread each steak onto three skewers using the flat-skewering (*hira-gushi*) technique.

**4** Grill as shown at right.

**5** Cut into thick slices and transfer to a serving dish. Add a dollop of mustard to each slice and garnish with the char-grilled *manganji* peppers.

### Cooking Procedure

#### Cooking in oven

| HEAT SOURCE | TEMPERATURE | FAN SPEED | COOKING TIME |
|---|---|---|---|
| Steam convection oven (Setting: Hot air) | 136°F (58°C) | 5 (of 5) | 25 min. |

**00:00** Start of cooking

**25:00** Cooking complete

Cross-section after roasting in steam convection oven. The meat is cooked through.

100 120 140 160 180 200 °F
104°F (40°C)

### Grilling over charcoal

| HEAT SOURCE | DIRECTION OF HEAT | TEMPERATURE | DISTANCE FROM HEAT |
|---|---|---|---|
| Charcoal | From below | 1440°F (782°C) | 3.3 cm (1¼ in.) |

**00:00** Start of grilling (either side may be grilled first)

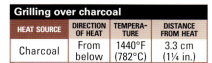

**00:55** Turning to grill on reverse side

**01:41** Grilling complete

The technique of immersing food in a *yuan-ji* or miso *yuan-ji* marinade is effective for meat as well as fish. The salt-soluble proteins dissolve, which promotes the retention of juices during cooking. This technique uses far infrared radiation from charcoal to heat just the surface, creating rich aromas. Although beef is not a traditional ingredient, this preparation serves it in a distinctly Japanese style.

YAKIMONO VARIATIONS   169

# Yakitori—Cuts of Meat

**Breast (*shio*)**

**Boneless thigh (*shio*)**

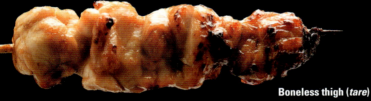

**Boneless thigh (*tare*)**

**Chicken oyster (*shio*)**

**Chicken oyster (*tare*)**

**Wing flat (*shio*)**

**Chicken and long onion (*shio*)**

**Chicken and long onion (*tare*)**

*Yakitori* meat cuts are cooked to impart an attractive color and satisfying firmness to the outer surface while locking in the juices to keep the meat succulent. Excess fat and fibrous tissue are carefully removed in the preparation stage. To cook *yakitori* well, it is essential to grill quickly to avoid overheating, since this can cause the meat to shrink and become tough. Because it is eaten straight from the skewer and consumed from the tip of the skewer down, the pieces at the tip of the skewer should not be salted too heavily. Salt should be sprinkled over the meat so that the flavor is somewhat stronger toward the base.

**Neck meat (*shio*)**

**Tenderloin (*shio*)**

# Breast
## (*mune; shio*)

While browning the surface, care should be taken to finish the meat so that the core temperature does not rise too high and dry out the meat.

**SAMPLE:**
Length: 9.5 cm (3¾ in.)
Width: 3.8 cm (1½ in.)
Thickness: 2.8 cm (1⅛ in.)
**WEIGHT:** 49.6 g (1.7 oz.)

*Serves 1*

4 portions chicken breast (*mune*)
Salt, as needed

1. Remove skin from the chicken breast, along with any fat attached to the flesh.
2. Divide the meat into thirds, then cut
3. into bite-sized pieces.
4. Insert a skewer perpendicular to the muscle fibers. Place smaller pieces at the base of the skewer, since the heat is less intense at the front of the grill. This ensures that all the pieces on the skewer are cooked evenly.
5. Sprinkle salt all over.
6. Grill as shown at right.

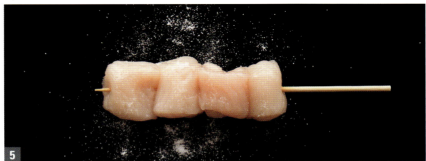

### Grilling Procedure

| HEAT SOURCE | DIRECTION OF HEAT | TEMPERATURE | DISTANCE FROM HEAT |
|---|---|---|---|
| High-intensity gas grill | From below | 993°F (534°C) | 3.5 cm (1⅜ in.) |

**00:00** Start of grilling (either side may be grilled first)

Turn four times during this interval

**05:44** Grilling complete

Cross-section when grilling is complete

The meat should be cooked inside and out so that the center is not raw or underdone, but care must be taken not to overcook.

YAKIMONO VARIATIONS  171

# Boneless thigh (*momo; shio*)

The skin side should be grilled to a slight crisp in such a way as to trap the juices of the meat and keep the inside moist.

**SAMPLE:**
Length: 11.2 cm (4⅜ in.)
Width: 4.8 cm (1⅞ in.)
Thickness: 2.3 cm (⅞ in.)
**WEIGHT:** 54.0 g (1.9 oz.)

Oyster   Thigh meat   Leg meat

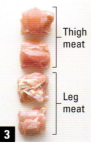

Thigh meat
Leg meat

*Serves 1*

2 portions deboned chicken thigh (*momo*)
2 portions deboned chicken leg meat (*sune*)
Salt, as needed

1. Separate a whole deboned chicken thigh into the oyster, thigh, and leg meat. Use two pieces each of thigh and leg meat. Trim the thickest part of the thigh so that all pieces are an even thickness.
2. Cut the thigh and leg meat into bite-sized pieces.
3. With the two pieces of leg meat at the base and the two pieces of thigh meat above, insert a skewer perpendicular to the muscle fibers. The smaller cuts are placed at the base of the skewer since the heat is less intense at the front of the grill. This ensures that all the pieces on the skewer are cooked evenly.
4. Sprinkle salt all over.
5. Grill as shown at right.

## Grilling Procedure

| HEAT SOURCE | DIRECTION OF HEAT | TEMPERATURE | DISTANCE FROM HEAT |
|---|---|---|---|
| High-intensity gas grill | From below | 891°F (477°C) | 2.7 cm (1⅛ in.) |

**00:00** Grilling skin side
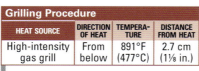

**05:17** Turning to grill on flesh side

Turn six times during this interval

**08:55** Grilling complete

Cross-section when grilling is complete

182°F (83.3°C)

# Boneless thigh (*momo*; *tare*)

The skin side should be grilled to a slight crisp in such a way as to trap the juices of the meat and keep the inside moist.

**SAMPLE:**
Length: 11.2 cm (4⅜ in.)
Width: 4.8 cm (1⅞ in.)
Thickness: 2.3 cm (⅞ in.)
**WEIGHT:** 54.0 g (1.9 oz.)

### Serves 1

2 portions deboned chicken thigh (*momo*)

2 portions deboned leg meat (*sune*)

*Tare* sauce, as needed

| 1.8 L (60.9 fl. oz.) *koikuchi* shoyu
| 1.8 L (60.9 fl. oz.) de-alcoholized mirin
| 500 g (17.6 oz.) sugar

Mix all ingredients together and simmer at low heat for 10 minutes, skimming any foam that rises to the surface. Remove from heat and allow to cool.

**1** Separate a whole deboned chicken thigh into the oyster, thigh, and leg meat. Use two pieces each of thigh and leg meat. Trim the thickest part of the thigh so that all pieces are an even thickness.

**2** Cut the thigh and leg meat into bite-sized pieces.

**3** With the two pieces of leg meat at the base and the two pieces of thigh meat above, insert a skewer perpendicular to the muscle fibers. The smaller cuts are placed at the base of the skewer since the heat is less intense at the front of the grill. This ensures that all the pieces on the skewer are cooked evenly.

**4** Grill as shown at right.

## Grilling Procedure

| HEAT SOURCE | DIRECTION OF HEAT | TEMPERATURE | DISTANCE FROM HEAT |
|---|---|---|---|
| High-intensity gas grill | From below | 891°F (477°C) | 2.7 cm (1⅛ in.) |

**00:00 Grilling skin side**

**02:11 Turning to grill on flesh side**

Turn twice during this interval

**07:36 Checking color**

**07:41 Dipping in *tare* sauce, grilling skin side**

Turn three times during this interval

**10:05 Dipping in *tare* sauce, grilling flesh side**

Since the *tare* sauce will scorch if it evaporates too much, the meat should be dipped in sauce again just before it begins to scorch.

Turn twice during this interval

**11:27 Dipping in *tare* sauce, grilling skin side**

**11:37 Grilling complete**

188°F (86.5°C)

**Finish by dipping in *tare* sauce once more**

Cross-section when grilling is complete

The meat is cooked inside and out.

# Chicken oyster
## (*soriresu*; *shio*)

For chicken oyster (Fr. *sot-l'y-laisse*), the skin side should be grilled to a slight crisp in such a way as to trap the juices of the meat and keep the inside moist.

**SAMPLE:**
Length: 9.5 cm (3¾ in.)
Width: 3.8 cm (1½ in.)
Thickness: 2.8 cm (1⅛ in.)
**WEIGHT:** 49.6 g (1.7 oz.)

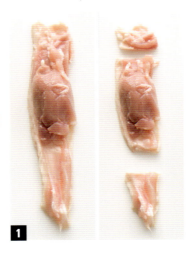

**Serves 1**

2 chicken oysters (*soriresu*)
Salt, as needed

**1** Separate the oyster from the thigh and cut off the thick, fatty pieces of skin on either side.

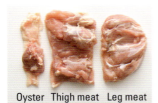
Oyster   Thigh meat   Leg meat

**2** Wrap the skin around the meat and skewer so it is held in place.

**3** Sprinkle salt all over.

**4** Grill as shown at right.

### Grilling Procedure

| HEAT SOURCE | DIRECTION OF HEAT | TEMPERATURE | DISTANCE FROM HEAT |
|---|---|---|---|
| High-intensity gas grill | From below | 1017°F (547°C) | 3.0 cm (1⅛ in.) |

**00:00  Grilling skin side**

Turn three times during this interval

**07:33  Grilling complete**

Cross-section when grilling is complete

184°F (84.5°C)

174  YAKIMONO VARIATIONS

# Chicken oyster
(*soriresu*; *tare*)

For chicken oyster (Fr. *sot-l'y-laisse*), the skin side should be grilled to a slight crisp in such a way as to trap the juices of the meat and keep the inside moist.

**SAMPLE:**
Length: 9.5 cm (3¾ in.)
Width: 3.8 cm (1½ in.)
Thickness: 2.8 cm (1⅛ in.)
**WEIGHT:** 49.6 g (1.7 oz.)

### Serves 1

2 chicken oysters (*soriresu*)
*Tare* sauce (see p. 173), as needed

1. Separate the oyster from the thigh and cut off the thick, fatty pieces of skin on either side.
2. Wrap the skin around the meat and skewer so it is held in place.
3. **Grill as shown at right.**

## Grilling Procedure

| HEAT SOURCE | DIRECTION OF HEAT | TEMPERATURE | DISTANCE FROM HEAT |
|---|---|---|---|
| High-intensity gas grill | From below | 882°F (472°C) | 3.0 cm (1⅛ in.) |

**00:00 Grilling skin side**

**03:16 Turning to grill on flesh side**

**07:15 Checking color**

**07:22 Dipping in *tare* sauce, grilling skin side**

**08:31 Turning to grill on flesh side**

**09:27 Dipping in *tare* sauce, grilling skin side**

Turn once during this interval

**09:54 Grilling complete**

171°F (77.2°C)

**Finish by dipping in *tare* sauce once more**

Cross-section when grilling is complete

YAKIMONO VARIATIONS 175

# Chicken and long onion (*negima; shio*)

Care should be taken to avoid scorching the long onion while keeping the meat juicy.

**SAMPLE:**
Length: 9.5 cm (3¾ in.)
Width: 3.7 cm (1½ in.)
Thickness: 1.9 cm (¾ in.)
**WEIGHT:** 39.0 g (1.4 oz.)

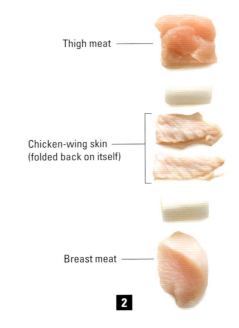

Thigh meat

Chicken-wing skin (folded back on itself)

Breast meat

**2**

**3**

### Serves 1

1 portion deboned thigh meat (*momo*)

2 pieces long onion (*naganegi*; white parts only)

2 pieces chicken-wing skin (*kawa*; see p. 179)

1 portion breast meat (*mune*)

Salt, as needed

**1** Cut the thigh and breast meat into bite-sized pieces, then cut the long onions and wing skin to match the width of the meat.

**2** Insert a skewer perpendicular to the muscle fibers in the following order, from the base: breast meat, long onion, wing skin, long onion, thigh meat (this ensures that the breast meat is cooked at the front of the grill, where the heat is less intense).

**3** Sprinkle salt all over.

**4** Grill as shown at right.

### Grilling Procedure

| HEAT SOURCE | DIRECTION OF HEAT | TEMPERA-TURE | DISTANCE FROM HEAT |
|---|---|---|---|
| High-intensity gas grill | From below | 941°F (505°C) | 3.5 cm (1⅜ in.) |

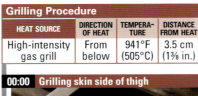
**00:00** Grilling skin side of thigh

**02:36** Turning to grill on flesh side

**05:10** Grilling complete

176    YAKIMONO VARIATIONS

# Chicken and long onion (*negima*; *tare*)

Care should be taken to avoid scorching the long onion while keeping the meat juicy.

**SAMPLE:**
Length: 9.5 cm (3¾ in.)
Width: 3.7 cm (1½ in.)
Thickness: 1.9 cm (¾ in.)
**WEIGHT:** 39.0 g (1.4 oz.)

*Serves 1*

1 portion deboned thigh meat (*momo*)
2 pieces long onion (*naganegi*; white parts only)
2 pieces chicken-wing skin (*kawa*; see p. 179)
1 portion breast meat (*mune*)
*Tare* sauce (see p. 173), as needed

**1** Cut the thigh and breast meat into bite-sized pieces, then cut the long onions and wing skin to match the width of the meat.

**2** Insert a skewer perpendicular to the muscle fibers in the following order, from the base: breast meat, long onion, wing skin, long onion, thigh meat (this ensures that the breast meat is cooked at the front of the grill, where the heat is less intense).

**3** Grill as shown at right.

| Grilling Procedure | | | |
|---|---|---|---|
| HEAT SOURCE | DIRECTION OF HEAT | TEMPERATURE | DISTANCE FROM HEAT |
| High-intensity gas grill | From below | 990°F (532°C) | 3.5 cm (1⅜ in.) |

**00:00** Grilling skin side of thigh

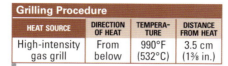

**02:16** Turning to grill on flesh side

**04:10** Checking color

**04:15** Dipping in *tare* sauce, grilling skin side

**05:23** Turning to grill on flesh side

**06:02** Dipping in *tare* sauce, grilling flesh side

**06:34** Turning to grill on skin side

**06:56** Grilling complete

Finish by dipping in *tare* sauce once more

YAKIMONO VARIATIONS

# Tenderloin
(*sasami*; *shio*)

Cook to lightly brown the surface while keeping the inside slightly rare, so that the meat does not dry out.

**SAMPLE:**
Length: 9.5 cm (3¾ in.)
Width: 3.8 cm (1½ in.)
Thickness: 2.8 cm (1⅛ in.)
**WEIGHT:** 49.6 g (1.7 oz.)

***Serves 1***

3 portions tenderloin (*sasami*)
Salt, as needed

1. Remove the tendon from the chicken tenderloin. Place the side with the tendon facing up, and use the tip of the knife to cut loose around 5 cm (2 in.) of visible white tissue.
2. Turn the tenderloin over. Holding the meat in place with the spine of the knife, pull the loose end and separate the tendon from the meat.
3. Cut the fillet into bite-sized pieces and skewer perpendicular to the muscle fibers. Place smaller pieces at the base of the skewer, since the heat is less intense at the front of the grill. This will ensure that all pieces on the skewer are cooked evenly.
4. Sprinkle salt all over.
5. Grill as shown at right.

### Grilling Procedure

| HEAT SOURCE | DIRECTION OF HEAT | TEMPERATURE | DISTANCE FROM HEAT |
|---|---|---|---|
| High-intensity gas grill | From below | 864°F (462°C) | 3.0 cm (1⅛ in.) |

**00:00** Start of grilling (either side may be grilled first)

During this interval, turn five times to grill in the following order: reverse, right, left, reverse, serving side (first side grilled).

**06:05** Grilling complete

Cross-section when grilling is complete

The meat should still be slightly rare at the end of grilling.

153°F (67°C)

178 YAKIMONO VARIATIONS

# Wing flat (*teba; shio*)

The skin side is grilled until it is crisp and fragrant; the flesh side is more lightly grilled to keep the meat juicy.

SAMPLE: Length: 10.0 cm (3⅞ in.)
Width: 8.0 cm (3⅛ in.)
Thickness: 1.6 cm (⅝ in.)
WEIGHT: 65.0 g (2.3 oz.)

### Serves 1

2 wing flats (*teba*; wingette, middle part of wing)

Salt, as needed

1. Use fish-bone tweezers to remove any pin feathers remaining on the wing. Cut the skin from the wingtip, reserving for use in *negima* (chicken and long onion) *yakitori*.
2. Cut off the wingtip, leaving the flat. Open the meat and remove the thinner bone (radius), leaving the larger ulna in place.
3. Place two chicken wing flats skin side down and skewer between bone and flesh. When skewering, gather up excess skin and thin parts of flesh so that they do not hang down from the skewer during grilling.
4. Sprinkle salt all over.
5. Grill as shown at right.

### Grilling Procedure

| HEAT SOURCE | DIRECTION OF HEAT | TEMPERATURE | DISTANCE FROM HEAT |
|---|---|---|---|
| High-intensity gas grill | From below | 954°F (512°C) | 3.3 cm (1¼ in.) |

**00:00 Grilling skin side**

**05:23 Turning to grill on flesh side**

**08:21 Grilling complete**

YAKIMONO VARIATIONS

# Neck meat (*seseri*; *shio*)

The juices are sealed in to keep the meat succulent and tender.

**SAMPLE:**
Length: 9.5 cm (3¾ in.)
Width: 3.7 cm (1½ in.)
Thickness: 1.9 cm (¾ in.)
**WEIGHT:** 39.0 g (1.4 oz.)

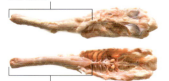
Neck meat on the dorsal side of the bone

Neck meat on the front/belly side

Neck meat cut away from the bone

Since neck meat is rich in collagen and fat, a reasonable amount of fat should be allowed to drip off during grilling. The meat should be salted generously, since salt is also likely to be lost with the drippings.

### Serves 1

8 portions neck meat (*seseri*)
Salt, as needed

1. Remove the neck meat from the bone. Use a knife to cut away the meat that runs from the neck on the dorsal side of the chicken down the back. Repeat the same process with the neck meat on the front/belly side.
2. Cut into bite-sized pieces and thread closely onto a skewer, rolling up the cut pieces by following the rounded contour of the neck meat.
3. Sprinkle salt all over.
4. Grill as shown at right.

### Grilling Procedure

| HEAT SOURCE | DIRECTION OF HEAT | TEMPERATURE | DISTANCE FROM HEAT |
|---|---|---|---|
| High-intensity gas grill | From below | 997°F (536°C) | 3.6 cm (1⅜ in.) |

**00:00** Start of grilling (either side may be grilled first)

Turn five times during this interval

**11:04** Grilling complete

182°F (83.2°C)

180 YAKIMONO VARIATIONS

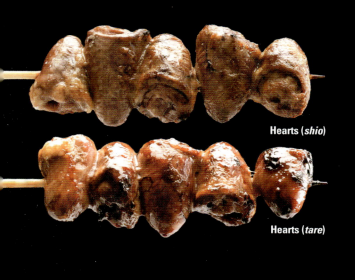

Hearts (*shio*)

Hearts (*tare*)

Liver (*tare*)

Tsunagi (connective tissue; *tare*)

Kidneys (*segimo*; *tare*)

Nankotsu (breastbone cartilage; *shio*)

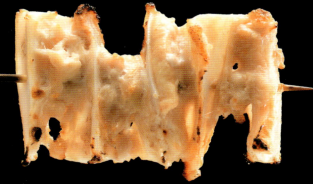

Skin (*kawa*; *shio*)   Skin (*kawa*; *tare*)   Bonjiri (uropygium, pope's nose; *shio*)

## *Yakitori* —Chicken Giblets and Rare Cuts

Giblets spoil more quickly than muscle, so it is important to obtain the freshest possible ingredients and to remove excess fat and blood before grilling. The softer meats are apt to fall apart during cooking, so they should be skewered securely to prevent them from dropping. In grilling, the heat must penetrate to the center to kill any microbes, but cooking should be halted before the meat becomes tough.

Gizzard (*sunagimo*; *shio*)   Meatballs (*tsukune*; *shio*)   Meatballs (*tsukune*; *tare*)

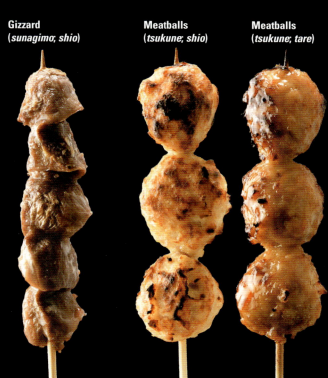

# Hearts (*shio*)

Grill to brown the outside while keeping the meat inside juicy. If fresh, leaving some blood can give a pleasant umami flavor.

SAMPLE: Length: 9.0 cm (3½ in.)
Width: 3.8 cm (1½ in.)
Thickness: 2.0 cm (¾ in.)
WEIGHT: 36.0 g (1.3 oz.)

### Serves 1

5 chicken hearts
Salt, as needed

1. Separate the heart from the liver, leaving a small amount of the base of the heart attached to the *tsunagi* connective tissue (this is used in skewering the *tsunagi*).
2. Remove visible blood from the blood vessels with the tip of a knife.
3. Thread the hearts onto a skewer, alternating the left-right orientation.
4. Sprinkle salt all over.
5. Grill as shown at right.

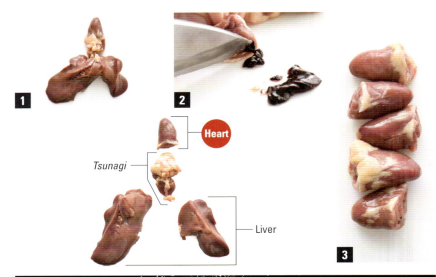

### Grilling Procedure

| HEAT SOURCE | DIRECTION OF HEAT | TEMPERATURE | DISTANCE FROM HEAT |
|---|---|---|---|
| High-intensity gas grill | From below | 610°F (321°C) | 3.0 cm (1⅛ in.) |

**00:00** Start of grilling (either side may be grilled first)

Turn eight times during this interval

**06:43** Grilling complete

Cross-section when grilling is complete

195°F (90.4°C)

# Hearts (*tare*)

Grill to brown the outside while keeping the meat juicy inside. If fresh, leaving some blood can give a pleasant umami flavor.

SAMPLE: Length: 9.0 cm (3½ in.)
Width: 3.8 cm (1½ in.)
Thickness: 2.0 cm (¾ in.)
WEIGHT: 36.0 g (1.3 oz.)

### Serves 1

5 chicken hearts
*Tare* sauce (see p. 173), as needed

1. Separate the heart from the liver, leaving a small amount of the base of the heart attached to the *tsunagi* connective tissue (this will be used in skewering the *tsunagi*).
2. Remove visible blood from the blood vessels with the tip of a knife.
3. Thread the hearts onto a skewer, alternating the left-right orientation.
4. Grill as shown at right.

## Grilling Procedure

| HEAT SOURCE | DIRECTION OF HEAT | TEMPERATURE | DISTANCE FROM HEAT |
|---|---|---|---|
| High-intensity gas grill | From below | 766°F (408°C) | 3.5 cm (1⅜ in.) |

**00:00 Start of grilling (either side may be grilled first)**

**Turn three times during this interval**

**05:35 Checking color**

Unless some degree of browning takes place, the *tare* will not adhere.

**05:39 Dipping in *tare* sauce and grilling**

**Turn twice during this interval**

**07:00 Dipping in *tare* sauce and grilling**

**Turn once during this interval**

**07:49 Grilling complete**

100 120 140 160 180 200 °F
176°F (80°C)

**Finish by dipping in *tare* sauce once more**

Cross-section when grilling is complete

YAKIMONO VARIATIONS

# Liver (*tare*)

Keep the meat juicy without browning the outer surface.

**SAMPLE:**
Length: 9.9 cm (3⅞ in.)
Width: 3.8 cm (1½ in.)
Thickness: 2.2 cm (⅞ in.)
**WEIGHT:** 29.0 g (1.0 oz.)

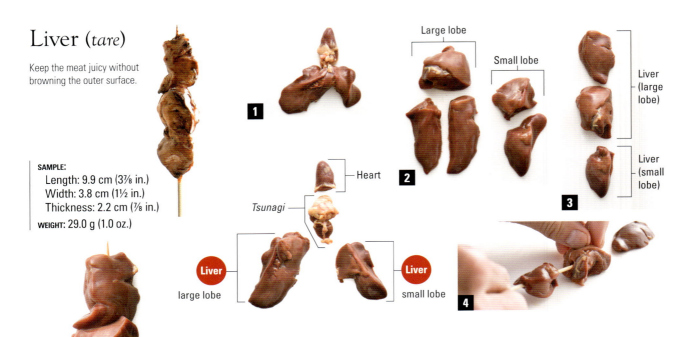

**Serves 1**

3 portions liver
*Tare* sauce (see p. 173), as needed

 Detach the large and small lobes of the liver from the vessels and connective tissue (*tsunagi*) attaching them to the heart. Carefully remove any remaining blood and fat and wash in water. Cut the large lobe into thirds and the small lobe in half to make bite-sized pieces.

 Since the liver is not fibrous, it is important to skewer the meat so that it does not come loose. The meat of the small lobe, which is slightly firmer, should be placed at the base of the skewer to secure the other pieces.

 **Grill as shown at right.**

## Grilling Procedure

| HEAT SOURCE | DIRECTION OF HEAT | TEMPERATURE | DISTANCE FROM HEAT |
|---|---|---|---|
| High-intensity gas grill | From below | 808°F (431°C) | 2.2 cm (⅞ in.) |

**00:00** Start of grilling (either side may be grilled first)

Turn twice during this interval

**02:30** Checking color

**02:36** Dipping in *tare* sauce and grilling

Turn once during this interval

**03:49** Dipping in *tare* sauce and grilling

Turn twice during this interval

**04:59** Grilling complete

185°F (85°C)

Finish by dipping in *tare* sauce once more

Cross-section when grilling is complete

184  YAKIMONO VARIATIONS

# *Tsunagi* (connective tissue; *tare*)

Since there is a lot of fat around the blood vessels of this connective tissue, grill thoroughly to brown while keeping the inside juicy.

**SAMPLE:**
Length: 10.2 cm (4 in.)
Width: 3.3 cm (1¼ in.)
Thickness: 2.2 cm (⅞ in.)
**WEIGHT:** 39.0 g (1.4 oz.)

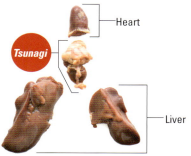

Heart — Liver — Tsunagi

### Serves 1

6 pieces *tsunagi* (connective tissue)
*Tare* sauce (see p. 173), as needed

**1** Separate the heart and liver from the vessels and tissue (*tsunagi*) that connect them, taking a small part of the base of the heart as well. If any blood remains in the blood vessels, remove it with the tip of a knife.

**2** Since *tsunagi* is a soft organ, insert the skewer into the meat of a heart base. After inserting the skewer, secure the soft flesh with the next heart base and continue adding pieces.

**3** Grill as shown at right.

### Grilling Procedure

| HEAT SOURCE | DIRECTION OF HEAT | TEMPERATURE | DISTANCE FROM HEAT |
|---|---|---|---|
| High-intensity gas grill | From below | 759°F (404°C) | 3.0 cm (1⅛ in.) |

**00:00 Start of grilling (either side may be grilled first)**

Any protruding parts should be removed with scissors, as they are likely to scorch.

**Turn twice during this interval**

**04:43 Checking color**

**04:47 Dipping in *tare* sauce and grilling**

Turn once during this interval

**06:21 Dipping in *tare* sauce and grilling**

Turn once during this interval

**07:05 Grilling complete**

185°F (85°C)

**Finish by dipping in tare sauce once more**

YAKIMONO VARIATIONS 185

# Kidneys
(*segimo*; *tare*)

Grill to brown the outside while keeping the meat juicy inside.

**SAMPLE:**
Length: 10.5 cm (4⅛ in.)
Width: 3.7 cm (1½ in.)
Thickness: 2.2 cm (⅞ in.)
**WEIGHT:** 37.7 g (1.3 oz.)

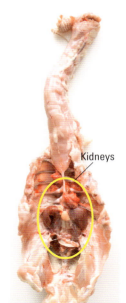
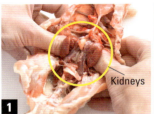
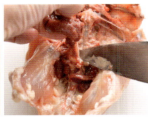
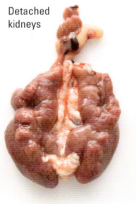

***Serves 1***

5 portions kidneys (*segimo*)
*Tare* sauce (see p. 173), as needed

**1** Detach the kidneys from the back. Insert the thumbs on the inner side of the backbone between the ribs and the kidneys to carefully separate the kidneys from the flesh. Insert the thumbs from the tail side and detach the kidneys, then pull them away and sever the attachment to the spine with the tip of a knife.

**2** Cut the detached kidneys apart vertically to make them easier to thread onto a skewer.

**3** Skewer five pieces together closely, threading through the thick parts of the meat.

**4** Grill as shown at right.

## Grilling Procedure

| HEAT SOURCE | DIRECTION OF HEAT | TEMPERATURE | DISTANCE FROM HEAT |
|---|---|---|---|
| High-intensity gas grill | From below | 811°F (433°C) | 2.4 cm (1 in.) |

**00:00** Start of grilling (either side may be grilled first)

Turn three times during this interval

**05:01** Checking color

**05:05** Dipping in *tare* sauce and grilling

Turn once during this interval

**06:34** Dipping in *tare* sauce and grilling

Turn once during this interval

**07:40** Grilling complete

188°F (86.5°C)

Finish by dipping in *tare* sauce once more

186 YAKIMONO VARIATIONS

# Gizzard
## (*sunagimo; shio*)

While browning, care should be taken to avoid over-grilling, which makes the meat tough. Cook through for a firm, rather chewy texture.

**SAMPLE:**
- Length: 9.8 cm (3⅞ in.)
- Width: 4.0 cm (1⅝ in.)
- Thickness: 2.0 cm (¾ in.)

**WEIGHT:** 25.0 g (0.9 oz.)

### Serves 1

5 gizzards (*sunagimo*)
Salt, as needed

1. Patches of fibrous tissue known as "silver skin" (*ginkawa*) are attached to the gizzard; they must be removed before grilling. Place the butterflied gizzard inner side down on the work surface. Insert the knife along the ridge of flesh (dotted line in photograph) and cut through.
2. Turn the gizzard over, so the silver skin is underneath, insert the knife between the silver skin and the meat and slice off the meat.
3. Skewer the meat so that the cut surface is on the outside, alternating thick and thin pieces.
4. Sprinkle salt all over.
5. **Grill as shown at right.**

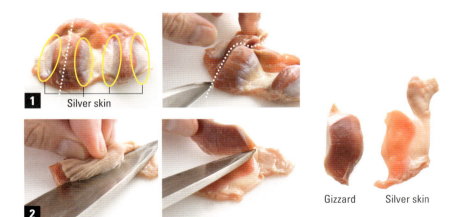

Gizzard    Silver skin

### Grilling Procedure

| HEAT SOURCE | DIRECTION OF HEAT | TEMPERATURE | DISTANCE FROM HEAT |
|---|---|---|---|
| High-intensity gas grill | From below | 770°F (410°C) | 3.6 cm (1⅜ in.) |

**00:00** Start of grilling (either side may be grilled first)

Turn six times during this interval

**06:00** Grilling complete

Cross-section when grilling is complete

The heart and gizzard are essentially muscle, and muscle fibers shrink during cooking. By contrast, the liver and kidneys contain no muscle fiber and are mostly protein-rich cells whose proteins are denatured during heating. Owing to the ferrous ions in the blood that these cuts contain, lipid oxidation is likely, which is often perceived as unpleasant. These can be masked by the products of the Maillard reaction that occurs when shoyu and similar ingredients are heated. For this reason, cuts like liver, *tsunagi*, and kidneys are often served with *tare* sauce.

YAKIMONO VARIATIONS

# Skin (*kawa; shio*)

The outside is grilled until crisp and lightly browned, while the inside remains tender and juicy.

**SAMPLE:**
Length: 9.0 cm (3½ in.)
Width: 3.0 cm (1⅛ in.)
Thickness: 2.0 cm (¾ in.)
**WEIGHT:** 36.0 g (1.3 oz.)

*Serves 1*

8 pieces neck skin (*kawa*)
Salt, as needed

1. Parboil the neck skin for about 2½ minutes to remove impurities and excess fat, then transfer to cold water. Carefully remove any remaining pin feathers.
2. Cut into bite-sized pieces. Roll up each piece and fold over, then thread on a skewer, taking care to align the folds. Treat the side with the folds as the serving side.
3. Sprinkle salt all over.
4. Grill as shown at right.

### Grilling Procedure

| HEAT SOURCE | DIRECTION OF HEAT | TEMPERATURE | DISTANCE FROM HEAT |
|---|---|---|---|
| High-intensity gas grill | From below | 975°F (524°C) | 3.6 cm (1⅜ in.) |

**00:00** Grilling serving side (side with folds)

**Turn five times during this interval**

**06:19** Grilling complete

Parts like the skin and the *bonjiri* contain large amounts of collagen and fats that liquefy when heated. If these parts are overcooked or exposed to heat for too long, the collagen will run off and the meat will shrink and lose its tenderness. If undercooked, by contrast, the collagen will not gelatinize and the texture will remain tough. Since salt is also lost with the fat, these parts should be salted more generously than others.

# Skin (*kawa; tare*)

The outside is grilled until crisp and lightly browned, while the inside remains tender and juicy.

**SAMPLE:**
Length: 9.0 cm (3½ in.)
Width: 3.0 cm (1⅛ in.)
Thickness: 2.0 cm (¾ in.)
**WEIGHT:** 36.0 g (1.3 oz.)

### Serves 1

8 pieces neck skin (*kawa*)
*Tare* sauce (see p. 173), as needed

1. Parboil the neck skin for about 2½ minutes to remove impurities and excess fat, then transfer to cold water. Carefully remove any remaining pin feathers.
2. Cut into bite-sized pieces. Roll up each piece and fold over, then thread on a skewer, taking care to align the folds. Treat the side with the folds as the serving side.
3. Grill as shown at right.

## Grilling Procedure

| HEAT SOURCE | DIRECTION OF HEAT | TEMPERATURE | DISTANCE FROM HEAT |
|---|---|---|---|
| High-intensity gas grill | From below | 770°F (410°C) | 3.6 cm (1⅜ in.) |

**00:00** Grilling serving side (side with folds)

**Turn three times during this interval**

**07:20** Checking color on serving side

**07:26** Dipping in *tare* sauce, grilling reverse side

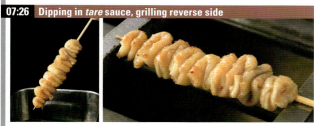

**Turn twice during this interval**

**09:17** Dipping in *tare* sauce, grilling reverse side

**09:38** Grilling complete

**Finish by dipping in *tare* sauce once more**

# *Bonjiri* (uropygium or pope's nose; *shio*)

This fleshy protuberance that supports the bird's tail feathers is quite fatty, so it needs to be grilled well to render out some of the lipids. The outside is cooked to a light crisp, while the inside should have a pleasant crunch.

**SAMPLE:**
 Length: 10.0 cm (3⅞ in.)
 Width: 4.5 cm (1¾ in.)
 Thickness: 1.8 cm (¾ in.)
**WEIGHT:** 39.0 g (1.4 oz.)

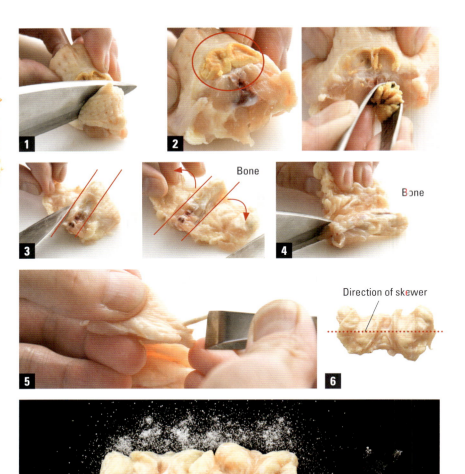

### Serves 1

2 portions *bonjiri* (uropygium or pope's nose)

Salt, as needed

1. Place the cut surface to the left and cut off the tapered part at the tip.
2. The yellow fat on the cut surface has a strong, distinctive smell, and should be carefully removed with fish-bone tweezers.
3. Place the cut surface facing up. Cut open the flesh to the left and right of the central bone.
4. Flip over to expose the bone; cut it away.
5. Use fish-bone tweezers to remove any pin feathers that remain in the skin.
6. Spread out the flesh on both sides and skewer as if stitching horizontally from left to right.
7. Sprinkle salt all over.
8. Grill as shown at right.

### Grilling Procedure

| HEAT SOURCE | DIRECTION OF HEAT | TEMPERATURE | DISTANCE FROM HEAT |
|---|---|---|---|
| High-intensity gas grill | From below | 945°F (507°C) | 3.7 cm (1½ in.) |

Turn five times during this interval

200°F (93.6°C)

# *Nankotsu* (breastbone cartilage; *shio*)

The outside surface is grilled to a light crisp, while the inside is fully cooked.

**SAMPLE:**
Length: 9.3 cm (3⅝ in.)
Width: 6.2 cm (2½ in.)
Thickness: 1.9 cm (¾ in.)
**WEIGHT:** 40.6 g (1.4 oz.)

1 — Chiai

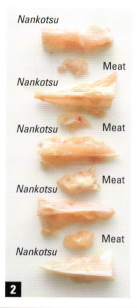

Nankotsu / Meat / Nankotsu / Meat / Nankotsu / Meat / Nankotsu / Meat / Nankotsu

2

⊗ Any parts of the skewer exposed in the gaps between the *nankotsu* may scorch.

3

***Serves 1***

5 portions *nankotsu* (breastbone cartilage)

Additional meat, as needed

Salt, as needed

1. Cut the part of the cartilage where blood (*chiai*) is visible through the thick parts of the cartilage.
2. Skewer the cartilage pieces, alternating the direction each time. To prevent exposed portions of the skewer from scorching, thread an extra piece of meat between each cartilage piece to cover the skewer. Use thin skewers, since the cartilage is delicate and easily broken.
3. Sprinkle salt all over.
4. Grill as shown at right.

### Grilling Procedure

| HEAT SOURCE | DIRECTION OF HEAT | TEMPERATURE | DISTANCE FROM HEAT |
|---|---|---|---|
| High-intensity gas grill | From below | 894°F (479°C) | 3.0 cm (1⅛ in.) |

**00:00** Start of grilling (either side may be grilled first)

**Turn twice during this interval**

**05:19** Grilling complete

YAKIMONO VARIATIONS

# Meatballs (*tsukune*; *shio*)

Since the meat is cooked in advance, grilling serves only to brown the outside and warm the inside.

**SAMPLE:**
Length: 9.2 cm (3⅝ in.)
Width: 3.3 cm (1¼ in.)
Thickness: 3.1 cm (1¼ in.)
**WEIGHT:** 41.0 g (1.4 oz.)

### Serves 1

3 meatballs (*tsukune*)
Salt, as needed

Meatball mix
- 500 g (17.6 oz.) ground chicken meat
- 500 g (17.6 oz.) onion, finely grated on an *oroshigane*
- 1 egg
- 30 ml (2 Tbsp.) *koikuchi* shoyu

Kombu dashi
- 2 L (67.6 fl. oz.) water
- 30 g (1.1 oz.) kombu

1. Wrap in the finely grated onion in gauze and squeeze tightly to remove excess moisture. Combine all ingredients and knead well until the mixture develops a sticky consistency.
2. Take an appropriate amount of the mixture and squeeze into a ball through a ring formed by the thumb and index finger; use a spoon to tidy the shape. Boil in the kombu dashi to cook. The cooking liquid will also serve as soup.
3. Skewer the meatballs through the center.
4. Sprinkle salt all over.
5. Grill as shown at right.

### Grilling Procedure

| HEAT SOURCE | DIRECTION OF HEAT | TEMPERATURE | DISTANCE FROM HEAT |
|---|---|---|---|
| High-intensity gas grill | From below | 930°F (499°C) | 3.0 cm (1⅛ in.) |

**00:00 Start of grilling (either side may be grilled first)**

Turn three times during this interval

**03:49 Grilling complete**

160°F (71°C)

192  YAKIMONO VARIATIONS

# Meatballs
(*tsukune*; *tare*)

Since the meat is cooked in advance, grilling serves only to brown the outside and warm the inside.

**SAMPLE:**
Length: 9.2 cm (3⅝ in.)
Width: 3.3 cm (1¼ in.)
Thickness: 3.1 cm (1¼ in.)
**WEIGHT:** 41.0 g (1.4 oz.)

*Serves 1*

3 meatballs (*tsukune*)
*Tare* sauce (see p. 173), as needed

Meatball mix
  500 g (17.6 oz.) ground chicken meat
  500 g (17.6 oz.) onion, finely grated on an *oroshigane*
  1 egg
  30 ml (2 Tbsp.) *koikuchi* shoyu

Kombu dashi
  2 L (67.6 fl. oz.) water
  30 g (1.1 oz.) kombu

**1** Wrap in the finely grated onion in gauze and squeeze tightly to remove excess moisture. Combine all ingredients and knead well until the mixture develops a sticky consistency.

**2** Take an appropriate amount of the mixture and squeeze into a ball through a ring formed by the thumb and index finger; use a spoon to tidy the shape. Boil in the kombu dashi to cook. The cooking liquid will also serve as soup.

**3** Skewer the meatballs through the center.

**4** Grill as shown at right.

## Grilling Procedure

| HEAT SOURCE | DIRECTION OF HEAT | TEMPERATURE | DISTANCE FROM HEAT |
|---|---|---|---|
| High-intensity gas grill | From below | 844°F (451°C) | 3.0 cm (1⅛ in.) |

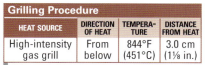

**00:00** Start of grilling (either side may be grilled first)

Turn once during this interval

**04:41** Checking color

**04:45** Dipping in *tare* sauce and grilling

**06:36** Dipping in *tare* sauce and grilling

Turn once during this interval

**07:50** Dipping in *tare* sauce and grilling

**08:49** Grilling complete

177°F (80.3°C)

# Garnishes and Other Accompanying Dishes

This section introduces recipes for the garnishes (*ashirai*) and small dishes served as accompaniments to the *yakimono* presented in this book. The function of garnishes in Japanese cuisine is to impart a sense of the season and add taste and color to the main dish. They are important accompaniments that represent seasonal themes and refresh the palate. The ingredients of most are vegetables or seaweed, but also include roots, beans, fruit, and nuts processed in various ways, and their names differ according to their use. They are arranged according to the recipes with which they appear, sometimes with slightly differing procedures depending on the dishes they are intended to accompany and the discretion of the chef. Ingredients are listed in easy-to-make amounts.

## Chapter 1  Introducing *Yakimono*

**p. 18** Salt-Grilled Striped Mackerel

### Vinegar-pickled *myoga* (*su-zuke myoga*)

25 *myoga* buds (in proportion with the sweet vinegar marinade below)
Salt

Sweet vinegar marinade (*ama-zu*)
  7 g (0.2 oz.) kombu
  600 ml (20.3 fl. oz.) water
  200 ml (6.8 fl. oz.) rice vinegar
  110 g (3.9 oz.) sugar

1. Place kombu in rice vinegar/water mix and leave for 12 hours.
2. Transfer to a saucepan, add sugar, and place over heat. Remove from heat just before the mixture comes to a boil; remove kombu; allow to cool.
3. Cut the *myoga* in half lengthwise; blanch in boiling water, then drain. Sprinkle with a scant amount of salt and leave to cool.
4. Immerse the *myoga* in the sweet vinegar marinade for 4 to 5 hours.

## Chapter 3  Basic Types of *Yakimono*

**p. 44** *Yuan* Style Butterfish

### Syrup-simmered yuzu rind (*amigasa-yuzu*)

1–2 yellow yuzu (*kiyuzu*)

Syrup
  200 ml (6.8 fl. oz.) water
  100 g (3.5 oz.) sugar

1. Remove the zest from the rind with a grater. Cut rind in half vertically and scoop out the pulp.
2. Blanch the rind briefly in boiling water, then douse in cold water. Repeat several times until bitterness is removed. Carefully remove the white pith.
3. Heat the rind for 5 minutes in a convection oven, on steam setting, at 212°F (100°C), level 3 (of 5), until the moisture has evaporated.
4. Combine the water, sugar, and yuzu rind in a saucepan. Bring to a boil, then reduce until all liquid is gone. Turn off the heat, cover with a drop-lid (*otoshibuta*), and leave to cool.

**p. 56** Miso-Marinated Grilled Beltfish

### *Shimeji* mushrooms, simmered *tosa-ni* style (*shimeji no tosa-ni*)

*Shimeji* mushrooms, as needed

Marinade
  150 ml (5.1 fl. oz.) *ichiban* dashi
  10 ml (2 tsp.) *usukuchi* shoyu
  10 ml (2 tsp.) mirin

Powdered katsuobushi, as needed

1. Place the dashi and the mushrooms in a saucepan.
2. Bring to a boil, add the mirin and *usukuchi* shoyu, and simmer for 5 to 6 minutes. Skim if necessary.
3. Allow to cool in the liquid.
4. Once cooled, remove the mushrooms from the liquid and dredge in the powdered katsuobushi.

**p. 60** Salted and Grilled Tilefish

### Pickled turnip, cut "chrysanthemum" style (*kikka-kabura*)

1 turnip

Sweet vinegar marinade (*ama-zu*)
  600 ml (20.3 fl. oz.) water
  200 ml (6.8 fl. oz.) rice vinegar
  80 g (2.8 oz.) sugar
  7 g (0.2 oz.) kombu

Salt, as needed

1. Mix together the water, vinegar, and sugar, then add the kombu and allow to stand for one day.
2. Transfer to a saucepan, heat, and remove from the heat just before the boil. Allow to cool in the pan, then remove the kombu.
3. Cut the turnip into 2-cm (¾ in.) thick rounds, leaving the skin on. Peel a wide layer from the circumference using the *katsuramuki* technique to remove the tough, fibrous skin on the outside.
4. Score the face of the turnip round at very thin intervals down to about two-thirds of the thickness. Turn 90 degrees and cut the turnip again at very thin intervals to the same depth.
5. Turn the cross-scored turnip upside down. Trim the sharp edges and cut into 2-cm (¾ in.) wide strips. Cut squares from the strips.
6. Place the squares in a 0.8 percent salt water bath. When the "petals" soften and open up, remove from the salt water and squeeze out moisture.
7. Immerse in the sweet vinegar marinade for 2 hours. Remove and drain, then arrange the petals in a chrysanthemum-flower shape.

**p. 69** Overnight-Dried Whiting

### Early-harvested lotus root with crushed edamame beans (*shin-renkon no zunda-ae*)

Early-harvested lotus root, as needed
Kombu dashi, as needed

Vinegar

Crushed edamame beans (*zunda*), as needed

1. Peel the lotus root, slice, and trim into flower shape. Combine a dash of vinegar with water in a saucepan, add the lotus root, and bring to a boil.
2. Transfer the lotus root to the kombu dashi with a dash of vinegar added, and leave to soak.
3. Drain the lotus root, cut slices into quarters (*icho-giri*), and mix with the crushed edamame beans.

**p. 69 Overnight-Dried Whiting**

Vinegar-pickled Moriguchi radish (*Moriguchi daikon no su-zuke*)

Moriguchi daikon

Marinade

Combine seven parts *niban* dashi, two parts rice vinegar, and one part each *usukuchi* shoyu and mirin in a saucepan and bring to a boil, then remove from heat.

Moriguchi daikon is a radish that can be marinated without peeling. Cut the daikon into 1.5-cm (⅝ in.) cubes. Pierce the center of each piece and thread onto the pine needles. Immerse pieces in the marinade, cover with plastic wrap, and leave overnight.

**p. 72 Grilled Yellowtail**

Pickled turnip, cut "chrysanthemum" style (*kikka-kabura*)

→See recipe for Pickled turnip, cut "chrysanthemum" style, under p. 60 Salted and Grilled Tilefish, above p. 194

**p. 80 Grilled Quail**

Syrup-simmered yuzu rind (*amigasa-yuzu*)

1 yellow yuzu (*kiyuzu*)
30–40 g (1.1–1.4 oz.) sugar

1. Remove the zest from the yuzu with a grater. Cut the rind in half crosswise and scoop out the pulp (remnants of pith may be left).
2. Blanch the yuzu rind in boiling water for 1 to 2 minutes, then discard the water. Repeat this process two or three times, then transfer the rind to 500 ml (16.9 fl. oz.) cold water. Bring to a boil and cook until just a slight tang remains.
3. Add the sugar and bring to a boil again, then continue cooking to reduce the liquid by one-third.

**p. 84 Grilled Sweetfish (Electric grill)**

Boiled *satoimo* taro (*kinu-katsugi*)

5 *satoimo* taro corms
Salt, as needed
*Daitokuji* natto, finely chopped, as needed

1. Wash the taro corms, then steam for 20 to 25 minutes, or until easily pierced with a bamboo skewer.
2. Remove the corms from the steamer and sprinkle lightly with salt.
3. Cut a slice off the bottom of each corm and hollow out a small cavity. Roll the natto into small balls and insert into the cavity of each corm.

**p. 90 Grilled Sweetfish (Charcoal grill)**

Vinegar-pickled *myoga* (*su-zuke myoga*)

3 *myoga* buds
Salt, as needed

Sweet vinegar marinade (*ama-zu*)
300 ml (10.1 fl. oz.) water
200 ml (6.8 fl. oz.) rice vinegar
50 g (1.8 oz.) sugar
5 g (0.2 oz.) kombu
Salt

1. Combine all marinade ingredients and mix.
2. Cut the *myoga* in half lengthwise, parboil, and drain in a sieve. Sprinkle lightly with salt and allow to cool.
3. Immerse the *myoga* in the sweet vinegar marinade for about 2 hours.

**Chapter 4  *Yakimono* Variations**

**p. 108 *Awayuki* Grilled Sea Bream**

Grilled bamboo shoot (*yaki-takenoko*)

1 bamboo shoot

1. Cut the bamboo shoot in half lengthwise, then into pieces 5-cm (2 in.) wide. Thread the pieces onto skewers.
2. Grill thoroughly over direct heat until the surface browns, then cut into bite-sized pieces.

**p. 114 *Kenchin* Style Grilled Sea Bream**

Simmered *shimeji* mushrooms and soused spinach (*shimeji to horenso no ohitashi*)

*Shimeji* mushrooms, as needed

*Saka-shio* (salted sake/water mixture), as needed

Combine one part sake with three parts water and add salt (3% by weight). No heating required.

Spinach, as needed

Marinade
200 ml (6.8 fl. oz.) *ichiban* dashi
15 ml (1 Tbsp.) *usukuchi* shoyu
15 ml (1 Tbsp.) mirin
Mix to combine (no heating required)

1. Cut the *shimeji* mushrooms to desired size and immerse in the *saka-shio*. Blanch the spinach for approximately 2 minutes, then transfer to an ice bath. Drain and cut into bite-sized lengths.
2. Place the *shimeji* mushrooms and spinach in the marinade and let stand for 10 minutes.

**p. 116 Sea Bream Grilled with Oil**

Marinated lotus root (*renkon no sanbaizu-zuke*)

Lotus root, as needed
Vinegar, as needed

*Sanbai-zu* dressing
90 ml (3.0 fl. oz.) vinegar

GARNISHES 195

30 ml (2 Tbsp.) *usukuchi* shoyu

60 g (2.1 oz.) sugar

Combine all *sanbai-zu* ingredients in a saucepan, bring to a boil, then allow to cool.

1. Peel the lotus root and slice into thin rounds. Place in hot water with a small amount of vinegar and bring to a boil.
2. Simmer the lotus root for 2 to 3 minutes, until pleasantly firm and crunchy, then transfer to cold water.
3. Drain well, then immerse in the *sanbai-zu* and leave for 5 to 6 hours.

**p. 120** Grilled *Sawara* Mackerel with *Natane* Topping

## Soused *nanohana* (rape blossom) shoots (*nanohana no ohitashi*)

2 *nanohana* shoots (trim off the hard part of the stem)

Salt, as needed

### Marinade

180 ml (6.1 fl. oz.) *niban* dashi

18 ml (1¼ Tbsp.) sake

18 ml (1¼ Tbsp.) *usukuchi* shoyu

9 ml (2 tsp.) salt water, fully saturated with around 26% salt

7 g (0.2 oz.) katsuobushi flakes

Combine all marinade ingredients except the katsuobushi flakes and bring to a boil. Turn off the heat, add the katsuobushi flakes, and allow to cool, then strain.

1. Add salt (1% by weight) to warm water, bring to a boil, and blanch the *nanohana* shoots for 30 seconds to 1 minute.
2. Transfer to cold water and allow to cool. Let stand for 30 minutes to reduce bitterness (*nanohana* greens tend to be particularly bitter).
3. Immerse in the marinade for 3 hours.

**p. 124** Sea Bass Roasted in Green *Hoba* Leaves

## Vinegar-pickled *myoga* (*su-zuke myoga*)

→See recipe for "Vinegar-pickled *myoga*" under p. 18 Salt-Grilled Striped Mackerel, above p. 194

**p. 126** *Tade-Miso* Grilled Sea Bass

## Mustard-filled lotus root (*karashi renkon*)

Early harvested lotus root, as needed

### Marinade

800 ml (27.1 fl. oz.) kombu dashi

40 ml (2 Tbsp. plus 2 tsp.) vinegar

20 ml (1 Tbsp. plus 1 tsp.) *usukuchi* shoyu

Salt

Mix to combine (no heating required)

*Kimi-garashi* (egg-yolk mustard filling)

1 egg yolk

Pinch sugar

5 g (0.2 oz.) *karashi* mustard dissolved in lukewarm water, as needed

Mix the egg yolk, sugar, and mustard. Heat slowly until the mixture thickens, then strain through a fine-mesh sieve.

1. Peel the lotus root and cut into chrysanthemum-flower shape (*kikka-renkon*). Slice to desired width and parboil until just tender.
2. Immerse in the marinade for 1 hour.
3. Fill the holes in the lotus root slices with the *kimi-garashi* mixture.

**p. 126** *Tade-Miso* Grilled Sea Bass

## Simmered wild butterbur (*yama-buki kyara-ni*)

1 stalk wild butterbur (*yama-buki*)

Salt, as needed

### Simmering liquid

500 ml (16.9 fl. oz.) sake

500 ml (16.9 fl. oz.) water

200 ml (6.8 fl. oz.) *koikuchi* shoyu

100 ml (3.4 fl. oz.) mirin

1. Sprinkle the butterbur stalk with salt, then place on a cutting board and roll until the salt coats the surface.
2. Let stand for 30 minutes to 1 hour, until moisture forms on the surface of the stalks, then immerse in boiling water.
3. When the water returns to a boil, transfer the butterbur to a sieve. (Butterbur harvested in early spring may be soft enough to use without peeling.) If the outside of the stalk is tough and fibrous, peel and allow to dry for about one day in the shade.
4. Combine the sake and water in a saucepan. Cut the butterbur in bite-size lengths and add to the liquid.
5. Simmer until the liquid is reduced by half, then add the *koikuchi* shoyu.
6. Continue to simmer until the liquid is reduced by half again, then remove the butterbur so it does not become tough.
7. Add the mirin to the liquid in the saucepan and boil once more. When the liquid has boiled down to the point bubbles appear, add the butterbur, and stir to coat thoroughly.

**p. 132** Tilefish Grilled with *Karasumi* Powder

## Soused spinach (*horenso no ohitashi*)

Spinach, as needed

### Marinade

180 ml (6.1 fl. oz.) *ichiban* dashi

2.5 ml (½ tsp.) *usukuchi* shoyu

2.5 ml (½ tsp.) mirin

1 g (scant ¼ tsp.) salt

Mix to combine (no heating required). Divide into two portions.

1. Blanch the spinach in boiling water for 20 to 30 seconds; remove and chill in ice water.
2. Drain the spinach, then immerse in one portion of the marinade to remove excess water.
3. Drain the spinach, place in the remaining marinade, and let stand for 3 hours. Before serving, gather the spinach into a bundle and squeeze gently to remove moisture, then cut into lengths.

**p. 134** Tilefish, *Shiba-yaki* Style

## *Aomi* (green) radish pickled in miso (*aomi daikon no miso-zuke*)

1 *aomi* daikon radish

### Marinade

White miso, as needed

Sake, as needed

Mirin, as needed

Mix to combine.

1. Bring water to a boil, then add the *aomi*

196    GARNISHES

daikon and cook until the root is tender but not soft. Blanch the leaves.
2. Transfer to the marinade and let stand for 2 hours.

### p. 136 Grilled *Kinmedai* Marinated in Sake Lees
## Candied walnuts (*kurumi ame-ni*)

300 g (10.6 oz.) walnuts

Simmering syrup 200 ml (6.8 fl. oz.)
  1 L (33.8 fl. oz.) sake
  100 ml (3.4 fl. oz.) *koikuchi* shoyu
  40 ml (2 Tbsp. plus 2 tsp.) *usukuchi* shoyu
  300 g (10.6 oz.) *mizuame* syrup
  70 g (2.5 oz.) sugar

Rice oil, as needed

Powdered sugar, as needed

1. Deep-fry the walnuts in the rice oil at 266°F (130°C) for 10 minutes.
2. Mix together simmering syrup ingredients in a saucepan and bring to a boil to de-alcoholize.
3. Lower the heat and simmer until large bubbles form and the mixture thickens. Add the walnuts and stir to coat; remove from heat.
4. Spread out and allow to cool and set, then dust with powdered sugar.

### p. 138 Koji Grilled Salmon
## Syrup-simmered yuzu rind (*amigasa-yuzu*)

→ See recipe for "Syrup-simmered yuzu rind" on p. 194, accompanying the recipe for *Yuan* Style Butterfish.

### p. 140 Rikyu Style Sesame-Grilled Flounder
## Soused butterbur (*fuki no ohitashi*)

1 stalk butterbur (*fuki*)

Salt, as needed

Marinade
  180 ml (6.1 fl. oz.) *niban* dashi
  18 ml (1¼ Tbsp.) *usukuchi* shoyu
  5 g (0.2 oz.) katsuobushi flakes

Add the *usukuchi* shoyu to the *niban* dashi and bring to a boil. Add the katsuobushi flakes and remove from heat.

1. Bring salt water (2% salinity) to a boil. Add the butterbur and blanch, then transfer to cold water to cool.
2. Peel the butterbur and cut into 4-cm (1⅝ in.) lengths.
3. Immerse the butterbur in marinade for 5 hours.

### p. 146 Grilled Pike Conger with *Tare* Sauce
## Yam-and-egg sauce (*tamago imo*)

50 g (1.8 oz.) *yama-imo* yam

2 egg yolks

10 ml (2 tsp.) *ichiban* dashi

Salt

1. Peel and grate the yam, then mash well in a *suribachi*.
2. Add the egg yolks and mix well.
3. Add the *ichiban* dashi in small amounts, mixing well, and season with salt.

### p. 154 Grilled Cuttlefish, *Ro-yaki* Style
## Pickled turnip, cut "chrysanthemum" style (*kikka-kabura*)

1 turnip

Salt, as needed

Sweet vinegar marinade (*ama-zu*)
  500 ml (16.9 fl. oz.) rice vinegar
  500 ml (16.9 fl. oz.) water
  200 g (7.1 oz.) sugar

1. Combine all sweet vinegar marinade ingredients in a saucepan and bring to a boil; remove from heat and allow to cool.
2. Score the turnip with a knife (see p. 60 garnish recipe for details), immerse in salt water (3% salinity), and let soak for 4 hours.
3. Drain well, then immerse in the sweet vinegar marinade for one day.

### p. 158 Abalone Grilled in a Salt Crust
## Abalone liver sauce (*awabi-kimo-dare*)

100 g (3.5 oz.) abalone liver

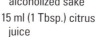

30 ml (2 Tbsp.) *koikuchi* shoyu

60 ml (2.0 fl. oz.) de-alcoholized sake

15 ml (1 Tbsp.) citrus juice

1. Briefly parboil the abalone liver, then pass through a sieve.
2. Combine the liver with the *koikuchi* shoyu, sake, and citrus juice and stir well.

### p. 158 Abalone Grilled in a Salt Crust
## Citrus sauce (*kankitsu-shio*)

100 ml (3.4 fl. oz.) citrus juice

3 g (¾ tsp.) salt

Add the salt to the juice and stir well to dissolve.

### p. 162 Kamo Eggplant *Dengaku*
## *Chamame* (edamame) pods

*Chamame* pods (unshelled beans), as needed

Kombu dashi, as needed

Salt, as needed

1. Place the *chamame* pods in a *suribachi*, sprinkle with salt, and rub well to remove the fuzz from the pods.
2. Bring water to a boil and cook the pods.
3. Add salt (1% by weight) to the kombu dashi and refrigerate. Drain the *chamame* pods and transfer them to the dashi to cool. Let stand for 1 hour, then drain.

### p. 166 Roast Duck Breast
## Egg and vinegar dressing (*kimi-zu*)

3 egg yolks

Kombu dashi, same amount as egg yolks

Sugar, as needed

Rice vinegar

Taihaku (untoasted) sesame oil

Combine the egg yolks, kombu dashi, sugar, and rice vinegar in a pan over low heat, stirring continuously. Once the mixture thickens, stir in the sesame oil. Pass the dressing through a sieve while it is still hot.

GARNISHES 197

# Skewering Techniques (*Kushi-uchi*)

The practice of skewering ingredients for grilling over direct heat is the defining characteristic of Japanese *yakimono*. Chefs employ numerous techniques; a few of the most common are introduced here.

As a general rule, skewers are inserted in the back-to-belly direction, perpendicular to the line between the head and tail of the fish. Exceptions to this rule include sweetfish (*ayu*), which is skewered whole, and pike conger (*hamo*), which is skewered in the head-to-tail direction after preparing by the *honekiri* technique. The thickness and length of the skewers, as well as the number used, depends on the size, shape, and weight of the fillet. Care is taken to apply the skewers in a way that prevents the flesh from coming apart or fragmenting when food is moved or turned during grilling.

Another important consideration is determining which side will be served face up. To ensure that no skewer holes are visible when the food is served, skewers are typically inserted from the reverse side (the side that will be served face down), and thin skewers are selected to minimize the visibility of the perforations. The skewers are inserted in a fan pattern, which allows the ends to be grasped in one hand. This arrangement also prevents the flesh from breaking apart when handling during cooking.

**Types of skewers**

Length 60 cm (23⅝ in.), thickness 3.0 mm (⅛ in.)
Length 51 cm (20⅛ in.), thickness 2.5 mm (1/10 in.)
Length 42 cm (16½ in.), thickness 2.0 mm (/16 in.)

Skewers are made from either bamboo or metal. Bamboo skewers are generally used for eel (*unagi no kaba-yaki*) and *yakitori*, while stainless steel skewers are preferred for most other ingredients. Skewers come in various lengths and thicknesses, and chefs select the number of skewers and the technique based on the shape, size, and other qualities of the ingredients, as well as the grilling method to be used.

## ■ Flat-skewering (*hira-gushi*)

This is the most basic technique. The skewers are inserted so that the ingredients lie flat and the heat penetrates the surface of the food evenly throughout.

### Tilefish (*amadai*) fillet  **3 skewers**

Since tilefish flakes easily when heated, skewers are inserted at equal intervals so that each skewer bears roughly the same weight.

**1** The skin side is treated as the serving side, which will be served face up. The fillet is placed with the skin side down, belly end to the front.

**2** Begin skewering from the right edge. With the left hand lightly supporting the fillet, insert the tip of a skewer into the flesh. When inserting the skewer, use the fingers of the left hand to ascertain its position inside the fish.

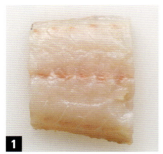

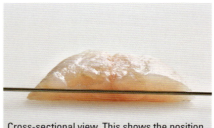

Cross-sectional view. This shows the position of the skewer as it passes through the flesh.

3. Insert the second and third skewers in the same way.
4. Fillet after insertion of the third skewer.

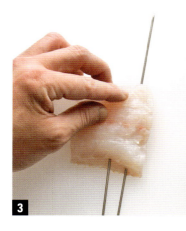

## Biwa gudgeon (*moroko*)

**4 skewers**

With fish that are grilled whole rather than being filleted, the skewers should be inserted so that they are below the central bones when the fish is turned. This prevents the flesh from falling off the side that is heated first.

1. The side of the fish that is face up when the head is to the left is used as the serving side. Arrange three fish in a line with the heads to the right, bellies toward the front. Since the skewers are inserted in a fan shape, arrange the fish in order of increasing size, with the smallest at the bottom.
2. Insert the first skewer around the pectoral fin, the fourth close to the anal fin, and the other two at equal intervals between. All skewers should pass above the central bones.
3. After inserting the fourth skewer, make sure there is sufficient space between the three fish to allow heat to penetrate evenly.

View from the ends of the skewers. The skewers pass over the central bones.

SKEWERING TECHNIQUES 199

# Wave-skewering (*uneri-gushi*)

The skewering of a fillet by the *uneri-gushi* "wave" technique derives from the way whole fish are skewered to evoke the appearance of vigor and movement. As the skewering makes the tail stand up as if vigorously swimming, the technique is known as *odori-gushi* (literally, "dancing"). (See skewering of *ayu* sweetfish, pp. 85, 93.)

## Butterfish (*managatsuo*) fillet — 3 skewers

The *uneri-gushi* skewering technique is introduced here using the *uwami* and *shitami* fillets of butterfish (*managatsuo*). Arrange a butterfish filleted *sanmai-oroshi* style with the head end to the right, skin side down. Cut the portions along the grain of the muscle (*junme*, see p. 19), starting from the tail. Basically, the portion is placed with the wider part of the fillet at the far end and the narrower part at the near end, and the skewers inserted starting from the belly side to the dorsal side. However, since inserting the first skewer through skin makes it easier to maintain the shape of the portion and ensure an attractive final appearance, sometimes the wider part is placed at the near end and the narrower part at the far end. Here we introduce the techniques for (1) inserting the first skewer into the skin of an *uwami* portion, (2) inserting the first skewer into the belly side of an *uwami* portion, and (3) inserting the first skewer into the skin side of a *shitami* portion.

### *Uwami* fillet: Inserting the first skewer into the skin of an *uwami* portion

**1** Treat the skin side as the side to be served face up. Place the skin side down with the dorsal edge at the front.

**2** Insert a skewer from below through the skin on the serving side at the dorsal edge and push it until it emerges above. Inserting the first skewer through the skin makes it easier to maintain the wave shape.

**3** Re-insert the skewer in front of the *chiai* flesh and thread midway through the flesh until the point emerges on the far side of the *chiai*. Take care that the skewer does not go through to the serving side. Re-insert the skewer into the flesh at the belly edge and push through to the serving side.

**4** Insert the second skewer in the same way. The skewers should be slightly fanned; the third skewer may not necessarily pass through the belly edge.

**5** View after insertion of the third skewer.

View from the side. To preserve the appearance, make sure that skewers do not emerge from the serving side along the length of the fillet.

***Uwami* fillet: Inserting the first skewer into the belly side of an *uwami* portion**

1. Treat the skin side as the side to be served face up. Place the skin side down and the belly edge at the front.
2. Insert a skewer into the flesh on the serving side of the belly end and push it until it emerges above. Take special care in inserting the first skewer, as it passes through soft flesh.
3. Re-insert the skewer in front of the *chiai* flesh and thread midway through the flesh until the point emerges on the far side of the *chiai*. Take care that the skewer does not go through to the serving side. Re-insert the skewer into the flesh at the dorsal edge and push through to the serving side.
4. Insert the second and third skewers in the same way.

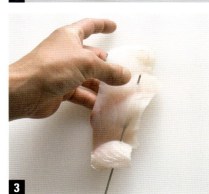
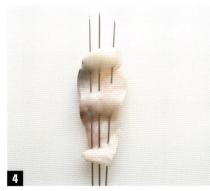

***Shitami* fillet: Inserting the first skewer into the skin of a *shitami* portion**

1. Treat the skin side as the side to be served face up. Place the skin side down and place the belly edge at the front.
2. Insert a skewer from the serving side on the belly edge and push it until it emerges above. Inserting the first skewer through the skin makes it easier to maintain the wave shape.
3. Insert the second and third skewers in the same way.

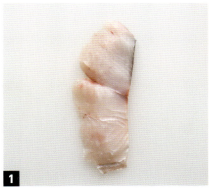

SKEWERING TECHNIQUES 201

## ■ Single-tuck (*katazuma-ori*) skewering

In this technique, the thinner flesh at the tail end is rolled up and held in place on the skewer. This reduces exposure of the thin parts of the flesh to heat and prevents overcooking and scorching.

### Barracuda (*kamasu*) fillet
**2 skewers**

1. Treat the skin side as the side to be served face up. Place the fillet skin side down with the head end at front.
2. Roll up the tail end of the flesh.
3. Insert a skewer at the head end from the serving side.
4. Press the skewer through the roll to fix it in place at the tail end.
5. Insert the second skewer in the same way.

Shown from above and from the side. The thin part of the flesh is tucked under itself so that it is not exposed to direct heat.

## ■ Double-tuck (*ryozuma-ori*) skewering

In this technique, both ends are rolled up, leaving only the thick part of the belly exposed to direct heat. This avoids exposing the thinner parts of the flesh to excessive heat and avoids overcooking.

### Barracuda (*kamasu*) fillet
**2 skewers**

1. Treat the skin side as the side to be served face up. Place the fillet skin side down with the tail end at the front.
2. Curl and tuck the flesh at both head and tail ends.
3. Insert a skewer to fix both curled ends in place. Insert the second skewer in the same way.

Shown from above and from the side. The rolls at both ends of the flesh are well secured, ensuring that the ends are not directly exposed to heat.

# Stitch skewering (*Nui-gushi*)

Squid (*ika*) **5 skewers**

This method is used to prevent the seafood from curling as it is heated. Metal skewers are inserted at regular intervals, while bamboo support skewers are inserted horizontally to keep the flesh flat during grilling.

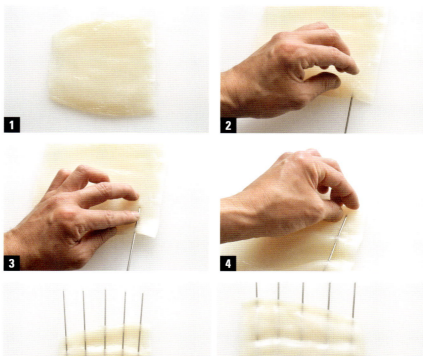

The serving side seen from above. The skewers do not emerge from the serving side.

From the side. In cross section, the skewers are seen entering the upper surface, running through the flesh as if picking up stitches at regular intervals.

1. The squid should be cut open and cleaned. Place the mantle flesh with the serving side down (i.e., the side with the skin before removal), with the tapered end facing left.
2. Insert the tip of a skewer into the cut edge of the flesh on the near side and push it into the flesh to emerge after approximately 1 cm (⅜ in.). Be careful to not let the skewer go through to the serving side.
3. Lightly support the tip of the skewer and insert it into the flesh again, pushing it through to emerge after approximately 1 cm (⅜ in.).
4. Continue to thread the skewer through the flesh as if stitching.
5. Insert all five skewers in the same way. Thread them so that the places where the skewers emerge are aligned. This will make placement of the horizontal bamboo skewers (*yoko-gushi*) easier.
6. Insert the bamboo skewers under the main skewers and above the flesh.

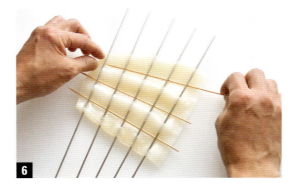

SKEWERING TECHNIQUES 203

# Tsubo-nuki

When fish is served at celebrations and other auspicious occasions, the preference is often to serve it in a state as close to its natural appearance as possible—without removing the head and tail or cutting into the belly. On such occasions, the *tsubo-nuki* technique is used, whereby the gills and internal organs are removed through the gill opening without cutting into the belly.

## Using the *tsubo-nuki* technique to clean a sea bream (*madai*)

### Detaching organs from the anal vent end

1. Descale the sea bream and place it with the head to the left.
2. Use a knife to make a hole large enough to insert a finger at the anal vent.
3. Insert a finger and gently trace around the outside of the internal organs to separate them from the body. Taking care not to damage the flesh or organs, detach carefully as far as your finger can reach.

### Detaching the gills

4. The upper part of the gills is attached to the spine on either side, while the lower part is fixed to one spot at the tip of the collar (*kama*). Open the gill cover and use a knife to cut the tissue connecting the gills to the spine.
5. Cut the membrane between the gills and the belly meat. The esophagus and other organs lie inside this membrane, so be careful to cut only the membrane without damaging the organs.
6. Turn the fish over, open the gill cover on the opposite side, and use a knife to sever the tissue connecting the gills to the spine above, as well as to cut the membrane between the gills and belly.
7. Use the knife to detach the lower part of the gills from the tip of the collar.
8. The gills will now be free to be removed along with the organs.

### Separating and removing the internal organs on the collar side

9. Insert a finger through the gill opening and trace around the outside of the internal organs to separate them from the body. At the same time, insert a finger through the hole at the anal vent and separate the organs entirely from the body of the fish. Confirm that the fingers meet inside the body of the fish.
10. If the fish is too big to allow the fingers to meet, use a cooking chopstick to carefully detach the organs. Insert a finger into the gill opening from one side to guide the chopstick.
11. Gently and slowly pull out the gills and organs through the gill opening, being careful not to allow any parts to separate and remain inside the fish.

# *Yawata-maki*
## (long-fish-wrapped burdock)

This technique uses eel (*unagi*), conger eel (*anago*), or other long, thin fish filleted *sanmai-oroshi* style. The tails of the *uwami* and *shitami* fillets are tied together in an interlocking knot (*aioi-musubi*) to form a single long piece. This is then wrapped around burdock or a similar root. The technique takes its name from the Yawata region of Kyoto, which was once famous for burdock production.

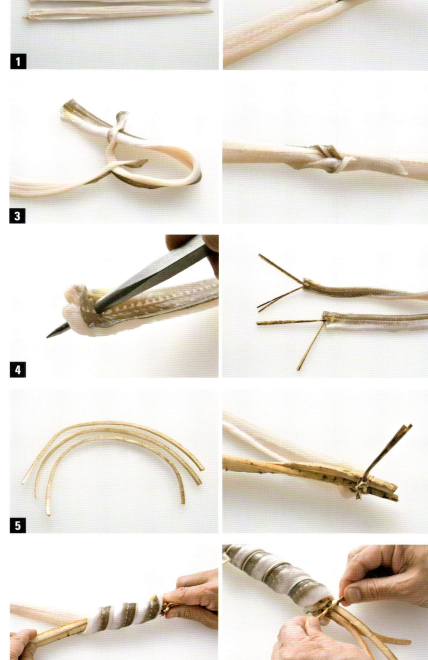

### Knotting the fillets

1. Clean and prepare the fillets in the *sanmai-oroshi* style. Make vertical incisions about 3-cm (1⅛ in.) long in the tail sections of the *uwami* and *shitami* fillets.

2. Insert one tail section through the hole made in the other tail piece.

3. Take the section that has passed through the hole and thread the head end through the hole in its own tail. Pull both head ends in opposite directions to tighten the knot.

### Wrapping around burdock

4. Pierce a hole in the head end of both the *uwami* and *shitami* fillets. Pass a cord through each hole and tie securely. Use bamboo-sheath cord if possible, since it will hold even if singed during grilling.

5. If the burdock root is thick, cut it lengthwise into as many as six strands. Two or three strands can be used together. Use the cords from step 4 to attach one end of the eel securely to the burdock.

6. Coil the flesh around the burdock in a spiral with the skin side facing outward (the surface to be grilled). Once all the flesh is wrapped around the burdock, use the other cord to tightly bind it and the burdock together.

YAWATA-MAKI 205

# Types of Grills

In Japanese cuisine today, the equipment used for grilling has been developed to suit the tradition of cooking food directly over charcoal, which has been the preferred method since it emerged in the Edo period (1603–1868). The following is a brief introduction to some of the main types of grills used in the *yakiba* section of Japanese restaurants today.

There are two main styles of grill: those that heat from below and those that heat from above. Each has its own characteristics. With heat from below, the air warmed by the heat source cooks the food as it rises, making for efficient cooking. However, fats and moisture released from the food drip onto the heating surface, so it takes skill to give the finished food a clean, attractive surface. Additionally, the dripping of fats and moisture adds to the difficulty of maintaining and cleaning the heat source. With heat from above, fats and other liquids drip onto a surface opposite the heat source, keeping the surface of the food and the heating element clean. However, since air warmed by the heat source rises and escapes, this style is less efficient than heating from below.

A salamander broiler is sometimes used in place of a grill that heats from above. Unlike a traditional grill, a salamander is not used for cooking ingredients from a raw state to completion, but to impart color and texture for finishing dishes after they have already been cooked. It is less powerful than a regular grill, but it can be used effectively as a grill by skewering the ingredients and placing them closer to the heat source.

## ■ Electric grill

An electric grill uses infrared radiation emitted from the heated surface of the grill to cook the ingredients. Some electric grills allow ingredients to be placed both above and below the heat source for flexibility. The advantages of this type of grill are that it does not produce combustion gases, since the heat is generated by electricity, and that it is easy to heat food at a specific temperature.

**Heating from below**

**Heating from above**

## ■ Charcoal grill

This type of direct-heat grill, developed in the middle of the Edo period (seventeenth century), makes it easy to reach high temperatures by fanning the embers. Charcoal provides long-lasting, steady heat, making it a popular, easy-to-use grilling method. (See also "Heat Sources for Cooking," p. 34.)

## ■ Gas grill

When a metal plate is heated on a gas burner, it produces infrared radiation that cooks the food. Some gas grills use a special burner to heat the metal plate to temperatures similar to those obtained with charcoal (around 1480°F/800°C), and certain models emit far infrared radiation with a wavelength in the 5 to 10 micrometers range. These grills allow food to be cooked at the same kind of high temperatures as charcoal.

# GLOSSARY

**Ame-ni**
This method of simmering is used mostly with river fish. The food is placed in a simmering liquid made with water, sake, shoyu, sugar, and *mizuame* syrup and cooked slowly until it takes on a dark color and glossy sheen. *Ame-ni* simmering is sometimes used for the purpose of preservation.

**Amino acids**
Amino acids are important components of the proteins from which the body is built and that determine its level of activity. Animal proteins are made from combinations of more than 10 different amino acids; it is said that there are approximately 20 amino acids that make up the body. Each amino acid tastes slightly different, and the combination of these amino acids with their individual tastes is one of the key elements that determines the flavor of foods.

**Ashirai (garnishes)**
The preparations served with a main dish to add aroma, color, or a sense of the season are called *ashirai*. They may also function to refresh the palate. Most *ashirai* consist of vegetables or seaweed, but they also include roots, beans, fruit, and nuts processed in various ways.

**Caramelization reaction**
A type of non-enzymatic browning in which heating sucrose leads to browning and the release of sweet aromas. Distinct from the Maillard reaction (see p. 16).

**Collagen**
A protein that is a principal component of the intercellular substances of animal connective tissue such as bones. Becomes soluble in water when heated.

**Furi-yuzu**
Sprinkled yuzu zest. Yuzu is grated on an *oroshigane* grater, and a bamboo tea whisk (*chasen*) or similar implement is used to sprinkle the zest on a finished dish. Imparts a brisk, refreshing, citrusy color and aroma to the food.

**Hazard analysis and critical control points (HACCP)**
A system of regulations that analyzes sanitation and quality-control hazards that may be present in food production and processing, sets out a list of critical control points that must be monitored to ensure food safety, and controls and records them. This internationally recognized system is used in many countries.

**Himono (dried seafood)**
*Himono* are made by drying fish and other seafood. Reducing water moisture content helps to preserve food; this approach is used all over the world. The drying process imparts distinctive mellow flavors to the dried food.

**Hoba leaf**
The leaf of the *ho* tree (*Magnolia obovata*; Japanese bigleaf magnolia). The leaves, which are large and resistant to scorching, have an appealing aroma, and have been used since ancient times to wrap ingredients when cooking. Fresh green leaves, harvested from May to July, are used to wrap ingredients, while the dried leaves are used as a cooking vessel with heat from below.

**Honekiri (literally, "bone-cutting")**
A cutting technique for finely scoring fish with fine bones too numerous to remove, making it palatable with the bones left in the flesh. Pike conger (*hamo*) is well known for being prepared with this technique. Fine incisions are made perpendicular to the line between head and tail. When skewering pike conger prepared with the *honekiri* technique, four skewers are inserted in the head-to-tail direction.

**Horaku**
A flat unglazed earthenware pot historically used for roasting tea, beans, or salt. Today, it is also used in *horaku-yaki*, in which ingredients are laid on a bed of salt and cooked, as well as for other kinds of dishes. For *denpo-yaki*, a small *horaku* pot called a *kawarake* is used.

**Jikabi-yaki (direct heat)**
A method of grilling in which the ingredients are directly exposed to the heat source. This term also refers to dishes prepared in this way. (See also *kansetsu-yaki*.)

**Ji-zuke**
The process of marinating.

**Jomi**
The choice parts of a fish after it has been cleaned and filleted, and the blood, veins and other inedible parts removed. Also may refer to processed fish ready to be served as sashimi or used in other recipes.

**Kaba-yaki**
Originally, eel was grilled without filleting, with skewers inserted in the head-to-tail direction; the name came from its resemblance in shape and color to the "cattail" seedpods of bulrushes (*gama no ho*; also called *kaba*). Today, it refers to the standard method of grilling eel, in which they are cut open from the back or belly and grilled with *tare* sauce.

**Kansetsu-yaki (indirect heat)**
A method of preparation in which ingredients are cooked by indirect heat using a pot, metal or ceramic plate, aluminum foil, or other vessel. The Japanese term *kansetsu-yaki* is sometimes used to describe dishes prepared in this way. (See also *jikabi-yaki*.)

**Karasumi-ko**
*Karasumi* is mullet roe that has been preserved by salting and drying. The hardened roe is cut into thick slices for serving as an appetizer. The leftover end parts are grated on an *oroshigane* to produce *karasumi* powder.

**Kesho-jio**
Salt applied to fish or other ingredients immediately prior to grilling to give them an attractive appearance. The areas where the salt is applied will stand out with a whitish tinge. A generous amount of salt on the tail and fins inhibits scorching.

**Koji**
Steamed rice, wheat, soybeans, or other grains inoculated with spores of koji mold (*Aspergillus oryzae*) and fermented to produce sake, miso, shoyu, and other foods.

**Kurozumi (black charcoal)**
A type of charcoal made by firing *kunugi*, *kashi*, or *nara* oak wood in an earthen kiln and allowing the fire to extinguish naturally inside the kiln by closing all the openings of the kiln. Black charcoal, which is used for *chanoyu* tea gatherings, is softer than white charcoal (see *shirozumi*).

**Kushi-mawashi (skewer rotation)**
Rotating the skewers within the fish during grilling is essential, as otherwise the meat or fish may stick to the skewers, making them hard to remove when cooking is complete.

**Kyara-ni**
In this method of cooking, used for butterbur (*fuki*), burdock root (*gobo*), and spikenard (*udo*), ingredients are simmered in shoyu, sake, sugar, and other ingredients. The brown color that is imparted is called *kyara-iro*, from the *kyara* or aloeswood tree used for making incense.

**Miso yuan-ji**
A marinade made by adding miso to a basic *yuan-ji* marinade (see also *yuan-ji*, *yuzu*).

**Muscle cells (muscle fibers)**
General name for the spindle-like contractable cells that form the muscle structures in animal anatomy.

**Nikiri (de-alcoholization)**
Removal of the alcohol from sake or mirin by bringing to a boil.

**Nimono-wan (clear soup dishes)**
A dish consisting of combinations of fish, chicken, vegetables, and rehydrated dried ingredients immersed in clear soup (*sumashi-jiru*) and served in a large lidded lacquer bowl. In *kaiseki* cuisine, it is the most important dish in the basic *ichiju sansai* (one soup, three dishes) meal; in other words, it is not simply a clear soup but one of the main courses of the meal. The ingredients are substantial and the amount of soup is plentiful, making it one of the main dishes in the meal.

**Onigara-yaki**
Grilling in the shell. Used to cook shrimp, turban shell, and similar crustaceans in their hard shells.

**Osmosis and osmotic pressure**
When a solvent (e.g., water) and a solution (e.g., salt water) are separated by a semipermeable membrane (e.g., cell membrane), parts of the solvent (water) permeate the membrane and move toward the solution, seeking to balance the concentration of the two liquids. Osmotic pressure is the difference in pressure between two such liquids at a given time. When fish are sprinkled with salt, the salt dissolves in the surface moisture, forming a concentrated brine that creates osmotic pressure between the inside and outside of the cell membranes. This osmotic pressure difference causes water in the flesh to seep out.

The osmotic pressure generated when salt comes into contact with the flesh of a fish (which has a salt concentration of 0.9%) causes the cells to break down and salt to permeate the flesh, thereby denaturing the flesh components. (See also "The Science of *Yakimono*," pp. 14–17.)

**Radiation**
Radiation occurs when thermal energy is emitted from an object in the form of electromagnetic waves. The higher the temperature of the object, the greater the energy of the electromagnetic waves emitted. The emission of electromagnetic waves with wavelengths ranging from visible light to the infrared spectrum is also known thermal radiation; when an object is exposed to electromagnetic waves in this wavelength range, its temperature rises. For example, when fish is grilled over charcoal, it is heated by thermal radiation from the charcoal.

**Ro-yaki**
A style of *yakimono* using egg yolk to create a wax-like finish. Similar finishes include *kimi ro-yaki* (egg yolk-grill) and *uni ro-yaki* (sea urchin grill).

**Sake kasu (sake lees)**
*Sake kasu* are the lees left over after pressing the fermentation mash (*moromi*) during the sake-making process. Because of their high nutritional value, the lees are used in cooking and soups. Sake lees contain enzymes that break down starches and proteins.

**Salinity/salt concentration**
The density of salt dissolved in water or other liquid, usually expressed as a percentage of the content.

**Salt-soluble proteins**
Proteins that are insoluble in water but dissolve in salt water solutions. In fish flesh, myofibrillar proteins are salt-soluble proteins.

**Serving side**
The side of a food that is facing up and toward the diner when served. Which side is made the serving side determines how the portion will be finished. The basic rule is to make it look both appetizing and attractive.

**Shiogama-yaki**
A *yakimono* dish in which a fish is scaled, gutted by drawing the gills and internal organs out through the gill opening (*tsubo-nuki*, see p. 204), then wrapped in a mixture of salt and egg white and baked in an oven.

**Shirotsubu miso (unstrained white miso)**
Miso is made from soybeans, rice koji mold, and salt. White *shirotsubu* miso has a higher proportion of rice koji and a lower salt content than other types of miso, giving it a sweeter taste. It is mostly made in the Kansai region around Osaka and Kyoto. The miso is made without crushing or straining the steamed soybeans, koji, and other grains, giving it a stronger flavor than types in which straining is part of the process.

**Shirozumi (white charcoal)**
A type of charcoal made by firing wood from *kashi*, *nara*, or other species of oak at high temperatures in a kiln, then removing it and covering it with a mixture of earth, ash, and charcoal dust to smother the fire and allowing it to cool. The white color comes from ash that adheres to the surface. *Shirozumi* is hard and dense, and gives a metallic sound when tapped. It burns steadily for a long time. *Binchotan* charcoal made from the *ubamegashi* oak is considered to be of particularly fine quality. (See also *kurozumi*.)

**Shitabi (heat from below)**
This refers to heating food ingredients from below with a heat source such as charcoal, gas flame, or an electric grill placed below the food (see also *uwabi*). This heats ingredients by convection heat as well as radiation. (See also p. 206.)

**Shitami**
The side of the flesh that is facing down when a fish is placed with its head to the left and belly toward the front. The side that faces up is called the *uwami* side. (See also *uwami*.)

**Steam convection oven**
An oven equipped with a device that generates steam and forced convection of hot air inside a sealed chamber. Setting the humidity, temperature, and convection speed of the hot air inside the chamber allows for various heating processes, and a large amount of food can be cooked at once.

**Sukibiki**
A method of scaling a fish with small and delicate overlapping scales. With the *yanagiba* knife facing in the reverse direction toward the head (*sakasabocho*), insert the blade under the scales but over the skin, and skim off the scales. Slide the blade back and forth, moving from the tail end toward the head end.

**Tade (water pepper)**
An annual herb, also called *yanagitade*, with a distinctive aroma in its leaves and stems. There are red and green varieties. The *tade-miso* used with *yakimono* is made by mixing crushed green *tade* leaves with miso and thinning with sake. *Tade* is also combined with *tosa-zu* to make *tade-su* and with shoyu to make *tade-joyu*. Red *tade* (*benitade*) leaves are frequently used as a garnish for sashimi.

**Taihaku sesame oil**
Sesame oil squeezed from high-quality untoasted sesame seeds using the cold pressing method. Despite its neutral color and aroma, the oil brings out the umami flavors of the sesame.

**Tamari shoyu**
This is a type of shoyu produced during the process of making miso from soybeans. It is less salty than *koikuchi* shoyu, but is dark in color and somewhat thick, with a strong, rich umami flavor.

**Tare**
A seasoning sauce made from a shoyu base, often by adding sake and mirin. *Tare* is used for basting or pouring over fish while grilling. The same sauce may be used as a marinade. The flavor of *tare* sauce may differ slightly depending on how it is used, for example as sauce for *teriyaki*, for basting grilled *unagi*, or for flavoring *yakitori*.

**Tate-jio**
A saline solution with a slightly lower salt density (around 2%) than seawater. Ingredients are immersed in *tate-jio* solution when a chef wants to allow salt to penetrate evenly into all parts of an ingredient.

**Tekkyu (grilling bars)**
Long, thin square metal bars placed parallel to the length of a heat source in order to support fish and other ingredients on skewers during cooking.

**Tsuke-ji**
A marinade used to flavor fish and other ingredients before grilling (see also *yuan-ji*, miso *yuan-ji*).

**Usui-endo peas**
A variety of green peas. Compared to ordinary green peas, they tend to have thinner skin and a distinctive crisp, yet moist texture.

**Uwabi (heat from above)**
This refers to cooking on a grill with the heat source above the ingredients, so that the heat comes into contact with the food from above. (See also *shitabi*.) Since the heat source emits infrared radiation in all directions, the food is adequately cooked even though the heat comes from above. (See also p. 206.)

**Uwami**
The side of a fish that faces up when the fish is placed with the head to the left and the belly toward the front. The side that faces down in this position is called the *shitami*. (See *shitami*.)

**Yoko-gushi**
The practice of inserting a bamboo support skewer perpendicular to the other skewers in order to prevent the skewered flesh from turning or curling up when cooked.

**Yuan-ji**
A marinade made by mixing shoyu, mirin, and sake. Slices of yuzu or yuzu juice are also sometimes added (*see also* yuzu).

**Yubeshi**
A *wagashi* confection made by filling the hollowed-out rind of a yuzu fruit with sweetened miso, which is then steamed and dried. Nuts may be added to the miso filling.

**Yuzu**
A citrus fruit related to limes and clementines. The color and size vary through the year, from small *hana-yuzu* in the spring to green *ao-yuzu* harvested in summer, to the mature yellow fruit harvested in autumn and winter. The fruit, which has a characteristic fragrance and acidity, is used in *yuan-ji* and miso *yuan-ji* marinades to impart its distinctive aroma and flavor. (See also *yuan-ji*, miso *yuan-ji*.)

# Causes and Prevention of Food Poisoning (Focus on "Grilling")

| Category | Toxic substance | Main causes and sources of infection | Preventive measures, etc. |
|---|---|---|---|
| Bacteria and other microbes | Enterohemorrhagic *E. coli* | Fecal matter, raw liver | Heat (at least 1 minute at core temperature of 167°F/75°C) |
| | *Campylobacter* | Undercooked chicken, meat, eggs | Heat (at least 1 minute at core temperature of 167°F/75°C) |
| | *Salmonella* | Chicken, eggs, processed egg products | Heat (at least 1 minute at core temperature of 167°F/75°C) |
| | *Staphylococcus aureus* | Problems can occur when food prepared with bare hands is consumed after a lapse of time. *S. aureus* is routinely present on human and animal skin and in the mucus membranes of the nostrils and throat. It is particularly prevalent in infected cuts. When *S. aureus* proliferates in food, it produces toxins known as enterotoxins. | *S. aureus* can be killed by heating to 140°F (60°C) for 30 minutes, but if enterotoxins are present, these cannot be neutralized even after heating to 212°F (100°C) for 30 minutes. Since enterotoxins are produced between 50 and 115°F (10 and 46°C), food should be kept at 50°F (10°C) or below at all times. Gloves should be worn when any cuts or infections are present on the hands. |
| | *Vibrio parahaemolyticus* | Uncooked fish and shellfish | *V. parahaemolyticus* proliferates at salinity concentrations of 1–8 percent, so washing food in fresh water is effective. Since it proliferates in saltwater at temperatures of 59°F (15°C) and above, food should be kept at 50°F (10°C) or below. Heat (to core temperature of at least 149°F/65°C). |
| | *Clostridium botulinum* | Canned and bottled foods, and foods in vacuum packs. (*C. botulinum* produces spores that proliferate and create toxins in oxygen-deprived environments.) | Heat (the toxins are rendered inactive by heating to a core temperature of 212°F/100°C for 1–2 minutes or to 176°F/80°C for 20 minutes, and are killed by heating to 248°F/120°C for 4 minutes.) |
| Viruses | Norovirus | Bacillus carriers, bivalve mollusks (oysters, various species of hard clams, scallops, etc.) | Careful maintenance of good health and hygiene practices (including thorough handwashing) not only by staff in the kitchen but throughout the restaurant. All cooking utensils must be disinfected and heated (to core temperature of 185–194°F/85–90°C for at least 90 seconds). Kitchen staff working in food preparation should be encouraged to take a stool test at least once a month. Those found to be asymptomatic carriers of the norovirus should not work on preparation jobs involving direct contact with food until they are confirmed through a clear stool test to be no longer carrying the virus. |
| Chemicals | Histamine | Fish with large amounts of dark-meat flesh including tuna, mackerel (*saba*), sardines, and saury (when histamine-producing bacteria proliferate in the gills, body surface, and internal organs, the histidine decarboxylase in these microbes produces histamine from free histidine). | Once produced in the flesh, histamine is resistant to heat and cannot be broken down even by heating. It is necessary to control the amount of histidine decarboxylase by preventing histamine-producing bacteria from attaching to the fish (by removing gills and organs) or proliferating (by storing at low temperatures). |
| Parasites (saltwater fish) | *Anisakis* | Mackerel (*saba*), horse mackerel, saury, bonito, sardines, salmon, squid, and others | Choose fresh fish and gut promptly. Since the parasite is also present in the muscles, either freeze (core temperature at least −4°F/−20°C for at least 4 hours) or heat (core temperature of 167°F/75°C for at least 5 minutes). The parasite is not killed by vinegar or wasabi. |
| | *Kudoa* | Fresh flounder (*hirame*) sold to be consumed uncooked | Parasitic in the muscles of fish. Freeze (−4°F/−20°C for at least 4 hours) or heat (core temperature 167°F/75°C for at least 5 minutes). |
| Parasites (freshwater fish) | *Metagonimus yokogawai* (Yokogawa fluke) | Freshwater and brackish water fish including sweetfish (*ayu*), big-scaled redfin (*ugui*), and icefish (*shira-uo*) | Cook thoroughly and do not eat raw. |
| Natural toxins | Paralytic shellfish poisoning / Diarrheic shellfish poisoning | Bivalve mollusks (clams, scallops, oysters, mussels, and *shijimi* clams) | The toxins are resistant to heat and are not broken down by cooking. In Japan, regular testing for shellfish toxins is carried out in line with public regulations to prevent bivalves and other shellfish containing amounts exceeding designated levels from being harvested or distributed. At present, choosing reputable distribution channels is the most important precaution. |
| | Ciguatera fish poisoning | Muscles and inner organs of fish, mostly coral reef fish. Main species that may contain this toxin include great barracuda and other species of the family Sphyraenidae; brown-marbled grouper, yellow-edged lyretail, squaretail grouper, and other species of family Serranidae, subfamily Epinephelinae; and red snapper and other species of the family Lutjanidae subfamily Lutjaninae. | The ciguatera toxin is not broken down even by cooking at high temperatures. In Japan, the distribution of species that might harbor the toxin is subject to regulations. At present, choosing reputable distribution channels is the most important precaution. |
| | Tetrodotoxin | Inner organs (ovaries, liver, etc.) of pufferfish (*fugu*) | Pufferfish toxin cannot be rendered harmless by cleaning in fresh water, heating, or any other preparation method. It is a highly potent toxin with a fatality rate of 5–10 percent. In Japan, regulations govern the species and parts that can be sold for food, and only chefs with special qualifications are allowed to prepare the fish for consumption. The sale or supply of any pufferfish species or parts other than those set out in the regulations is forbidden by the Food Sanitation Act. |

Compiled with reference to the official websites of the Ministry of Health, Labour and Welfare; Ministry of Agriculture, Forestry and Fisheries; Food Safety Commission of Japan; Bureau of Public Health, Tokyo Metropolitan Government; Osaka and Hokkaido prefectural government websites; and the reference work *Sakana no kagaku* (The Science of Fish; Asakura Shoten, 1994).

# INDEX

Page numbers in *italics* refer to a recipe. Titles of dishes are also in *italics*.

## A

abalone (*awabi*)
   *Abalone Grilled in a Salt Crust 158*
   abalone liver sauce (*awabi-kimo-dare*) 159, *197*
*abura-yaki* 22, 116
*aigamo*, see duck
*aioi-musubi* knotting 148, 205
*amadai*, see tilefish
*ama-zu*, see sweet vinegar marinade
*ame-ni* 137, *197*, 207
*amigasa-yuzu*, see yuzu citrus
amino acids 14–17, 19–21, 73, 79, 139, 207
*anago*, see conger eel
*Anisakis* parasite 210
aroma 12–13, 37, 169
   due to Maillard reaction 14–17, 19, 21, 61, 62, 73, 77, 91–93
   "kaba-yaki" 77
   of shoyu (in marinade) 39
*ashirai* (garnishes) 8, *194–197*, 207
asparagus 167
*awabi*, see abalone
*awayuki* topping 108, *109*
*ayu*, see sweetfish

## B

bamboo
   *sasa* leaf 85
   sheath cords 125, 205
   shoot (*takenoko*), grilled (*yaki-takenoko*) 23, *109*, *195*
barracuda (*kamasu*)
   ciguatera toxin in 210
   *Grilled Marinated Barracuda 52*
   skewering 202
Beef
   *Beef Tenderloin in Miso Yuan-ji Marinade 168*
beltfish (*tachiuo*)
   *Miso-Marinated Grilled Beltfish 56*
burdock root (*gobo*) 115, 149, 205, 208
*buri*, see yellowtail
butterbur (*fuki*) 208
   soused (*fuki no ohitashi*) 141, *197*
   wild, simmered (*yama-buki kyara-ni*) 127, *196*
butterfish (*managatsuo*) 39
   skewering 200–201
   *Yuan Style Butterfish 44*
butterfly cut, see cutting techniques

## C

*Campylobacter* microbe 210
caramelization 16, 207
carrot 115, 135
*chamame*, see edamame
*chanoyu* tea culture 23, 34, 100
charcoal 12–13, 14–17, 22–26, 34
   *arazumi* rough charcoal 98–100
   arranging, for grilling sweetfish 91–93
   *binchotan* white charcoal 23, 34, 96–104
   for *chanoyu* 100
   grills using 206
   *irizumi* refined charcoal 98–100
   Kishu Binchotan production 102–104
   *kurozumi* black charcoal 34, 100, 208
   *nikozumi* soft charcoal 98–99
   purity of 100
   radiation in cooking 35–37
   *shirozumi* white charcoal 34, 96, 100, 209
   vs. other heat sources 37
cherry blossoms
   petals *121*
   salt-pickled *109*
*chiaibone* bloodline bone 129
chicken, grilled, see *yakitori*
chrysanthemum-cut turnip, see turnip
chrysanthemum leaf 57, 61, 70, 73
ciguatera toxin 210
citrus juice *197*
citrus sauce (*kankitsu-shio*) 159, *197*
clam (*hamaguri*)
   *Clam Grilled in the Shell 156*
   norovirus in 210
*Clostridium botulinum* toxin 41, 210
collagen 16, 21, 38–39, 41, 85, 93, 147, 180, 207
   gelatinization of 77, 188
coloring 7, 9, 12, 21, 35, 37, 46, 54, 58, 63, 75, 91, 92, 130
   anthocyanin 163
   due to Maillard reaction 14–17, 20
   of shoyu (in marinade) 45, 53, 73, 81
conger eel (*anago*)
   *Grilled Conger Eel, Yawata Style 148*
   *Yawata-maki* preparation 205
cutting techniques
   butterfly cut (*sebiraki*) 61, 77, 81, *133*
   filleting
      *gomai-oroshi* 141
      *nimai-oroshi* 61, 127
      *sanmai-oroshi* 19, 45, 49, 53, 57, 65, 70, 73, 125, 129, 200, 205
   *honekiri* bone-severing 147, 207
   *sukibiki* scaling 135, 141, 209
cuttlefish (*ika*)
   *Grilled Cuttlefish, Ro-yaki Style 154*

## D

daikon, *see* radish
dashi
   *ichiban* dashi 115, 161, *194*, *195*, *196*, *197*
   *niban* dashi 115, 121, *195*, *196*, *197*
   katsuobushi flakes 12, *196*, *197*
   kombu dashi 12, 129, *192*, *193*, *194*, *196*, *197*
   stock from sea-bream bones 115
*dengaku*, see miso
*denpo-yaki* 24, 26, 207
duck (*aigamo* or *kamo*)
   *Roast Duck Breast 166*
duck, mallard (*magamo*)
   *Pan-Grilled Mallard Breast 164*

## E

edamame soybeans (*chamame* or *zunda*) 70, 163, *194*, *197*
eel (*unagi*) 22, 25
   *Grilled Eel on Rice 76*
   skewering, see skewering techniques
   *Yawata-maki* preparation 205
eggplant, Kamo
   *Kamo Eggplant Dengaku 162*
egg(s) (*tamago*) 115, 151, *192*, *193*
   *Campylobacter*, salmonella in 210
   soft-boiled *151*
   whites *109*, *111*, *113*, *133*, *135*, *141*, *159*, *161*, 208
   yolks *121*, *123*, *127*, *155*, *163*, 208
      egg and vinegar dressing (*kimi-zu*) 167, *197*
      egg-yolk mustard filling (*kimi-garashi*) *196*
      yam-and-egg sauce (*tamago imo*) 147, *197*

electricity
  cooking with  35
  grills using  206
  vs. charcoal  37
*engawa* fringe  141, 161
*Escherichia coli* microbe, enterohemorrhagic  40, 41, 210

## F
flounder (*hirame*)
  *Kudoa* parasite in  210
  Rikyu Style Sesame-Grilled Flounder  140
food poisoning, *see* hygiene and sanitation
French cuisine vs. Japanese  12, 20
*fugu, see* pufferfish
*fuki, see* butterbur
*furishio-yaki*  14, 15, 84, 90, 112, 114, 128, 144

## G
garnishes, *see ashirai*
gas
  cooking with  34–35
  grills using  206
  vs. charcoal  37
ginger shoots, pickled (*hajikami*)  117
ginkgo nuts  123
*gomai-oroshi, see* cutting techniques
*goyo-matsu, see* pine
grilling bars (*tekkyu*)  87, 91, 94, 133, 209
grills, types of  206
gudgeon, Biwa (*moroko*), skewering  199
*guji, see* tilefish

## H
HACCP  40, 207
*hamachi, see* yellowtail
*hamaguri, see* clam
*hamo, see* pike conger
*hassun*  6, 154
heat
  conduction heat transfer  16–17, 30–32, 33
  convection heat transfer  30, 32, 33, 34, 209
  direct (*jikabi-yaki*)  12–13, 24, 30, 32, 207
  effects of  15–16, 38–39, 92
  from above (*uwabi*)  66, 109, 113, 121, 127, 133, 135, 153, 155, 163, 206, 209
  from below (*shitabi*)  12, 206, 209

indirect (*kansetsu-yaki*)  24, 32, 207
  oven  32, 34
  residual, cooking with  111, 119, 167
  sources of  22–23, 34–35, 37
*himono* dried foods  65, 69, 207
*hira-gushi, see* skewering techniques
*hirame, see* flounder
histamine poisoning in fish  210
*hoba* leaf  207
  *aohoba-yaki*  124
  dried  123
  green *hoba* leaf  125
  *hoba* miso  123
  *hoba-yaki*  122
*honekiri, see* cutting techniques
*horaku* pot  26, 27, 30, 32, 123, 151, 207
*horaku-yaki*  24, 26, 122, 150
*horenso, see* spinach
horned turban shell (*sazae*)
  Tsubo-yaki Style Grilled Horned Turban Shell  160
*hosho-yaki*  128
*hozuki* fruit (Chinese lantern)  149
hygiene and sanitation  40–41, 210

## I
*ichiban* dashi, *see* dashi
*ichiya-boshi* overnight drying  69
*ika, see* cuttlefish; *see* squid
*Ise ebi, see* lobster

## J
Japanese pepper, *see* peppers, *sansho*
*jikabi-yaki, see* heat, direct
*ji-zuke, see* marinating
*jomi*  207
*junme*  19, 200

## K
*kaba-yaki* grilled eel  22, 25, 77, 207
*kabuto-yaki*  112
*kaji no ha, see* paper mulberry leaf
*kake-dare* sauce for eel  77
*kamasu, see* barracuda
*kamo, see* duck
*Kamo nasu, see* eggplant
*kansetsu-yaki, see* heat, indirect
*karasumi-ko* dried mullet roe powder  133, 157, 207
*kasu, see* sake lees
*katazuma-ori, see* skewering techniques

*katsuobushi*
  flakes, *see* dashi
  powdered  194
*kenchin*  114
*kesho-jio, see* salting
*ki-dare* sauce for eel  77
*kikka-kabura, see* turnip
*kikurage* wood ear  115
*kinmedai* (snapper)
  Grilled Kinmedai Marinated in Sake Lees  136
*kinome, see* peppers, *sansho*
*kisu, see* whiting
*koji* mold  137, 139, 208
  bed (*koji doko*)  139
  marinade, effects of  139
  *shiokoji*  138, 139
*kombu* dashi, *see* dashi
*kombu* (kelp)  12, 129, 147, 194, 195
*Kudoa* parasite  210
*Kujo negi, see* onion, long
*kunugi* sawtooth oak  34, 100, 208
*kuruma-ebi, see* prawns
*kurumi, see* walnuts
*kushi-mawashi* (skewer rotation)  20, 77, 147, 208
*kuwai* arrowhead bulb  135
*kuwa-yaki*  164
*kuzu*
  leaves  151
  starch  115, 165
*kyara-ni*  127, 196, 208

## L
lemon  113, 119
lobster (*Ise ebi*)
  Grilled Lobster in the Shell  152
lotus root (*renkon*)
  early harvested, with crushed edamame (*shin-renkon no zunda-ae*)  70, 194
  marinated (*renkon no sanbaizu-zuke*)  117, 195
  mustard-filled (*karashi renkon*)  127, 196

## M
mackerel
  histamine and anisakis parasites in  210
  *sawara*
    Grilled Sawara Mackerel with Natane Topping  120

*Sawara* Mackerel *Hoba-yaki* 122
*Yuan* Style *Sawara* Mackerel 118
striped (*shima-aji*) 16–17
Salt-Grilled Striped Mackerel 18
*madai*, see sea bream
*magamo*, see duck, mallard
Maillard reaction 14–17, 19, 20, 21, 61, 62, 65, 73, 75, 77, 92, 187, 207
*maitake*, see mushrooms
*managatsuo*, see butterfish
*manganji*, see peppers
maple leaves *70, 85, 133, 149*
marinades (*tsuke-ji*) 13, 14–16, 24, 27, *53, 73, 81, 121, 123, 125, 145, 167, 194, 195, 196, 197,* 209
*koji*, see *koji* mold
*miso* marinade 57
*miso yuan-ji* marinade 14, *49, 141, 169,* 208
*sake kasu*, see sake lees
*shoyu* marinade *141*
*yuan-ji* marinade 14, *39, 45, 119,* 209
marinating (*ji-zuke*), effects of
in *tare-yaki 73, 74, 81, 83*
in *yuan-yaki 45, 47, 49, 51, 53, 55, 57, 59, 137, 139, 169*
*masu*, see salmon
*matsuba*, see pine needles
*matsutake*, see mushrooms
*mirin*, de-alcoholized *53, 141, 145, 167, 173,* 208
*miso*
*dengaku* 25, 27, *126, 163*
*hoba miso*, see *hoba* leaf
red *163*
Sendai *123*
*shiro surimiso 169*
*shirotsubu 49, 57,* 208
*tade-miso*, see *tade* water pepper
*taki-miso 127*
white *121, 123, 127, 141, 163, 196*
*miso yuan-yaki* 48, 168
*misozuke-yaki* 56
*mitsuba 115, 161*
*mizuhiki* cords *128*
Moriguchi daikon, *see* radish
muscle cells (fibers) 7, 14–17, 19, 21, 40–41, *45, 51, 57, 59, 65, 73, 83, 119, 137, 139,* 187, 208
gelatinization *47, 55*
proteins in, *see* proteins

mushrooms
*maitake 123*
*matsutake 151*
*shimeji*
simmered *tosa-ni* style (*shimeji no tosa-ni*) 57, *194*
with soused spinach (*shimeji to horenso no ohitashi*) 115, *195*
*shiitake 115, 161*
mustard *165*
*karashi 167, 169*
*karashi renkon*, see lotus root
*myoga 147*
vinegar-pickled (*su-zuke myoga*) 19, *93, 125, 194, 195, 196*

## N

Nachiguro slate stones *151*
*naganegi*, see onion
nandina (*nanten*) *145*
*nanohana* rape blossoms, soused (*nanohana no ohitashi*) *121, 196*
*natane-yaki 120*
*natto, Daitokuji 195*
*niban* dashi, see dashi
*nikiri* (de-alcoholization) *121, 123, 127, 147, 163, 197,* 208
*nimai-oroshi*, see cutting techniques
*nimono-wan* 11, 12, 208
norovirus poisoning 40–41, 210
*nui-gushi*, see skewering techniques

## O

*odori-gushi*, see skewering techniques
oil
rice oil *135, 163, 197*
sesame oil 22, 25, 26, *143*
Taihaku (untoasted) sesame oil *61, 117, 197, 209*
vegetable oil *165*
okra *129*
*onigara-yaki* 25, *152,* 208
onion
globe (*tamanegi*) *192, 193*
long (*naganegi*) *165, 176, 177*
osmosis or osmotic pressure 14, 15, 17, 19, 208
oven, convection 34, *125, 139, 159, 167, 169, 194,* 209

## P

paper mulberry leaf (*kaji no ha*) *117, 127, 163*

peas
*kinusaya 135*
*usui-endo 121,* 209
peppers
*manganji 149, 169*
*sansho* (Japanese pepper) 22, 24, 25
*kinome 109, 157*
peppercorns *125*
powder *73, 81, 165*
*togarashi* (red chili) 25, 26, *155*
persimmon leaves *73*
pike conger (*hamo*) 207
Grilled Pike Conger with Tare Sauce *146*
skewering, see skewering techniques
pine
needles (*matsuba*) *70, 111, 123, 151, 159, 195*
sprigs *113*
five-needle pine (*goyo-matsu*) *155*
poppy seeds *163*
potatoes
white *135*
sweet *135*
prawns, tiger (*kuruma-ebi*) *151*
proteins 12, 14–17, 38, 40–41, 51, 161, 187, 207
in muscle fibers 19, *57, 59, 73, 137, 139*
proteolytic enzymes 49, *57, 59, 137, 139*
salt-soluble 14, 17, 19, *45, 51, 59, 65, 81, 169,* 208
pufferfish (*fugu*)
Grilled Pufferfish *144*
tetrodotoxin poison of *145,* 210

## Q

quail
Grilled Quail 80

## R

radiation, infrared (thermal) 14, 15, 30, 34–37, 92, *117, 169,* 206, 208
radish (*daikon*) *165*
green, pickled in miso (*aomi daikon no miso-zuke*) *135, 196*
red *167*
vinegar-pickled Moriguchi (*Moriguchi daikon no su-zuke*) *70, 195*
*renkon*, see lotus root
*rikyu-yaki 140*
*ro-yaki* "wax" grill 25, *154,* 208
*ryozuma-ori*, see skewering techniques

INDEX 213

## S

*sakame* 19
*saka-shio* 195
*saka-yaki* 64
sake, de-alcoholized 45, 49, 57, 125, 137, 139, 167, 197
sake lees (*sake kasu*) 24, 136, 208
    marinating effects 137
    sake lees bed (*kasu-doko*) 137
salmon (*masu* or *sake*)
    Grilled Salmon in Miso Marinade 48
    Koji Grilled Salmon 138
salmonella bacteria 210
salting 13
    concentration of (salinity) 208
    effects of
        in *shio-yaki* 19, 63, 65, 67, 70
        in *yuan-yaki* 45, 47, 53, 55, 57, 59
    for preparing fish 13, 14–15, 17
    *kesho-jio* 85, 113, 151, 207
    *tate-jio* 14, 209
    technique for 8
*sanbai-zu* dressing 195
*sanmai-oroshi*, see cutting techniques
*sansho*, see peppers
*satoimo* taro
    boiled (*kinu-katsugi*) 85, 195
*sawara*, see mackerel
*sazae*, see horned turban shell
sea bass (*suzuki*) 27, 38
    Grilled Sea Bass with Hosho Paper 128
    Sea Bass Roasted in Green Hoba Leaves 124
    skewering, see skewering techniques
    Tade-Miso Grilled Sea Bass 126
sea bream (*madai* or *tai*) 22, 23, 26, 27
    Awayuki Grilled Sea Bream 108
    cleaning, see *tsubo-nuki*
    Grilled Sea Bream and Shrimp Roasted in a Horaku 150
    Grilled Sea Bream Head 112
    Kenchin Style Grilled Sea Bream 114
    Salt-Crust Baked Sea Bream 110
    Sea Bream Grilled with Oil 116
sea urchin (*uni*) 153, 159
*sebiraki*, see cutting techniques
serving side 198, 208
sesame seeds 119, 141, 143, 147
shellfish poisoning 210
*shiba-yaki* 134
*shichimi* spice mixture 147
*shiitake*, see mushrooms
*shima-aji*, see mackerel, striped

*shimeji*, see mushrooms
*shiogama-yaki* 22, 27, 110, 158, 208
*shio-yaki* 14, 15, 18, 24, 60, 64, 69, 108, 110, 132, 134
shiso leaf (*oba*) 147
*shitabi*, see heat
*shitami* face-down side 85, 93, 200, 201, 205, 209
skewering techniques 198–203
    for eel 77
    for pike conger 147
    for sea bass 125
    for sweetfish 85, 93
    *hira-gushi* flat 65, 81, 117, 121, 123, 127, 129, 135, 141, 151, 169, 198
    *katazuma-ori* single-tuck 19, 57, 61, 73, 133, 137, 139, 202
    *nui-gushi* stitch 203
    *odori-gushi* "dancing" 12, 85, 93, 200
    *ryozuma-ori* double-tuck 45, 53, 155, 202
    *uneri-gushi* wave 49, 109, 119, 151, 200
spinach (*horenso*)
    soused (*horenso no ohitashi*) 133, 196
    soused, with *shimeji* mushrooms (*shimeji to horenso no ohitashi*) 115, 195
sprouts, broccoli 167
sprouts, red cabbage 167
squid (*ika*), skewering 203
*Staphylococcus aureus* microbe 210
*sudachi* 19, 117, 145, 153, 161
sugars (saccharides) 14–17, 57, 137, 139
    fructose 16
    glucose 15, 16, 73
    lactose 16
    reducing 16
*sukibiki*, see cutting techniques
*su-zuke myoga*, see *myoga*
*suzuki*, see sea bass
sweetfish (*ayu*) 91–93
    Ayu no shio-yaki 12, 24
    Grilled Sweetfish (Charcoal grill) 90
    Grilled Sweetfish (Electric grill) 84
    parasites in 210
    skewering, see skewering techniques
sweet vinegar marinade (*ama-zu*) 194, 195, 197

## T

*tachiuo*, see beltfish

*tade* water pepper 24, 84, 209
    leaves 127
    *tade-miso* 127, 207
    *tade-su* 24, 27, 84, 209
*tai*, see sea bream
Taihaku sesame oil, *see* oil
*takenoko*, see bamboo shoot
*taki-miso*, see miso
*tamago*, see eggs
*tamari* ("rich") shoyu 26, 27, 73, 149, 209
*tare* sauce 15, 16, 24, 27, 74–75, 79, 147, 209
    variations in eel 79
*tare-yaki* 14, 15, 72, 76, 80, 126, 146, 148, 164
*tate-jio*, see salting
*te-gaeshi* in grilling eel 78, 79
*tekkyu*, see grilling bars
tetrodotoxin poisoning 145, 210
tilefish (*amadai* or *guji*) 38
    Grilled Tilefish Flavored with Sake 64
    Salted and Grilled Tilefish 60
    skewering 198–199
    Tilefish Grilled with Karasumi Powder 132
    Tilefish, Shiba-yaki Style 134
tofu 23–27, 115, 119, 143
*togarashi*, see peppers
*tsubo-nuki* cleaning, of sea bream 22, 27, 111, 204
*tsubo-yaki* 24, 160
*tsuke-dare* sauce for eel 77
*tsuke-ji*, see marinades
*tsuke-yaki* 24, 52, 80
*tsukune-imo*, see yam
turnip, pickled
    cut "chrysanthemum" style (*kikka-kabura*) 61, 73, 155, 194, 195, 197

## U

*ubame-gashi* oak 34, 37, 96–98, 100, 209
    coppicing of 104–105
umami 13, 17, 49, 57
*umeboshi* paste 61, 73
*unagi*, see eel
*uneri-gushi*, see skewering techniques
*uni*, see sea urchin
*urajiro* fern 113, 153
*uwabi*, see heat
*uwami* face-up side 85, 93, 200, 201, 205, 209

## V

*Vibrio parahaemolyticus* microbe 210

## W

wakame seaweed 159, 161
walnuts, candied (*kurumi ame-ni*) 137, 197
whiting (*kisu*)
    Overnight-Dried Whiting 69

## Y

*yakitori* (grilled chicken)
    cuts of 170–180
    giblets and rare cuts 181–193
yam
    *tsukune-imo* 109
    *yama-imo* 115
    yam-and-egg sauce (*tamago imo*) 147, *197*
*yama-buki*, see butterbur
*Yawata-maki* (long-fish-wrapped burdock) 148–149, 205
yellowtail (*hamachi* or *buri*) 25, 26, 27, 38
    Grilled Yellowtail 72
Yokogawa fluke 210
*yoko-gushi* horizontal skewers 85, 93, 147, 151, 203, 209
*yuan-ji*, see marinades
*yuan-yaki* 14, 15, 44, 48, 52, 56, 118, 120, 122, 124, 136, 138, 140, 168
*yubeshi* 119, 209
    *yubeshi shira-su* dressing 119

yuzu citrus 25–27, *45*, *49*, *119*, *169*, 209
    green yuzu 49, *163*
    in *yuan-ji* 45, 49, *119*, *169*, 209
    rind, simmered in syrup (*amigasa-yuzu*) 45, 81, 139, *194*, *195*, 197
    yuzu zest (*furi-yuzu*) 45, 137, *163*, 207

## Z

*zunda*, see *edamame*

## CONVERSIONS

Measurements in this book are given in accordance with the metric system; conversions using standard U.S. measures are given in parentheses.
E.g.: 200 ml (6.8 fl. oz.), 50 g (1.8 oz.)

For small amounts, metric quantities are converted to tablespoons (Tbsp.) and teaspoons (tsp.). Please use the conversion table below as a guide.

### Volume

| Metric | USA |
|---|---|
| 5 ml | 1 teaspoon |
| 15 ml | 1 tablespoon |
| 50 ml | 3 tablespoons + 1 teaspoon |
| 60 ml | 2 fluid ounces |
| 80 ml | 2.7 fluid ounces |
| 100 ml | 3.4 fluid ounces |
| 240 ml | 8.1 fluid ounces |
| 400 ml | 13.5 fluid ounces |
| 480 ml | 16.2 fluid ounces |
| 1 L | 33.8 fluid ounces |

### Length

| Metric | USA |
|---|---|
| 3 mm | ⅛ inch |
| 6 mm | ¼ inch |
| 1.25 cm | ½ inch |
| 2.5 cm | 1 inch |
| 5 cm | 2 inches |
| 6.25 cm | 2½ inches |
| 7.5 cm | 3 inches |
| 10 cm | 3⅞ inches |
| 20 cm | 7⅞ inches |
| 40 cm | 15¾ inches |

### Weight

| Grams | USA |
|---|---|
| 10 g | 0.4 ounce |
| 15 g | 0.5 ounce |
| 20 g | 0.7 ounce |
| 30 g | 1.1 ounce |
| 50 g | 1.8 ounces |
| 100 g | 3.5 ounces |
| 150 g | 5.3 ounces |
| 200 g | 7.1 ounces |
| 500 g | 17.6 ounces |
| 1 kg | 35.3 ounces |
| 3 kg | 6.6 pounds |

### Temperature

| Celsius (°C) | Fahrenheit (°F) |
|---|---|
| 40°C | 104°F |
| 50°C | 122°F |
| 60°C | 140°F |
| 75°C | 167°F |
| 90°C | 194°F |
| 100°C | 212°F |
| 150°C | 302°F |
| 250°C | 482°F |
| 500°C | 932°F |
| 750°C | 1382°F |
| 1000°C | 1832°F |

**Editorial Supervisor:** Nakata Masahiro and Kawasaki Hiroya, Japanese Culinary Academy
**Art Direction and Design:** Miki Kazuhiko and Hayashi Miyoko, Ampersand Works
**Editing:** Nagai Sakiha
**Translation, copyediting, and proofreading:** Lynne E. Riggs, Paul Warham, Katherine Heins, Nakaishi Satoshi, Iguchi Haruko (Center for Intercultural Communication)

## PHOTO CREDITS

Saito Akira: pp. 8–9, 17–21, 31, 33, 44–55, 60–90, 93–105, 108–135, 140–193, 194 (other than bottom center), 195, 196, 197 (other than top and middle left), 198–205, 206 (top right)
Yamagata Shuichi: pp. 2–3, 10–11, 24–25, 28–29, 36, 39, 42–43, 56–59, 106–107, 136–139, 194 (bottom center), 197 (top and middle left), 206 (top and bottom left and bottom right)
Kuma Masashi: Jacket

## COOPERATION

The publisher thanks the following individuals and institutions for cooperation for this book:
pp. 23, 26: National Institute of Japanese Literature / Collection: Ajinomoto Foundation for Dietary Culture
pp. 24–25: Kenshoku, "Eating Life" Library
p. 34: Shoei Manufacturing Co., Ltd.
pp. 91–93: NHK (Japan Broadcasting Corporation)
pp. 96–105: Wakayama Charcoal Co-operative / Wakayama Prefecture, Forestry Promotion Department
p. 206 (top and bottom center): Tanico Corporation

## SPECIAL COLLABORATION

Ehara Ayako, specialist in food culture: *Yakimono* in History (pp. 22–27)

## CONTRIBUTORS

Kawasaki Hiroya, specialist in culinary science and sensory science: The Science of *Yakimono* (pp. 14–17); How Fish Changes Under the Effects of Heat (pp. 38–39)
Sugiyama Kuniko, specialist in cookery science: Types and Methods (pp. 30–37)
Koda Tomoko, specialist in nutrition science: Hygiene in Preparing and Cooking *Yakimono* (pp. 40–41), Causes and Prevention of Food Poisoning (Focus on "Grilling") (p. 210)

## CULINARY SCIENCE CONSULTANT

Kawasaki Hiroya, specialist in culinary science and sensory science

---

英文版 日本料理大全 焼場
焼く技法　塩焼き、ふり塩焼き、幽庵焼き、たれ焼き、焼き鳥

2025年4月18日発行

監　　　修　　特定非営利活動法人 日本料理アカデミー
　　　　　　　村田吉弘

発　行　者　　栗栖正博
制 作 責 任　　築地　正
発　行　所　　特定非営利活動法人 日本料理アカデミー
　　　　　　　〒604-8187 京都府京都市中京区東洞院通御池下ル
　　　　　　　　　　　　笹屋町436番地
　　　　　　　office@culinary-academy.jp
　　　　　　　https://culinary-academy.jp/
　　　　　　　Tel 075-241-4163／Fax 075-241-4168

印 刷・製 本　　日本写真印刷コミュニケーションズ株式会社

落丁本・乱丁本はお取替えいたします。本書のコピー、スキャン、デジタル化等の無断複製は著作権法上での例外を除き禁じられています。

© Japanese Culinary Academy
ISBN 978-4-911188-10-1